ROCK AND HAWK

Rock and Hawk

Robinson Jeffers and the Romantic Agony

WILLIAM H. NOLTE

The University of Georgia Press
ATHENS

Athens, Georgia 30602

Set in 10 on 13 point Mergenthaler Baskerville
Printed in the United States of America

Library of Congress Cataloging in Publication Data

Nolte, William Henry, 1928–
Rock and hawk.

Includes bibliographical references and index.
1. Jeffers, Robinson, 1887–1962—Criticism and interpretation. I. Title.

PS3519.E27Z69 811'.5'2 77-22982
ISBN 0-8203-0432-8

TO HUNTINGTON CAIRNS
AND ROBERT McHUGH

the falcon's
Realist eyes and act
Married to the massive

Mysticism of stone,
Which failure cannot cast down
Nor success make proud.

"Rock and Hawk"

Contents

Acknowledgments

Parts of this study appeared originally in an article entitled "Robinson Jeffers as Didactic Poet," in the *Virginia Quarterly Review* (Spring 1966); an article entitled "Robinson Jeffers, An Uncanny Prophet," in the *Alternative: An American Spectator* (May 1976); and in *Guide to Robinson Jeffers* (Columbus, Ohio: Charles E. Merrill Publishing Company, 1970). The author and the publisher are grateful to the editors for permission to reprint passages from these works. Grateful acknowledgment is also made to Random House, Incorporated for permission to quote from the following copyrighted works of Robinson Jeffers: *The Selected Poetry of Robinson Jeffers*, *Be Angry at the Sun*, *The Beginning and the End*, and *Selected Poems*; to W. W. Norton and Company for permission to quote from Jeffers's *The Women at Point Sur*, *Dear Judas*, and *The Double Axe*; and to the Macmillan Publishing Company for permission to reproduce five lines of "The Man Against the Sky" from the *Collected Poems* of Edwin Arlington Robinson.

ROCK AND HAWK

ONE Introduction

Though it is impossible to believe that the poets are the unacknowledged legislators of the world, Shelley spoke clearly and objectively of the major poets when he stated that they measured the circumference and sounded "the depths of human nature with a comprehensive and all-penetrating spirit, and they are themselves perhaps the most sincerely astonished at its manifestations; for it is less their spirit than the spirit of the age." Of course the great poet concerns himself with subjects of lasting importance or universal meaning, just as of necessity he interprets his materials from some philosophical viewpoint. In the work of every major poet there is a single world view apparent. The expression of that view is nothing more than a vehicle and a signature; only minor writers (or critics) believe that expression is all. If the vehicle cannot bear the freight of the philosophy, we have a misadventure of communication—an unfortunate failure. If the style of the poet cannot be distinguished from that of other poets, we may have a practiced eclectic, but no major poet.

Of all major modern poets, Robinson Jeffers came closest to expressing himself in a singular style. Among the many critics who have remarked about that style, George Sterling commented on its individuality as well as any: "One could pick, unerringly, a poem by him from a stack of thousands of others. In all that collection there would be no other that could be mistaken, by a discerning eye, for one of his." In like manner William Rose Benét wrote: "Given a short section of any Jeffers poem I think I could recognize his authorship without having any other indication that he has written it. . . . There are passages so intensely imbued with his own individuality that one could not mistake them for the work of anyone else." In *The Literary Notebooks of Winfield Scott*, published posthumously in 1969, Scott said of Jeffers that no other contemporary poet had "evolved a style expansive enough to manipulate all occasions, from personal to universal. He can say 'Moscow' or 'Munich' or 'Roosevelt' directly—just to cite one revealing characteristic. He does not make a poetry which depends upon symbol, innuendo, or any kind of double-talk. Of its kind there has been nothing successfully like it since Whitman. It is direct. It is a man speaking. Granted there are other graces and enviable ways for poetry, this way can be uniquely powerful in the hands of great talent."[1]

In saying that style is simply the vehicle of the poet's meaning, the expression of his weltansicht, I should perhaps add that the way a thing is said definitely contributes to what is being said and to how it will affect the reader. Even the manner in which the words are placed on the page affects their meaning, as the poetry of E. E. Cummings readily shows. But if we are more concerned with the manner of a poet than we are with his matter, then we can rest assured that we are not in the company of a writer who will long outlive his own day. He will become, at best, a historical curiosity. The effective style is born of strong personality in the artist and has little if anything to do with mannerisms. The supreme style blends so thoroughly with its subject that it all but disappears; which is to say, the greatest art *seems* artless. Mark Van Doren said as much in his excellent foreword to *The Selected Letters of Robinson Jeffers*:

> [Jeffers] was never wiser than when he insisted that the proper function of poetry was not to express but to present; or when he said: "Poetry does not necessarily have a 'message' except 'How beautiful things are'—or 'How sad, or terrible'—or even 'How exciting.' These are the only messages that Homer and Shakespeare have for us."
>
> Homer and Shakespeare. In what more fitting company could we leave him?[2]

II

The reader of Jeffers's poetry invariably wonders about the man. What was he like, this passionate solitary who loved mountains and ocean, trees and rock, and admired hawks more then men? This misanthropic individualist who loved and was loved by one woman for over forty years, and who formed a mystical relationship with stone while building outside the village of Carmel the granite edifices Tor House and Hawk Tower that pilgrims continue to visit half a century later. Who stated in a famous poem "Hurt Hawks" that he would "sooner, except the penalties, kill a man than a hawk," and yet shrank from the thought of giving pain to any living creature. Who insisted that he had paid his "birth-dues" by telling his reader how man might find that peace which he seeks, and who was hence "quits with the people"—and yet never ceased exhorting man to turn aside from his self-destructive ways.

The following biographical note, which Jeffers furnished his publisher in 1925, provides a partial outline:

> Born in Pittsburgh in 1887; my parents carried me about Europe a good deal; of the first visit I remember three things—a pocketful of snails loosed on the walls of a kindergarten in Zurich, paintings of Keats and Shelley hanging side by side somewhere in London and Arthur's Seat, the hill above Edinburgh. When I was fifteen I was brought home. Next year my family moved to California and I graduated at eighteen from Occidental College, Los Angeles. After that, desultory years at the University of Southern California, University of Zurich, Medical School in Los Angeles, University of Washington but with faint interest. I wasn't deeply interested in anything, but poetry. I married Una Call Kuster in 1913. We were going to England in the autumn of 1914; but the August news turned us to this village of Carmel instead; and when the stage-coach topped the hill from Monterey, and we looked down through pines and sea-fogs on Carmel Bay, it was evident that we had come without knowing it to our inevitable place.[3]

Some consider it worthy of note that Jeffers's father, Dr. William Hamilton Jeffers, was forty-nine when Robin was born. A second son, Hamilton, arrived seven years later. Hamilton, interestingly enough, became an astronomer and worked at Lick Observatory, one of the few places Robin condescended to visit after settling in his home by the sea. Evidence of Jeffers's interest in, and knowledge of, astronomy appears throughout the poetry. Although he never seriously considered becoming anything but a poet, as he remarked in the note quoted above, his knowledge in various scientific disciplines far exceeded that of any other American litterateur, past or present. He once wrote, "The happiest and freest man is the scientist investigating nature, or the artist admiring it; the person who is interested in things that are not human."[4]

Considering Jeffers's great interest in Christ-figures (and in the person of Jesus), as well as other saviors, both religious and secular, it is noteworthy that his father was a theologian of some renown, holding the chair of Old Testament Literature and Exegesis at Western Theological Seminary at the time of Robin's birth. At the age of five Robin received his first instruction in Latin from his father, who also insisted that the boy study Greek at a time when most children are still learning the rudiments of their native language. While in Europe with his parents in the summers of 1891 and 1892, Robin attended kindergartens and began learning German and French. In 1898, having become dissatisfied with American schools, Dr. Jeffers sent his wife and sons to Europe where they remained for five years. He joined his family during the summer months. From the age of eleven to fifteen, when he returned home with his mother and brother, Robin was sent to five different schools—in Leipzig, Vevey, Lausanne, Geneva, and Zurich—all carefully picked by his scholarly father. At the age of twelve he knew German and French as well as he did English, had a thorough knowledge of Latin, and could read Greek. Such a Spartan diet doubtless deprived him of anything resembling a normal childhood but did provide him with an excellent education. Because he never stayed in one place long enough to form, or expect to form, strong attachments with other children, he spent much of his time alone. He also developed those solitary traits—especially the addiction to long walks and to mountain climbing—that later were hallmarks of his personality. Like the young Wordsworth, his interest in the world of flora and fauna came almost as a matter of course. The nonhuman world would later appear as a major "character" in his poetry.

Various critics have wondered if Jeffers's rejection of Christianity in particular and his contempt for saviors in general were not tantamount to a rejection of his extremely religious father. I find no evidence to support such a contention, whereas a great deal flatly contradicts it. That Jeffers greatly admired his father is evident from his letters and the few poems which refer to him, particularly the sonnet "To His Father" and the long ode "The Year of Mourning," written in memory of his father and of his first child, who died the day he was born. There is also a moving tribute to Dr. Jeffers in "Come, Little Birds," written twenty-five years after his father's death. Although a somber figure—always restless, moving from place to place, impatient with human frailty, Victorian in his attitude toward duty and hard work—Dr. Jeffers was an extremely liberal theologian who never attempted to force religious belief on his son. Indeed, according to Lawrence Clark Powell, who wrote the first important book on Jeffers, the boy did not attend Sunday school, and his father taught him the Bible as oriental literature rather than as divine revelation. In a letter to Hyatt Waggoner (21 November 1937) Jeffers spoke of the need for writers to be at least aware of modern scientific thought. In answer to a question from Waggoner about his intellectual development, he confessed that he could not remember the first scientific books that had made an impression on him, adding (very importantly I think) that his own philosophical views entailed no "sudden readjustment": "My father was a clergyman but also intelligent, and he brought me up to timely ideas about origin of species, descent of man, astronomy, geology, etc., so that progress was gradual, none of the view-points of modern science came as a revelation. Studies in university and medical school gave me more room to move in, more points of support, but never, that I remember, any sudden readjustment."[5]

There are also those who think of Jeffers as a recluse, a kind of intellectual dropout, so appalled by industrial civilization that he retreated to his Carmel aerie from where, following Yeats's lead, he bade the mad world go by. In such an assessment there is at least a kernel of truth, but not much more than that. To see how little truth there is in the belief, one need only read his letters. In the little compilation of tributes to Jeffers, *Ave, Vale, Robinson Jeffers* (San Francisco: Grabhorn, 1962), the following inscription appears on the title page: "This little volume pays homage to a man who has left us a legacy that will be recorded in the annals of literature as one of the greatest. Robinson Jeffers had few friends, but those who knew him well have written these tributes in the knowledge that they have walked with a titan." The fact is that Jeffers was amiable enough to visiting writers and artists who sought him out, and he frequently invited such people to visit him in his home, but he was too much the artistic aristocrat to pay the least heed to polite society. As for celebrity hounds who were constantly appearing at his doorstep, he avoided them like the plague, even going so far as to place over his front gate a sign prohibiting visitors until after 4:00 P.M., by which time he was usually in the hills behind his home or walking on the shore below.

In answer to a questionnaire received in 1931, Una, who was in many ways a mediator between Jeffers and the world, outlined his daily schedule, or rather regimen since he adhered to it so strictly. In the mornings until around one in the afternoon he wrote in the long attic room of Tor House; weather permitting he worked in the turret of Hawk Tower. The afternoons were spent working with stone or planting and caring for the hundreds of trees surrounding the house and tower. At least one complete day a fortnight was spent with his wife and sons in the hills and canyons, closely examining rock formations, trees and flowers, water courses and animals. Usually he and Una took a brisk two- or three-mile walk along the shore just before sunset each day. Una remarked one invariable habit: "He never goes to bed without going outdoors about midnight and walking around the place—watching the stars in their courses, marking the rising or setting of the Constellations and feeling the direction of the wind and noticing the tides at ebb or flow. He observes the barometer closely in winter—one hangs by his bed—is exhilarated by storms. He passionately loves rain and wet weather, distrusts a blazing sun, thinks people overestimate the health in sun baths—points to the hardy races in Northern Europe who live in dark countries."[6]

In a letter to Una in 1938 Jeffers lamented that he was unable to write. For thirty years past, writing had been "one of the conditions of life for me," and now the well seemed to be dry. We know of course that the period passed and he wrote again; five volumes of verse, counting the adaptation of Euripides' *Medea*, were to follow. After the death of his beloved Una in 1950 he again found it impossible to compose a line of poetry. But that period also passed. Many consider *Hungerfield and Other Poems* (1954) one of his best volumes. To the end of his life, when his eyesight had failed to the point that he was unable to decipher his own handwriting, he continued to work at his trade, shaping thoughts into poetry.

III

When Gilbert Highet wrote twenty years ago that the critical neglect of Jeffers constituted the greatest shame in American letters, he was expressing a view that I have heard numerous times in the last decade. The constantly reiterated query why Jeffers is not more often read today makes me wonder if he is not the most widely read "unread" poet in world literature. While he is certainly not taught in colleges and universities as often as various others, there is ample reason to believe that he is read. I have had numerous students ask in astonishment and something close to outrage why they had not been introduced to him before. I have also known a few professors of English who did not know his poetry, but I have never known anyone interested in poetry who was unacquainted with his work.

Considering Jeffers's rejection of all mass beliefs and faiths, his extraordinary individualism, and his abhorrence of all intrusions on his privacy, one might marvel that he gained so large an audience in the 1920s and 1930s, when he was once featured on the cover of *Time* magazine and T. S. Eliot was his only competitor as our most popular serious poet. In an article in *Saturday Review of Literature* (9 March 1935), Niven Busch marveled at the sale of Jeffers's books: "Although he has never written anything designed for a restful afternoon in a hammock, he has not, in the last nine years, written anything which sold less than six editions, and *Tamar* zoomed through fourteen, and this month received the accolade of inclusion in the Modern Library." His manuscripts and the early editions of his books were then bringing higher prices than those of any other living poet.

After a sharp decline in popularity just before, during, and after World War II, Jeffers's stock has in recent years been on the rise again both at home and abroad. His out-of-print volumes are in great demand once more. One bookfinder (with the House of Books, Ltd.) wrote me in 1966 that "Jeffers books which a few years ago were found all over at fairly reasonable prices have suddenly disappeared and when available the prices have skyrocketed." New editions are appearing and then selling out almost at once. In the last ten years translations of his poetry have been very well received on the Continent, and especially in Iron Curtain countries where he is probably the favorite American poet. *The Selected Poetry of Robinson Jeffers*, which was first published in 1938 and has never been allowed to go out of print, is in its fifteenth printing. The times, I am convinced, are now catching up with what was most timeless in his verse.

In his rejection of all secular panaceas and his refusal to glorify the past or write hopefully of the future, Jeffers seems almost an anachronism in the modern world. Preeminently the advocate of disillusion, he remained steadfastly attached to the present while at the same time remaining detached from poetic fads and fashions. He was every bit as solitary and secure in his own majority of one as were Poe, Melville, Whitman, Thoreau, and Dickinson in the nineteenth century. In August of 1939 when even the wise were admonishing the multitudes to gather into herds, Jeffers in "The Soul's Desert" insisted that it was clearly time "To become disillusioned, each person to enter his own soul's desert / And look for God—having seen man." In "Wise Men in Their Bad Hours," first published in 1924, he remarked the peculiar envy which many intellectuals have for the sleepwalking masses. The rhythmic flow of the opening lines in particular perfectly complements the central idea of the poem—that to have made "Something more equal to the centuries / Than muscle and bone, is mostly to shed weakness." Read aloud the opening lines give off a somber music:

Wise men in their bad hours have envied
The little people making merry like grasshoppers
In spots of sunlight, hardly thinking
Backward but never forward, and if they somehow
Take hold upon the future they do it
Half asleep, with the tools of generation
Foolishly reduplicating
Folly in thirty-year periods; they eat and laugh too,
Groan against labors, wars and partings,
Dance, talk, dress and undress; wise men have pretended
The summer insects enviable;
One must indulge the wise in moments of mockery.[7]

Jeffers reminds us of Voltaire and the ancient Stoics, but we know that the symbolic spokesmen of our age are Rousseau and Marx, and their aberrant cousin, Bakunin.

It is nonetheless understandable why Jeffers should be given a second reading today. Even the most nearsighted among us knows that we live in a falling age, a period of crumbling values and intense introspection. And pessimism (except in political circles where optimism is mandatory) has become widespread—almost, indeed, an article of faith, a testament of one's sobriety and intelligence. Even we Americans, so long the apparent favorites of God and history that we had begun to mistake happy circumstance for enduring fact, have been touched by the chilling winds of doubt. Today where are the certitudes of our national destiny? Lodged in the shallow brainpans of hucksters and demagogues but fortunately no longer extant in the cerebellums of thinking citizens. In a recent study, John Lukacs, a Hungarian-born historian, described the spirit of the age in a way that now seems almost fashionable:

> By the middle of the 1960's most people of the Western World, even in America, felt the prevalence of despair. This was a new experience for civilized mankind, especially for Americans. In Europe there reigned cynicism and calculation, something that to many people of the Old World was at least not entirely unfamiliar. Americans were beset by the fatal flaw of their mental habits, their tendency to state human problems wrongly. They were preoccupied with the persistence of violence whereas their problem was the re-emergence of savagery. It seemed that this once Indian land may have left a curse on its conquerors. In more and more places American civilization was succumbing to the temptations of a motorized and drugged witches' sabbath, at the edges of which reappeared the impassive savage ghost of the Indian.
>
> In any event, the old things and beliefs were now beginning to go very fast. In many ways the end of the Modern Age, of the only civilization that some of us have known, began to set in. . . . The monstrosity of government, the impotence of Powers, the separation of races, the conformity of nations, the purposelessness of society, the fiction of prosperity, the dissolution of learning, the meaninglessness of letters, the senselessness of the arts, the destruction of nature, the decay of science, the faithlessness of religion, the mutation of morality were, all, at hand.[8]

Lukacs, who is much less the prophet than he is the reporter, summarizes in a matter-of-fact way what other historians in this century have predicted or envisioned. In the work of Henry and Brooks Adams there was gloomy prophecy—and some very bad guesses as to specifics. The Adams brothers saw the general direction of Western decay but were unable, of course, to see the details of decline. The same thing might be said of others, most notably Spengler. In the preface to his *Character and Opinion in the United States* (1921), George Santayana said serenely what others tend to say in anger and dismay: "Civilization is perhaps approaching one of those long winters that overtake it from time to time. A flood of barbarism from below may soon level all the fair works of our Christian ancestors, as another flood two thousand years ago levelled those of the ancients. Romantic Christendom—picturesque, passionate, unhappy episode—may be coming to an end. Such a catastrophe would be no reason for despair. Nothing lasts for ever; but the elasticity of life is wonderful, and even if the world lost its memory it could not lose its youth." My point is that the views of Lukacs, unlike those of the earlier previsionists, go beyond theory to faits accomplis. It is less the visions of tomorrow than it is the experiences of today that haunt the dreams of the civilized minority.

Though Jeffers has been proven an uncanny prophet, that fact would not in itself make him particularly important as an artist, though it would certainly give his work an interest of sorts. While we may read him for what he says, as we may read the historians and philosophers, we reread him for the manner in which he dramatizes his ideas. Poetry is not, needless to say, the same thing as history or philosophy or psychology or whatever. But if the poet is to sound the depths of human nature and/or express the spirit of his age, then certainly his poetry will embody elements of all those branches of knowledge. Jeffers said as much when he remarked that poetry, or at least great poetry, "gathers and expresses the whole of things," combining knowledge and experience in "one passionate solution."

It is possible, of course, to reject the philosophy expressed in the poetry while praising the poet for his presentation. I say this is possible since it has been done numerous times. Everyone, I suppose, has been delighted by the *expression* of views that nonetheless seemed absurd—most love poems, including several of Shakespeare's sonnets, are in this category. For obvious reasons this occurs more frequently in poetry than in prose, which lacks the emotional appeal of verse. That fact doubtless explains why many intelligent readers dismiss poetry as being childish, and on the other hand why some of poetry's most ardent proponents conclude that the poet should not be held accountable for his views, no matter how crackbrained they might be. I also think it apparent that some of the loveliest poetry verges on the meaningless—witness Coleridge's "Kubla Khan." But to believe that expression is all is to deny that poetry can ever be as important as prose. Since I believe that the best poetry can come closer to expressing the whole of things than can the best prose, I am forced to conclude that what is said is of paramount importance.

Though we cannot completely divorce expression from content since in each there must be an element of the other, we still constantly distinguish between the two. Indeed, only a child or a simpleton fails to make that distinction in everything he reads. In a notable passage, Louis Untermeyer, who has always been one of Jeffers's strongest advocates, comes dangerously close to making the fatal mistake of trying to differentiate completely between thought and expression; he does separate philosophy from poetry in criticizing this philosophical poet:

> The philosophy is negative, repetitious, dismal. The poetry, even when bitterest, is positive as any creative expression must be. It is varied in movement and color; it vibrates with a reckless fecundity; it is continually breaking through its own pattern to dangerous and unfathomed depths. This is not a work to be enjoyed without sacrificing that sense of ease dear to the casual reader; it is doubtful if, in the common sense, it can be "enjoyed" at all. But here is a full-throated poetry, remarkable in sheer drive and harrowing drama, a poetry we may never love but which we cannot forget.[9]

While I agree in the main with this assessment, I feel the same reservations might be applied to the poetry of Euripides. Certainly no reader would be well advised to read Jeffers in order to escape anything. When he wrote in "Boats in a Fog" that "it is bitter earnestness / That makes beauty; the mind / Knows, grown adult," he warned us, once and for all, that he would concern himself only with what is most serious in life. When we desire less than that, as we often do, we should go to someone else.

But Untermeyer is wrong when he says that the poetry cannot be enjoyed, since enjoyment derives not from what is said so much as from how it is said. Everyone, I think, enjoys Macbeth's famous lamentation beginning "Tomorrow and tomorrow and tomorrow . . ." even though the speech is a cry of blackest despair. One of Jeffers's fine poems, "Birth-Dues," begins:

Joy is a trick in the air; pleasure is merely contemptible, the dangled
Carrot the ass follows to market or precipice;

But limitary pain—the rock under the tower and the hewn coping
That takes thunder at the head of the turret—
Terrible and real. Therefore a mindless dervish carving himself
With knives will seem to have conquered the world.

The world's God is treacherous and full of unreason; a torturer, but also
The only foundation and the only fountain.
Who fights him eats his own flesh and perishes of hunger; who hides in the grave
To escape him is dead; who enters the Indian
Recession to escape him is dead; who falls in love with God is washed clean
Of death desired and of death dreaded.

No poet has more adamantly denied that joy was a proper concern for adults—or for poetry. In the fact that people seek joy, Jeffers could see only weakness. As in the poem "Joy":

Though joy is better than sorrow joy is not great;
Peace is great, strength is great.
Not for joy the stars burn, not for joy the vulture
Spreads her gray sails on the air
Over the mountain; not for joy the worn mountain
Stands, while years like water
Trench his long sides. "I am neither mountain nor bird
Nor star; and I seek joy."
The weakness of your breed: yet at length quietness
Will cover those wistful eyes.

Such poems unfortunately lend themselves to misinterpretation. Rather than read this as a denigration of joy, we should see that Jeffers is really concerned with placing that feeling in proper perspective. Joy is, after all, a transitory feeling, a "trick in the air," and not to be confused with such qualities as peace or strength. In seeking joy man consciously elevates a by-product to the position of value—that is, to the realm of substance or (relatively) permanent thing-in-itself.

This seems a good place to say something about Untermeyer's objections to Jeffers's pessimism and misanthropy, since those objections have been widely made by other critics and since in the following pages I shall concern myself very little with the critics. What is one to say about the following statement: "The idea dominating [*Thurso's Landing*] is the *idée fixe* which runs through all of Jeffers's volumes: Life is horrible"?[10] One can only say that the opposite is true. How anyone could arrive at such a conclusion after reading the poems is truly amazing since nowhere in the poetry is there support for such a view. If anything, Jeffers is too effusive in his praise of life. He always insisted, as in "Shine, Perishing Republic," that "life is good, be it stubbornly long or suddenly / A mortal splendor." He wrote dozens, if not hundreds, of poems in praise of life. Indeed, his entire aesthetic is founded on the premise that the poet engages in a celebration of the splendors and rhythms of life. Why Untermeyer, and others like him, should attempt to deny what is obviously undeniable is one of the great mysteries. Calling *The Double Axe and Other Poems* "Jeffers's most vehemently self-defeating work," Untermeyer quotes the following lines from the title poem to prove his assessment: "The human race is bound to defile" and "Whatever is public—land, thoughts, or women—is dull, dirty and debauched." Properly understood the poem is one of his most affirmative. I see nothing in either quotation to provoke argument; indeed both seem to me apodictic. I also wish Untermeyer had used the first quotation in toto:

> *"The human race is bound to defile, I've often noticed it,*
> *Whatever they can reach or name, they'd shit on the morning star*
> *If they could reach."* [11]

We need only be awake and moderately sentient to realize that such a statement, which has always struck me as being unintentionally humorous, is a good deal closer to platitude or truism than it is to misanthropy or pessimism. To find a much better example of misanthropy, Untermeyer should have turned to the next to last poem in the collection, "Original Sin." There Jeffers dates our remarkable penchant for evil from the time when "The man-brained and man-handed ground-ape, physically / The most repulsive of all hot-blooded animals / Up to that time of the world," discovered the keen delight of giving pain to other creatures. Cruelty is the original, and enduring, sin. After describing the capture and burning of the mammoth, Jeffers places the terrible scene against the Edenic beauty surrounding it:

> *Meanwhile the intense color and nobility of sunrise,*
> *Rose and gold and amber, flowed up the sky. Wet rocks were shining, a little wind*

Stirred the leaves of the forest and the marsh flag-flowers; the soft valley between the low hills
Became as beautiful as the sky; while in its midst, hour after hour, the happy hunters
Roasted their living meat slowly to death.

Then the final passage, the best example of misanthropy I know since it is all-inclusive, so nearly pure as to cancel even the tribute that loathing pays to its object:

These are the people.
This is the human dawn. As for me, I would rather
Be a worm in a wild apple than a son of man.
But we are what we are, and we might remember
Not to hate any person, for all are vicious;
And not be astonished at any evil, all are deserved;
And not fear death; it is the only way to be cleansed.

No need for me to point out that such a blanket indictment is irrational, or that extreme advocates of reason are usually the ones who in a bitter moment express such disgust for the human species.

To the end of his life, Jeffers pondered this essential problem of human evil, not only the evil of individuals, but the inherent cruelty of what Mark Twain called this "damned human race." In "The Beginning and the End," published posthumously in the volume of the same name, he theorized that man's behavior may be the result of some "wound" in the brain suffered in prehistoric times when man descended from his arboreal abode and began his trembling journey amidst the terrors of his daily existence. Filled with fear and visited by dreams of death, man invented weapons and used fire for defense. Against all odds he survived, and natural selection provided him with those ingrained traits that civilization has sought, with indifferent success, to suppress. The deeds that man celebrates are cruel and bloody: "Epic, drama and history, / Jesus and Judas, Jenghiz, Julius Caesar, no great poem / Without the blood-splash." Still, modern man is partially exonerated in that he is a prisoner of the past that made him:

But never blame them: a wound was made in the brain
When life became too hard, and has never healed.
It is there that they learned trembling religion and blood-sacrifice,
It is there that they learned to butcher beasts and to slaughter men,

And hate the world: the great religions of love and kindness
May conceal that, not change it.

"And hate the world" was for Jeffers the most inexplicable of all human traits. Obviously one cannot assume that his dislike for the human species is tantamount to a hatred of life or of the world. Only the man who detests life could possibly view with equanimity the wholesale fouling of the natural environment by the species. If critics have tended to be more optimistic and philanthropic than the artists they presume to judge, that is probably because the critic is farther removed from the sources of art than is the artist and much less perceptive of the ways of man. This also explains why the great critics have been primarily men of the world and only secondarily men of the study. Generally speaking, critics have been egalitarian in tastes, whereas the overwhelming majority of great artists over the last three thousand years have been aristocratic or elitist, and more than a little sniffish of the demos. In such goliaths as Shakespeare, Michelangelo, and Beethoven, that disdain becomes absolute contempt.

But I do not wish to give undue emphasis to the question whether Jeffers is pessimist or misanthropist, since that question is really of no importance whatever. It is nonetheless interesting that he should have seen fit to deny that he was either one or the other. Of one thing, however, there can be no doubt: he was deeply concerned for the human species. Although in some of his most memorable poems he damned it with a bitterness comparable to that of Swift, he was concerned for what it was doing to itself and for what it was doing to the world of which it is a small part. If mad Ireland hurt Yeats into poetry, then absurd humanity did the same for Jeffers. I say *if* since I have no doubt that Yeats would have been a poet had Ireland not been insane and that Jeffers would have celebrated the natural beauty of the wild world had man been perfectly rational. Although the First World War was probably an important catalyst in the formation of Jeffers's general attitude toward civilization, I think it likely that the history of the race would have brought him to the same place eventually. The war only hastened the day of his maturity, and the Second World War just demonstrated further what any student of history must know for a certainty. Those wars provided an emotional acknowledgment, since they were so close to home, of what was already an intellectual postulate.

In the opening paragraph of his preface to *The Double Axe and Other Poems* he made his feelings quite clear (italics mine):

> The first part ["The Love and the Hate"] of *The Double Axe* was written during the war and finished a year before the war ended, and it bears the scars; but the poem is not primarily concerned with that grim folly. Its burden, as of some previous work of mine, is to present a certain philosophical attitude, which might be called *Inhumanism, a shifting of emphasis and significance from man to not-man; the rejection of human solipsism and recognition of the transhuman magnificence.* It seems time that our race began to think as an adult does, rather than like an egocentric baby or insane person. This manner of thought and feeling is neither misanthropic nor pessimist, though two or three people have said so and may again. It involves no falsehoods, and is a means of maintaining sanity in slippery times; it has objective truth and human value. It offers a reasonable detachment as rule of conduct, instead of love, hate and envy. It neutralizes fanaticism and wild hopes; but it provides magnificence for the religious instinct, and satisfies our need to admire greatness and rejoice in beauty.

While an ecologist would have no trouble understanding and sharing such a view (it is fitting that Jeffers should now be one of the heroes of the conservation groups), the average human would doubtless find it difficult to get beyond the appellation Jeffers finally chose for his world view. While a few commentators still profess faith that all will be well tomorrow, or the day after, the vast majority of knowledgable men, I daresay, would subscribe to Aldous Huxley's sardonic remark: "I have looked into the future, and it won't work." Although he often qualified his own dark view, Jeffers was in general agreement with Huxley, particularly in "Diagram," a poem from *The Double Axe* volume:

> *Look, there are two curves in the air: the air*
> *That man's fate breathes: there is the rise and fall of the Christian culture-complex, that broke its dawn-cloud*
> *Fifteen centuries ago, and now past noon*
> *Drifts to decline; and there's the yet vaster curve, but mostly in the future, of the age that began at Kittyhawk*
> *Within one's lifetime.—The first of these curves passing its noon and the second orient*

All in one's little lifetime make it seem pivotal.
Truly the time is marked by insane splendors and agonies. But watch when the two
curves cross: you children
Not far away down the hawk's-nightmare future: you will see monsters.

What was once considered the aberrant view of a solitary and embittered individual is today, only twenty-five years later, very nearly the common outlook of intellectuals everywhere.

Certainly no one can fault him as man for offering advice (not comfort or hope, which he considered detrimental since they act as blinders to human reason) anymore than we can object to Nietzsche for his attempt, especially in *Thus Spake Zarathustra*, to show us the way out of the nihilism into which modern man has fallen. Actually *The Double Axe* resembles that work in its structure and manner of expression (the journey of the Old Man with the double axe is remarkably like that taken by Zarathustra), though it diametrically opposes the romantic philosophy of Nietzsche. Both works are "poems" written in agony, though not finally despair. Though neither protagonist can at all accept the common man, the great mediocrity, each is interested in killing the lies by which men live rather than destroying the suffering victim of those lies. Each work is a conscious effort to shed despair, to replace pity and hopelessness with affirmation, to locate in the midst of chaos and human agony a path that leads us out of self-hatred and self-destruction. In other words, each is centrally concerned with values, or with a transvaluation of values—with offering in place of outworn, and hence injurious, values a new ethic for the new age now amaking. I have no doubt that Nietzsche's prescription, were it taken (as it apparently is being taken by many who have never read one of his books), would compound the problem it seeks to resolve and kill the patient it presumes to cure. Nor do I have the slightest hope that Jeffers's values will ever be subscribed to by more than a handful of people; I doubt that he had any such hope himself. But that does not make his views any the less wise. Though Nietzsche was one of the great iconoclasts, whose demolition work has been in large part beneficial, I would never say his central constructive views, which in their own way are as anthropocentric as the views they propose to replace, are in any way wise or healthy. Only as a cultural pathologist does he deserve his great reputation. Though both men agree on what has happened and is happening to man (a creature both professed to dislike), they are poles apart in their therapeutics.

As Jeffers predicted (tongue in cheek, let us hope), "two or three people" still consider him a pessimist though he hardly fits any definition of pessimism. Though he took a gloomy view of things human, Jeffers always insisted that the world is well made, no matter what man does, and he took the naturalistic view of good and evil, which holds that though good and/or evil might be considered substantive in individual lives or cases, in the larger view they must be considered relative and transitive since an "evil" can effect a "good," or vice versa. While he did not deny the existence of absolutes in the transhuman world, he did view humanity in relativistic terms. The natural beauty of the world, for example, he considered an absolute, in no way dependent upon the eyes of any perceiver. He thus concludes his "Credo": "The beauty of things was born before eyes and sufficient to itself; the heart-breaking beauty / Will remain when there is no heart to break for it."[12] He would not, however, consider any one of life's species an absolute since all such outcroppings of nature are necessarily ephemeral. In a world of flux there can be no absolutes, except perhaps flux itself.

Most readers consider Jeffers pessimistic for the wrong reasons. Among these reasons are his lack of faith in that anomalous concept called "The American Dream," his anti-Christian views, his objections to democracy (which he considered only a phase of the fatal cycle all nations endure, and not one of the more happy or long-lived phases either), and finally his insistence that our civilization will inevitably decline into barbarism and will, indeed, breed that barbarism out of which, in all probability, the race will once more climb—only to stumble and unmake itself again. He wrote a number of poems on this subject of culture-ages—for example, *At the Fall of an Age* and *At the Birth of an Age* as well as "The Broken Balance," "Hellenistics," "Decaying Lambskins," and "Prescription of Painful Ends." From the natural sciences he took his determinism, which is generally considered (wrongly, to be sure) pessimistic. And like all naturalists, he accepted the cyclic theory of history, which effectually denies the existence of progress in the world—or in any case progress as permanent acquisition, as some kind of Hegelian synthesis towards which history inexorably and inevitably tends. For all his avowed belief in determinism, he never ceased exhorting man to *choose* rationally; note for example the sentences above that were taken from the preface to *The Double Axe*. At times he came close to saying that though humans are essentially irrational they are under no compulsion to act in accordance with their nature. No contradiction here: if it is possible for a person to act irrationally, then it is also possible for him to act rationally. The human animal is of course the only creature capable of acting either way; man is in short a rational animal, who usually acts irrationally. A remarkable example of how he could combine in one poem both freedom and necessity, playing one against the other without releasing his hold on either, is "The Answer," which begins:

Then what is the answer?—Not to be deluded by dreams.
To know that great civilizations have broken down into violence, and their tyrants come, many times before.

and ends:

Integrity is wholeness, the greatest beauty is
Organic wholeness, the wholeness of life and things, the divine beauty of the universe. Love that, not man
Apart from that, or else you will share man's pitiful confusions, or drown in despair when his days darken.

If there is acceptance here of the way things are, there is also resistance to, and even denial of, the belief that one can do nothing but resign oneself to evil. Though admitting that some things are ugly, he insists that we might through choice remain free from that ugliness, or at least be able to see that the ugliness is only partial. Such a view is almost Emersonian, except that Emerson considered history important as a reminder of man's greatness; in "Self-Reliance" he wrote that "all history resolves itself very easily into the biography of a few stout and earnest persons." Jeffers means something entirely different; he obviously uses history for what it teaches about ripening and decay, about cyclic patterns, above all about the human norms of behavior. Finally—and here he is poles apart from Emerson—he repeats his view that one must look beyond humanity in order to become truly human. In "Signpost," another exhortation, Jeffers prescribed a cure for those "civilized" people who were "crying how to be human again." After climbing "the great ladder out of the pit of yourself and man," then, and only then, would you be "free, even to become human, / But born of the rock and the air, not of a woman."

I fail to see how any of these beliefs, or a lack of belief, can be considered pessimistic. Most pessimists object not so much to man, one of life's spawn, as they do to life itself. They blame the world for not allowing a more equitable dispensation of benefits to fall upon the just and the unjust. In other words, the gloom of pessimism usually grows from a contemplation of the world and its irreversible rules, whereas Jeffers's "pessimism" concerns only mankind. The typical pessimist, after the fashion of Ecclesiastes (and most modern existentialists), objects to the rules of the game as being inherently unfair to mankind. (And yet where might one go to find more delicious despair than that contained in the Preacher's soaring strophes? Platitudes have never been burnished to brighter shining. It is heady stuff, indeed.) Though more knowing, perceptive, and infinitely more interesting (and entertaining) than their opposites, pessimists do not accept the world in which they live and die. Which is the same thing as saying they reject the world and seek to escape the conditions it inhumanly imposes on all matter. How does one escape? By turning inward, by drawing the world into the self, by reducing the world to idea after the fashion of Schopenhauer or Indian mystics. Jeffers stands as far from that incestuous and self-pitying solution as it is possible to stand.

If Jeffers at times lectured to us in verse—as in "The Answer" and "Signpost"—he more frequently mocked "our foibles, our dreams, our delusions," as Robert Boyers put it, without making any effort to stimulate our imagination. No doubt of that fact. But the critic then descends to something not far removed from critical gobbledygook when he adds: "The ideological content of Jeffers's fine poetry here hardens into a mannered response to experience, so that no valid experience is lived through in the poem. What we have is a system of response, but nothing valid or poetically real to respond *to*." Here one's patience necessarily ends: What is a "*valid* experience," and which responses are "poetically real"? In an otherwise good essay,[13] such preciosity stands out all the more. What he is really objecting to, in all probability, is Jeffers's penchant for clarity and at times direct statement.

Reading twentieth-century criticism one is tempted to conclude that it is more addicted to obtuseness and obscurantism than that of former periods. But a study of the second-rate critics of the past will show that we are no worse off in that area than any other period of the last five centuries. Our obscurantists are still visible whereas those of the past have been mercifully forgotten. I think it generally true, however, that modern critics have been more hospitable to experimentation in the arts than ever before. Which, though laudable in itself, is not without its dangers, the foremost of which is that the open-minded critic may finally be driven by his logic to conclude that only that which is different or difficult warrants serious attention. Nor can we overlook the part that the critic's egotism plays in the matter. Since elucidation of the work of art is a primary aim of criticism, it follows (logically but not very intelligently) that the more light the critic can shed upon the object the more important will be the critic. Given this premise it must follow that the more obscure the work of art, the more important the critic's analysis or interpretation will seem. It is equally obvious that somewhere in this syllogism the quality of the work of art has been shuttled into the background. Explication takes the place of judgment. If a poem is not "difficult" then it is, ipso facto, unsatisfactory. Or if it is clear but too famous to be dismissed as being trivial, then every effort is made to show that it actually contains hidden depths and obscure caves never before properly mined. The New Critics carried that sort of thing as far as it could go, and then a little beyond. For too long, poetry has been considered some kind of exotic plant to be nurtured in academic hothouses far from the madding crowd. Nor should poetry be relevant to anything we might recognize as concerning our daily lives. As Henri Peyre put it in his excellent study *The Failures of Criticism* (1967): "The relevance of poetry, and even of fiction, to everyday life is branded as a defacement of the nobility of 'literature as such.'"[14] Indeed, some critics (and poets) object to a poet's *saying* anything, insisting rather that poetry should do no more than *be*, or that it express only itself. This is foppish nonsense. No matter how bad or good, how stupid or intelligent the poet, he always tries to say something. If he is incapable of writing clearly, there will still be fools enough who will find hidden meanings in his outpourings. Moreover, the less he has to say, the more likely he will be consciously obscure, and the more likely he will insist that expression is all.

IV

In an address delivered at the Library of Congress, at Harvard, and various other places in 1941, Jeffers spoke on the "Themes in My Poems." That important document, which was published by the Book Club of California in 1956 and is now out of print, deserves more than passing notice since nowhere else did Jeffers comment so candidly on his poetic interests. He remarked six distinct though related themes to be found in his verse. In my brief summary of those themes both the breadth and depth of his central concerns should be apparent.

After admitting that he had "always disliked, and generally refused, to talk about" his poetry he spoke of one of the simplest and most frequently used themes: "the contemplation of death, and of death often desirable, but always to be resisted." The central theme of *Thurso's Landing*, one of his greatest long narratives, it is also central in the little book *Descent to the Dead*, generally accepted as among his best collections of brief lyrics. After reading a passage from *Thurso's Landing*, a lyric from *Descent to the Dead*, and "The Bed by the Window," which he called "household verses," he turned to a theme that was, he said, "congenial" to the death-theme: "this tragic war that obsesses all our minds now." He then quoted, most appropriately, these lines from Victor Hugo:

Soyez maudits, d'abord d'être ce que vous êtes,
Et puis soyez maudits d'obséder les poètes!

(Be accursed, first for being what you are;
and then be accursed for obsessing the minds of poets.)

Admitting that he had been obsessed for some years before the war began, he quoted his "Rearmament," written in 1934; "Air-Raid Rehearsals," written in March 1936; "Watch the Lights Fade," written in 1938, the year of Munich; "The Bloody Sire," written in the summer of 1940 in an effort to meet the war "with a kind of desperate optimism"; and, finally, one of the sonnets ("After all, after all we endured, who has grown wise?") of "The Truce and the Peace," a group of eleven sonnets written at the close of the First World War.

He then abruptly turned to a third theme: "The idea of culture-ages —culture-cycles—the patterned rise and decline of one civilization after another," an idea, he remarked, that was "nearly as commonplace as death or war" but one that had occupied his thoughts and been a frequent subject of his verses. The idea had been popularized by Oswald Spengler, of course, but Jeffers stated that "it came to me much earlier, from my own thoughts, and then I found it formulated by the English Egyptologist, Flinders Petrie, in a little volume called 'The Revolutions of Civilization,' first published in 1911. Of course it was developed long before that, notably by Vico of Naples, Giovanni Battista Vico, who published his book in 1725." Most important to our understanding of Jeffers are his remarks on "the spiritual conflict that lies at the heart of our culture, and creates a strain there." Here he touches on those values which are never far from the center of all his poetry:

> The religions and ethics of other civilizations were more or less home-grown; they adapted themselves to the people, and the people to the religions; but Christianity is Oriental and Near-Eastern in origin, and was imposed on the western races rather recently, as history goes; and we have never got used to it. We still hold two sets of ethics, pagan and Christian, simultaneously. For instance, we say that we should love our enemies and not resist evil; yet at the same time we believe in justice, and that criminals ought to be punished, and that we should meet force with force, violence with violence. Or another instance: we believe in humility; but we also believe in masculine pride and self-assertion. I think that this spiritual conflict creates a strain in our psychology and in the heart of our culture, that has been extremely fruitful both of good and evil, of greatness and intensity, as well as of self-contradiction and hypocrisy and frustration. This theme of spiritual civil war appears often in my verses, especially in the long semi-dramatic poem called "At the Birth of an Age." It appears also in the verses of my betters. Have you thought how many of Shakespeare's heroes, from Hamlet down, are at war in themselves, and in their own souls; whereas heroes of Greek tragedy struggle against fate or each other, but their souls remain simple and undivided?

Another theme that had often engaged his thought was "the expression of a religious feeling, that perhaps must be called pantheism, though I hate to type it with a name." Jeffers described this pantheism, which he at times employed as an antidote to humanism and narcissism, as the feeling, even "the certitude . . . that the world, the universe, is one being, a single organism, one great life that includes all life and all things; and is so beautiful that it must be loved and reverenced; and in moments of mystical vision we identify ourselves with it." He added that this was the "exact opposite of Oriental pantheism." Whereas the Hindu mystic found God in his own soul and considered the outer world illusion, Jeffers believed "the outer world is real and divine; one's own soul might be called illusion, it is so slight and transitory." I will return to this later.

As Jeffers said, his theme of the self-torturing God requires some explanation. Since I will say little about this particular theme, I shall quote at length Jeffer's comments:

> This divine outer universe is after all not at peace with itself, but full of violent strains and conflicts. The physical world is ruled by opposing tensions. The world of living things is formed by perpetual struggle and irreconcilable desires; and pain is an essential part of life. This is the old dilemma of religions. Some of them run away from it, by regarding the outer world as mere illusion; others explain it by inventing a devil, Satan or Ahriman, and the conflict becomes a struggle between good and evil. But clearly that is not true. The lion that kills is not a bit more evil than the lamb that is killed. The rock that falls on a man's head is no more evil than the rock he was standing on. Obscurely, and perhaps unconsciously, this is recognized in the dreams of many races. The Greek Prometheus, crucified on Caucasus: he was a Titan, of the race of the elder Gods: . . the Christian Jesus, the son of God, who assented to his own crucifixion: . . the Scandinavian Odin, the Chief of Gods, who hanged himself painfully for nine days, wavering in the wind, in order to learn the runes of wisdom: or, according to another story, because he demanded the greatest of sacrificial victims, and the greatest was himself: . . there is a tortured God in every mythology; and this seemed to me the fittest symbol to express something that is most beautiful, and painful, and true.

He turned then to "the simplest and commonest theme" in his verse: the landscape of the Monterey Coast-range, which he insisted was not just the scene for his narrative verse "but also the chief actor in it."[15] Though the coast is described throughout his narrative poems, he chose to read a short poem about a section of the coast he thought "too beautiful to be the scene of any narrative of mine." The stark lines of "The Place for No Story" express a reverence for the nonhuman world that can only be called Jeffersian:

The coast hills at Sovranes Creek:
No trees, but dark scant pasture drawn thin
Over rock shaped like flame;
The old ocean at the land's foot, the vast
Gray extension beyond the long white violence;
A herd of cows and the bull
Far distant, hardly apparent up the dark slope;
And the gray air haunted with hawks:
This place is the noblest thing I have ever seen.
No imaginable
Human presence here could do anything
But dilute the lonely self-watchful passion.

Jeffers remarked that when he was preparing his address it occurred to him that birds of prey appear so often in his lines that "hawk and falcon might be called a characteristic theme." Hawks appear often in his poetry "partly because there are so many in our mountains, and of so many kinds,—marshhawk and red-tail, Cooper's hawk and sparrowhawk and duckhawk—that is the American peregrine falcon—but I won't continue the list. And partly also because the hawk has symbolic values that are all the better for being diverse and multiform. And partly because I nursed a broken-winged hawk once and its savage individualism caught my fancy." Out of that experience he made one of the great poems of modern literature, "Hurt Hawks."

His themes then are the ancient ones. Living during a period of incredible change Jeffers sought always to focus on those things that abide. He focused not on that which resists change; nothing does or can stay the same in a dynamic world of ceaseless flow. Rather he looked for those shapers—call them principles, if you will—that lie behind the visible mask of nature. Though a philosophical materialist, he believed that the atomic presence depended on and was impelled by an essence (or in any case a force) that possesses neither shape nor weight. (There are similarities between Jeffers's primary mover and the Platonic theory of ideas.) Hence his interest in myths, "the phantom rulers of humanity" as he called them in *Roan Stallion*:

That without being are yet more real than what they are born of, and without shape, shape that which makes them:
The nerves and the flesh go by shadowlike, the limbs and the lives shadowlike, these shadows remain, these shadows
To whom temples, to whom churches, to whom labors and wars, visions and dreams are dedicate. . . .

Still, there is always in Jeffers a counterpoint to the central point, a relative permanence in a sea of change. Even in periods of greatest social and philosophical change, human nature remains essentially unchanged, so far anyhow as the mind can discern from history. In "The Beaks of Eagles," he remarks the incredible changes that have occurred during the lifetime of the she-eagle, insisting that though it is better for man to try all changes rather than "go down the dinosaur's way" he needs also "to know that his needs and nature are no more changed in fact in ten thousand years than the beaks of eagles."

At the beginning of this introduction I quoted Van Doren's approval of Jeffers's remark that the proper function of the poet was not to express but to present. I think it obvious that Jeffers does present his reader with a world, certainly a larger world than any other poet of his time has given us. But in his presentation there is also interpretation. Like all great writers he wants us to understand as well as appreciate. Thus Jeffers was less than candid when he insisted that all he, or his reader, needed to do was look on, and admire. After all, art is one thing, life another. Art attempts to make static some aspect of what can never be at rest. Moreover, the artist must give shape and meaning to a part of the cosmic flow that would otherwise be shapeless and meaningless. H. L. Mencken stated the case against "simple representation" with admirable precision: "Art can never be simple representation. It cannot deal solely with precisely what is. It must, at the least, present the real in the light of some recognizable ideal; it must give to the eternal farce, if not some moral, then at all events some direction. For without that formulation there can be no clear-cut separation of the individual will from the general stew and turmoil of things, and without that separation there can be no coherent drama, and without that drama there can be no evocation of emotion, and without that emotion art is unimaginable."[16] In his "Apology for Bad Dreams," Jeffers says essentially the same thing.

In the following pages I shall be concerned almost solely with the meaning of various of Jeffers's poems. I am more interested in what Jeffers said than in how he said it. Neither shall I be much concerned with the influences on his thought or style—for two reasons: one, other writers have examined at length and in depth the influences; and two, even when we can say for sure that this or that writer influenced him in this or that way, we still say nothing substantive about Jeffers. I know for instance that Milton and Pope were favorites of, respectively, Wordsworth and Byron, but that fact contributes precious little to my understanding of the two later poets. It is also easy to be misled by so-called influences. We know that Jeffers was an early admirer of Shelley and Nietzsche. Are we then to assume that he adopted their views concerning poetry, God, nature, man, morality, etcetera? Assume any of that and you would be entirely wrong—as I think his poetry abundantly proves.

Critics have nevertheless insisted on calling Jeffers a Nietzschean. Once a critical estimate, about influences anyhow, has become well known it is taken for granted—in part, perhaps, because influences are not after all very important. I have no doubt that many people who have called Jeffers a Nietzschean know very little about the philosopher; they simply repeat what seems unworthy of challenge like schoolboys repeating a textbook lesson. Moreover there are similarities to be found in the two writers, particularly in their central concern for values. Both were deeply imbued with a historical sense that enabled them to place in perspective our (unhappy, they called it) age. Each was pagan or, more precisely, Greek in associating the Good with knowledge and in rejecting the a priori reasoning that has been basic to Christian theology. Moral certitudes are thus the progeny of ignorance. Instead of viewing life in moral terms, they saw it as primarily aesthetic experience. Each was iconoclastic, as much concerned with exploding false (outworn and hence harmful) values as he was interested in proposing new values. The values they propose are, however, quite different. There are similarities in their temperaments. Though neither possessed much sense of humor, each displays a bitter, caustic wit, and neither is at all averse to using his wit to attack the sacred cows of the most popular of all modern faiths—democracy. If democracy really is rule by the common man, either directly or through representation, then it is too much to hope that democratic governments should do other than reflect the fear and greed that are the hallmarks of average men. Moreover the rulers of a democratic state are compelled to practice an art that is essentially degrading. Mencken put it bluntly (and I think irrefutably) in *Notes on Democracy* (1926):

> There is the art of the demagogue, and there is the art of what may be called, by a shot-gun marriage of Latin and Greek, the demaslave. They are complementary, and both of them are degrading to their practitioners. The demagogue is one who preaches doctrines he knows to be untrue to men he knows to be idiots. The demaslave is one who listens to what these idiots have to say and then pretends that he believes it himself. Every man who seeks elective office under democracy has to be either the one thing or the other, and most men have to be both.[17]

That Nietzsche and Jeffers share certain general views is obvious, but in their specifics they are far apart. Radcliffe Squires noted various of their oppositions in his *The Loyalties of Robinson Jeffers* (1956) and so, at least one would hope, helped open the way to a more judicious reading of Jeffers. But unfortunately Squires substituted an even worse mistake for the Nietzschean error when he attempted to show that Jeffers was really a Schopenhaueran. In other words, we are asked to believe that Jeffers was really an extreme Cartesian—an idealistic supporter of the insane belief that everything is emanation of the ego. Schopenhauer's one important book begins with this famous absurdity: " 'The world is my idea': this is a truth that holds good for everything that lives and knows, though man alone can bring it into reflective and abstract consciousness." No statement could be farther from the world view of Robinson Jeffers, who considered consciousness little more than atomic residue, a kind of fortuitous eyelet through which, momentarily, we might perceive the eternal magnificence of the Real. Jeffers made the Stoic identification of God with the world, whereas Schopenhauer, and most other romantics, subscribed to a neo-Platonic theory of ideas which treated the world of sense and its miseries as being unreal—or, in any case, as being dependent upon a conceptualizing mind or perceiver. Schopenhauer sought to reconcile men to their fate through denial of the sensual world; Jeffers shows us that men should appreciate their fate through acceptance of that world. He is thus much closer to the Nietzschean *amor fati* than he is to its opposite—Schopenhauer's abnegation of the sensual world and his retreat into Idea. I must add that Squires, whose book is actually quite good in most ways, stands almost alone in his view.

In a recent study, *Robinson Jeffers: Poet of Inhumanism* (Madison: University of Wisconsin Press, 1971), Arthur B. Coffin attempts to refute Squires's claim that Jeffers was heavily influenced by Schopenhauer. He prefers the more popular error about influences and devotes three of his eight chapters to "Jeffers and Nietzsche, the Beginning," "Jeffers and Nietzsche, the Middle Period," and "Jeffers and Nietzsche, the Final Period." Coffin concludes his study with this sentence: "The proper study for the reading of Jeffers, then, is *Thus Spoke Zarathustra* and *De Rerum Natura*." One might as well say that the proper study for reading Shakespeare is Plutarch and Hollingshead. Actually the latter statement makes more sense than does Coffin's since, as we all know, Shakespeare borrowed various of his stories from those writers. But the proper study for reading Shakespeare is, of course, Shakespeare; just as the proper study for reading Jeffers is Jeffers. All else is ancillary—helpful perhaps but subordinate. The matter of influences I happily leave to others.

And I shall be, as I remarked above, as little concerned with other critics of Jeffers as with possible influences. It would be simple enough to show that this or that writer has written perceptively about some aspect of his work, while that other critic foolishly misinterpreted what should have been obvious. If I do not always resist that temptation—so enticing because it is so self-complimentary—I hope at least to keep it to a bare minimum. For those readers interested in the scholarship, I highly recommend the annotated bibliographical study by Alex A. Vardamis, *The Critical Reputation of Robinson Jeffers* (Hamden, Conn.: Archon Books, 1972).

TWO The Business of Poetry

Passion is the sum-total of humanity. Without passion, religion, history, romance, art, would all be useless. —Balzac

Like most American poets—the important ones in any case—Robinson Jeffers was slow in reaching his artistic maturity. One recalls that Whitman wrote nothing of note before the age of thirty-five; that Dickinson, who wrote a few fine poems in her twenty-eighth year, was past thirty before composing those lyrics which put her among the world's greatest poets; that E. A. Robinson, though one of our most precocious poets, certainly did his best work after reaching the age of thirty; that Edgar Lee Masters was forty-five when it was suggested to him that he use *The Greek Anthology* as a model for what was to be his single important volume; that Frost was thirty-nine when his first volume, *A Boy's Will*, was published; that Wallace Stevens's *Harmonium* appeared in 1923 when he was forty-four; that Pound was in his mid-thirties before finding a voice of his own; that Eliot's few published poems (about three dozen in all) did not begin appearing until 1917 when he was nearly thirty. Though the list is hardly complete, I think it instructive that Americans, with rare exceptions (Poe and Millay being probably the leading examples), have been late-bloomers.

Reading Jeffers's early verse (now seldom read by anyone but the specialist) one is astonished at how far removed it is from the later work. When his first poems saw print in the *Aurora*, an undergraduate monthly literary magazine of Occidental College, he was sixteen and already convinced that he would be a poet. The following year he sold his first poem, "The Condor," to the *Youth's Companion.* His first volume, *Flagons and Apples*, was published at his own expense in 1912. Four years later Macmillan published *Californians.* It would be impossible to recognize the verse in those first volumes as that of Jeffers, whereas almost every line of poetry written after about 1920 bears his stamp clearly.

Though he had written what might be called nature poetry from the beginning, Jeffers chose to fill his first volume with love poems. *Flagons and Apples* brims with all that is dear to sad young Werthers. Lovers quarrel and part, women are praised for their beauties of form and face, a jejune cynicism informs verses that speak of eternal love that lasts but a season, the author refers to himself as "a mad and drunken poet," summer loves are ever on the wane, and so on. Childe Harold come home to roost on the Pacific coast. There are poems "To Helen, Whose Remembrance Leaves No Peace" and "To Aileen-of-the-Woods," and "To Canidia," and one called simply "Nyssa."

In *Californians* Jeffers employed more elaborate verse forms, such as terza rima and ottava rima, than he did in *Flagons*, but the poetry remains remarkable for its respectable mediocrity. There are, however, notable differences between the two volumes. Extreme subjectivity begins to give way to a more objective stance; the poet concentrates more on the world outside than on his personal aches and laments. Love of the natural world replaces love of individuals. Later this "loving outward" will be transformed into a commandment and will occupy a major place in the philosophic poetry. By the time we get to *Tamar and Other Poems* (1924), the first volume of truly Jeffersian verse, the youthful experiments, with an exception or two, have been left forever. In the Swinburnean embarrassment he entitled "Songs of the Dead Men," there is an unhappy remembrance of things past. For example, the second of the songs, "To Death," begins in this tripping fashion:

Was it lovely to lie among violets ablossom in the valleys of love on the breast of the south?
It was lovely but lovelier now
To behold the calm head of the dancer we dreaded, his curls are as tendrils of the vineyard, O Death
Sweet and more sweet is your dancing.

To quote more would be unkind. Incredible though it may seem, these three songs are placed cheek by jowl with such lyrics as "To the Stone-Cutters," "Gale in April," "Wise Men in Their Bad Hours," and "Continent's End."

As early as 1912 Jeffers had commented (in a letter to Una Call Kuster, whom he would marry the following year) on his poetic theory, saying that "poetry should be a blending of fire and earth—

should be made of solid and immediate things, of the earth earthy, which are set on fire by human passion."[1] Needless to say, nearly a decade would pass before theory and practice coalesced. Though he rephrased and revised that early view several times during his life, he never changed its essential message. Thirty-six years later, in one of his most important statements on the wellsprings of great poetry, he spoke of that extreme passion which lies beyond good and evil:

> Lately I had occasion to read more attentively the *Medea* of Euripides, and considering the reverence that cultivated people feel toward Greek tragedy I was a little shocked by what I read. Tragedy has been regarded, ever since Aristotle, as a moral agent, a purifier of the mind and emotions. But the story of *Medea* is about a criminal adventurer and his gun-moll; it is no more moral than the story of Frankie and Johnny; only more ferocious. And so with the yet higher summits of Greek tragedy, the Agamemnon series and the Oedipus Rex; they all tell primitive horror-stories, and the conventional pious sentiments of the chorus are more than balanced by the bad temper and wickedness, or folly, of the principal characters. What makes them noble is the poetry; the poetry, and the beautiful shapes of the plays, and the extreme violence born of extreme passion.
>
> That is to say, three times, the poetry—the poetry of words, the poetry of structure and the poetry of action. These are stories of disaster and death, and it is not in order to purge the mind of passions but because death and disaster are exciting. People love disaster, if it does not touch them too nearly—as we run to see a burning house or a motor crash— and also it gives occasion for passionate speech; it is a vehicle for the poetry.[2]

In a preceding paragraph Jeffers made it clear that he did not consider poetry a moral agent, and certainly not a replacement for religions, which once provided us with moral dicta. Many writers of the past hundred years have insisted that art can, and should, perform the office of moralizer. In other words, Art (with a capital A) has for such people become not only a religion but *the* religion—something to be worshiped, and something that might provide us with ethical criteria. To accomplish this, art would of necessity cease to be an interpretation and criticism of life. For example, Wallace Stevens, who at times mistook the imagination—that is, his imagination—for the voice of God or the gods, once remarked that when one ceased to believe in God, then poetry "takes [God's] place as life's redemption." He then added, "Poetry is a purging of the world's poverty and change and evil and death."[3] Jeffers would doubtless have dismissed such extravagant claims as extreme romantic nonsense. He considered such preciosity almost as bad as proposing that we make the average educated man the arbiter of poetry—the sort of man who may have an uneasy respect for poetry and who "associates it vaguely with 'ideals' and a better world, and may quote Longfellow on solemn occasions. This piety without instinct or judgment is a source of boredom, insincerity and false reputations; it is as bad as the delusions of the little groups; it is worse, because more constant." Among the "delusions of the little groups" he would have placed the belief that art was a moralizer or that it might take the place of religion. In a short paragraph he deplored, through implication, such views as being little more than absurd attempts at self-aggrandizement:

> I write verses myself, but I have no sympathy with the notion that the world owes a duty to poetry, or any other art. Poetry is not a civilizer, rather the reverse, for great poetry appeals to the most primitive instincts. It is not necessarily a moralizer; it does not necessarily improve one's character; it does not even teach good manners. It is a beautiful work of nature, like an eagle or a high sunrise. You owe it no duty. If you like it, listen to it; if not, let it alone.

Certainly Plato knew that great poetry appeals to "the most primitive instincts," and for that reason he banned the poets from his visionary Republic. After all, he wished to establish an orderly society founded on reason. And to do that, he considered it mandatory to protect the populace from their irrational propensities, which he sought to do by simply censoring much that is human in humanity. Realizing the impossibility of any such prohibition, Aristotle sought to make art, particularly poetic and dramatic art, work toward the end of civilizing the people. He wished to turn poetic drama into a means of civilizing the people, or at least allowing them an expedient valve through which they might vent their emotional drives. At the Dionysian festivals the poets (at least according to the Aristotelian poetic ideal) were to uncover those hidden depths of the unconscious in order to cleanse the audience through a partial infection and thus immunize them against emotional excess in their daily lives. There is no evidence whatsoever that such a vaccination was effective in Greece or elsewhere. Today various behavioral psychologists, B. F. Skinner for one, advocate even more stringent means of depriving the human animal of his animalistic urges, and of his freedom no less.

Jeffers would never propose that poetry should be turned into the handmaiden of society, nor was he at all in favor of restricting human freedom, which is limited in any case. It should be pointed out, however, that though he believed poetry was as amoral as the unreasoning beauty of the universe, he felt it could be nonetheless instructive. Rather than enable people to escape their true natures poetry should, he believed, provide insight into human nature. *To understand*—that is the most important verb in the language to Jeffers. Only through understanding, which is uniquely human, might man go beyond the self to the nonhuman world and discover beauty. Poetry is thus a means of discovery. In the final analysis, it is not so much men's relation to other men that matters as it is man's relation to the natural world. Begin with the latter relationship, Jeffers says, and the former will take care of itself, or will in any case be less a neurotic preoccupation.

The fact is, however, that twentieth-century man has been more interested in such wholly human "sciences" as psychology and sociology than in the infinitely more important natural sciences. It should surprise no one that the more neurotic a person or a people are the more likely they will be concerned with the pseudosciences; it matters little if the neurosis is cause or effect of the concern. I do not mean that the problem is peculiarly modern, only that it has grown vastly in the last few decades. Or perhaps I should say the last three or four centuries. Before ever looking very closely at the world and learning its language, we were stuck on the problem, Hamlet's problem, of how to look. When empiricism took an introspective turn, as George Santayana has pointed out, it began to doubt that anything could be known. "Far from being an exercise of intelligence, [British empiricism] retracted all understanding, all interpretation, all instinctive faith; far from furnishing a sure record of the truths of nature, it furnished a set of pathological facts, the passive subject-matter of psychology. . . . The irony of logic actually made English empiricism, understood in this psychological way, the starting-point for transcendentalism and for German philosophy."[4] In its exclusive concern for states of mind and body-mind relationships, psychology finally succeeds in withholding or in any case obscuring that knowledge which is gained sensually—our knowledge of the natural world. Indeed, the world to such idealism ceases to be thing-in-itself and becomes mere mental construct. It is easy to see how this sort of skepticism began to affect, or infect, even the natural sciences. "The higher superstition," as Santayana wrote, "the notion that nature dances to the tune of some comprehensive formula or some magic rhyme, thus reappeared among those who claimed to speak for natural science. In their romantic sympathy with nature they attributed to her an excessive sympathy with themselves; they overlooked her infinite complications and continual irony, and candidly believed they could measure her with their thumb-rules." I can imagine no better critique of romantic inversion. Think of Wordsworth's belief in "natural sympathy" or the psychological narcissism of Coleridge or the "Nature" of Emerson (either the essay of that name or his concept of nature). It should be noted, however, that in the half century since Santayana wrote his critique the natural sciences have, or so it seems to me, moved away from the stultifying effect of psychology. Philosophy, on the other hand, as Huntington Cairns remarked, seems almost hopelessly lost in the endless maze of epistemology and the severely logical analysis of categories.

II

Near the end of Jeffers's long apprenticeship, or, as he would put it, his belated maturation, he wrote an important statement on his poetic principles. In giving permission to S. S. Alberts to publish the two fragments that survived, he remarked that the writing seemed to him "very bad—smart and over-emphatic"; he did say, however, that it might have been useful as a form of writing to himself.[5] Actually the statement provides insight, as Alberts knew, into Jeffers's mind at a time when he was reaching poetic maturity. In later prose commentary he did little more than expand on ideas enunciated here, but the rock of his poetics was clearly formed and described. Indeed, his infrequent prose statements from that time forward (the fragments are dated June 1922) are so clear and emphatic that criticism in the sense of elucidation is disarmed and seems superfluous. In one of the fragments he wrote, "The poet is not to make beauty but to herald beauty; and beauty is everywhere; it needs only senses and intelligence to perceive it." Secondly, since the poet "does not write chiefly for his own generation," he must necessarily concern himself only with permanent things, "or things that are permanent because they are perpetually renewed, like grass and humanity. The most important part of a poem is the subject; and permanence is the one essential element in the subject of poetry." In the fragments he says little that is in any way original, but there is one remark that catches the eye: "In our world where all things are beautiful it is the poet's business to choose what is abiding." This surely was written in a moment of extreme euphoria, since it is obvious that all things are not beautiful. When Jeffers exaggerated, it was nearly always in his praise of life. Here he verges dangerously close to the indiscriminate yea-saying of Emerson, the difference (and it is quite an important difference) being that he found beauty where Emerson found moral good. Jeffers's extraordinary delight in life helps explain his view that the importance or value of a thing is in direct ratio to the degree of its permanence.

It is amazing how many times the word *permanence* recurs in Jeffers. And all the more amazing since he depicts a world that is in flux, a world in which nothing abides or retains shape. As he remarked in *Roan Stallion*, that which stays, and which shapes the phenomenological world, is itself without shape. Permanence then is to be found less in things than it is in relations. But it is the tangible thing, whose essence lies within the reach of our sense organs, that the poet must celebrate. In "Point Joe," from his first important volume, *Tamar and Other Poems* (1924), Jeffers reiterated his view concerning the proper subject matter of poetry:

Permanent things are what is needful in a poem, things temporally
Of great dimension, things continually renewed or always present.

Grass that is made each year equals the mountains in her past and future;
Fashionable and momentary things we need not see nor speak of.

Contemporary events mattered only insofar as they revealed some aspect of what was constantly renewable and therefore always present. Even when he wrote of the impending war in the thirties, Jeffers clearly showed that he was examining events that were new only in the sense that those living at the time had never experienced them. Those aspects of modern life that were ephemeral or exceptional he relegated to the province of prose. Such a view explains his interest in myths, whose meaning remains essentially unchanged from one age to the next. In his foreword to *The Selected Poetry of Robinson Jeffers* (1938), he spoke of the happy accident that brought him and his bride to the Monterey coast mountains, where he could "see people living—amid magnificent unspoiled scenery—essentially as they did in the Idyls or the Sagas, or in Homer's Ithaca."

In his narrative poems he showed humans performing acts that had been performed since man began. His characters react here and now to pressures and movers that have been present in the genes throughout the life span of the species. In *Roan Stallion* he explains an act of California, his central character, by showing first that the microcosm recapitulates the macrocosm:

The atom bounds-breaking,
Nucleus to sun, electrons to planets, with recognition
Not praying, self-equaling, the whole to the whole, the microcosm
Not entering nor accepting entrance, more equally, more utterly, more incredibly conjugate
With the other extreme and greatness; passionately perceptive of identity. . . .

In the next lines Jeffers describes the unwilling (in the sense that California does not will to act in a particular way, but is rather willed upon) and unconscious desire of his character as being the expression of "the phantom rulers of humanity" which are in time contiguous and in strength coequal with the present as it grows from out of the past and slides into the future. Which is to say, Jeffers reverses the normal view of loss and gain: we do not lose anything to time-past (except, momentarily, the shapes of matter and events); rather, we grow out of time-past and, in turn, pass on that which we inherit to time-future. The lines are most important, I feel, to any discussion of Jeffers's poetry and to any understanding of the principles which underlie his concept of beauty and the art of the poet whose sole mission is to express that beauty. The "fire" of the opening lines glows and throbs within the skull of California, described as "a small round stone, that smelt human, black hair growing from it":

The fire threw up figures
And symbols meanwhile, racial myths formed and dissolved in it, the phantom rulers of humanity
That without being are yet more real than what they are born of, and without shape, shape that which makes them;
The nerves and the flesh go by shadowlike, the limbs and the lives shadowlike, these shadows remain, these shadows
To whom temples, to whom churches, to whom labors and wars, visions and dreams are dedicate:
Out of the fire in the small round stone that black moss covered, a crucified man writhed up in anguish;
A woman covered by a huge beast in whose mane the stars were netted, sun and moon were his eyeballs,
Smiled under the unendurable violation, her throat swollen with the storm and blood-flecks gleaming
On the stretched lips; a woman—no, a dark water, split by jets of lightning, and after a season
What floated up out of the furrowed water, a boat, a fish, a fire-globe?
It had wings, the creature,
And flew against the fountain of lightning, fell burnt out of the cloud back to the bottomless water. . .
Figures and symbols, castlings of the fire, played in her brain; but the white fire was the essence,
The burning in the small round shell of bone that black hair covered, that lay by the hooves on the hilltop.

The "crucified man" is of course Jesus, the god of California. The vision of a woman being "covered" by a huge beast incorporates elements of nearly all anthropomorphic religions; his cosmic proportions ("sun and moon were his eyeballs") are also typical of human concepts of God. The flashes of light—that is, symbols and racial myths—in this ignorant girl's brain are really no different in kind from most other mystical experiences of man-made divinities. If the desire for sexual union with a beast appears perverse, we must remember that the love of man or woman for a beast produced most of the gods of Egypt and many of the demigods of Greece. Moreover, the myth of Europa probably occasioned the naming of California.

The lines which obviously refer to that essence, shadowy and difficult to articulate though it is, remind one of Ahab's exhortation in *Moby-Dick*: "All visible objects, man, are but as pasteboard masks. But in each event—in the living act, the undoubted deed—there, some unknown but still reasoning thing puts forth the mouldings of its features from behind the unreasoning mask. If man will strike, strike through the mask!" Jeffers would object to but one word in this speech—*reasoning*. His God, unlike Ahab's, was in no sense reasoning, unless one believes that the molecule reasons. Moreover, Jeffers would say, as he does in the second stanza of "Birth-Dues," that he who fights God, as did Ahab, "eats his own flesh and perishes of hunger." That God exists is as apparent to Jeffers as is the world we inhabit and the worlds that extend into infinity. His being we know sensuously; His essence manifests itself in beauty, which the poet or artist celebrates. And, as we shall see, the artist mimics God, is the ape of God, when he translates that beauty, human or nonhuman, for others to behold.

III

In an unpublished preface written in August 1923, which he intended to include in *Tamar and Other Poems*,[6] Jeffers objected to those who regarded poetry as a refuge from life (though he would say in "Apology for Bad Dreams" that the poet, in the act of creation, engaged in a catharsis whereby he might partially escape the fates which befell his "imagined victims"). While admitting that "poetry has been in fact refuge and ornament and diversion," he insisted that it was, in its higher forms, none of these: "not a refuge but an intensification, not an ornament but essential, not a diversion but an incitement. As presenting the universal beauty poetry is an incitement to life; an incitement to contemplation, because it serves to open our intelligence and senses to that beauty." Here, as in later comments on poetry, Jeffers aired discontents with modern verse. While admitting that many "laws" of poetry were "too basic to be conscious," he listed three of the attributes that were most ignored by his contemporaries: the need of poetry to deal with permanent things, to be rhythmic, and to avoid affectation. While there is little here to arrest the attention of the reader. Jeffers's forthright criticism clearly reveals the direction his own poetry would henceforth take and at the same time provides insight into why he seemed and still seems an isolate in modern literature. The following three paragraphs show, above all else, that he considered the sources of poetry to lie outside the mind. With Donne he might well have written that "the body makes the minde." I quote the following selection from the unpublished preface at length, first of all, because of its central importance in our understanding Jeffers and, secondly, because contemporary poetry has, if anything, moved even further from the reality that Jeffers insists is central to all great poetry:

> The superfluousness of imitative poetry is quite recognized nowadays (in principle) by everyone who thinks on the subject; and this is a gain; but a second-rate mind is sure to confuse eccentricity with originality; its one way of saying something new is to deform what it has to say; like the bobbed fox it sets a fashion for third-rate minds; and these are inevitably imitative, only now they follow a bad model instead of a good one. Here, I believe, is the origin of those extraordinary affectations which distinguish so much of what is called modern poetry. But this is not a disease of adults; and all there is to say further on the subject is that one's clearest thinking is not certain enough, nor one's most natural choice of words appropriate enough, for the passionate presentment of beauty which is poetry's function. If we alter thought or expression for any of the hundred reasons: in order to seem original, or to seem sophisticated, or to conform to a fashion, or to startle the citizenry, or because we fancy ourselves decadent, or merely to avoid commonplace: for whatever reason we alter them, for that reason they are made false. They have fled from reality.
>
> As to the necessity of dealing with permanent things I have spoken in the verses called "Point Joe," in this volume; and need but add that permanence is only another aspect of reality; a railroad, for example, is not real as a mountain is; it is actual, in its fantastic way, for a century or two; but it is not real; in most of the human past and most of the human future it is not existent. (Novelty is in itself no bar to poetic quality; permanence is the condition. An airplane is as poetic as a plow or a ship; it is not existent in the human past except as a most ancient of dreams, but it is existent, in some form or other, in all the human future. It is a real thing, not a temporary expedient, but the incarnation of metal and tissue of a permanent human faculty.) Most of our inventions are mere expedients, or the possible essential in them remains hidden; and here is what makes the life of modern cities barren of poetry; it is not a lasting life; and it is lived among unrealities. A life immensely fantastic is not poetic; and what is romantic is not usually poetic, though people think it is.
>
> This poetry must be rhythmic. By rhythm I do not mean the dissolved and unequal cadences of good prose, nor the capricious divisions of what is

> called free verse, (both these being sometimes figuratively spoken of as rhythmic), but a movement as regular as meter, or as the tides. A tidal recurrence, whether of quantity or accent, or of both, or of syllables and rhyme as in French verse, or of syllables and rhyme and tone as in Chinese verse, or of phrase and thought as in old Hebrew verse, has always been the simplest and inevitably one of the qualities of poetry. A reason is not far to seek. Recurrence, regular enough to be rhythmic, is the inevitable quality of life, and of life's environment. Prose belongs rather to that indoor world where lamplight abolishes the returns of day and night, and we forget the seasons. Human caprice, the volatile and superficial part of us, can only live sheltered. Poetry does not live in that world but in all the larger, and the poetry cannot speak without remembering the turns of the sun and moon, and the rhythm of the ocean, and the recurrence of human generations, the returning waves of life and death. Our daily talk is prose; we do not often talk about real things, even when we live with them; but about fictitious things; expedients, manners, past times, and aspects of personality that are not real because they are superficial and exceptional.[7]

The eternally recurring rhythms of reality. Almost, indeed, Nietzsche's eternal recurrence, which so effectively removed purpose (and with it God and judgment) from the world. Certainly Jeffers would agree with the German prophet that there is no "end of things," no future goal toward which history or nature tends. Moreover such a view invests life with heightened quality in so far as its end or purpose is existential, in the here and now. Although any such cyclic theory of life will not deny the casual properties of the past, it will remove from both past and future any static quality at the same time it denies all moral absolutes, a denial which intensifies and makes more immediate the problem of right and wrong.

During this period Jeffers made the vow "to shear the rhyme-tassels" from his verse because he considered them largely extraneous and sometimes injurious. In place of metric measure, he substituted a system of stressed and unstressed syllables. The accentual lines control the tempo, marking time like meter but allowing a freedom not possible to any verse encased in a metric corset. In an early study of Jeffers's prosody, Herbert Klein discussed this use of stress as a means of defining and limiting a line. The line is limited by the number of stresses, sometimes as many as ten, often as few as three. The tempo depends upon the line's quantity, which may be attained by the length of the vowels or by the complex of consonants following a short vowel which causes the syllable to appear long. Jeffers wrote Klein that he wanted his poetry to be "rhythmic and not rhymed, moulded more closely to the subject than older English poetry is, but as formed as alcaics if that were possible too." He remarked that the unstressed syllables played a part in the quantity of a line and that the rhythm had several sources—physics, biology, the beat of the blood, "the tidal environments of life," and a "desire for singing emphasis that prose does not have."[8] Occasionally Jeffers returned to traditional forms, particularly the sonnet form, which he handled extremely well. Reading those later poems, one is hardly aware of the rhyme or the metrics.

IV

In the introduction to the Modern Library edition of *Roan Stallion, Tamar and Other Poems* (1935), Jeffers discussed his early poetry. He recalled there the bitterness he felt when he was twenty-seven over not having produced any poetry of worth. Already older than Keats when he died, Jeffers had written many verses, "but they were all worthless." He spoke of the need for originality, "without which a writer of verses is only a verse-writer," and of the manner in which his contemporaries were attaining it—"by going farther and farther along the way that perhaps Mallarmé's aging dream had shown them, divorcing poetry from reason and ideas, bringing it nearer to music, finally to astonish the world with what would look like pure nonsense and would be pure poetry." He guessed that his fellow poets had been merely imitating each other, as he had been imitating Shelley and Milton. Certainly in imitation lay confession that one was not original, particularly if one imitated Mallarmé and his followers, who renounced intelligibility in order to concentrate on the music of poetry. As for their successors, they "could only make further renunciations; ideas had gone, now meter had gone, imagery would have to go; then recognizable emotions would have to go; perhaps at last words might have to go or give up their meaning, nothing be left but musical syllables. Every advance required the elimination of some aspect of reality, and what could it profit me to know the direction of modern poetry if I did not like that direction?"

In effect, much modern poetry strove to gain originality through amputation, by almost literally cutting itself off from reality, by shutting out the world. Since to Jeffers the world was all, individual consciousness being one of the phenomena, such a course seemed suicidal; hence his decision not to become "modern." In short, he "did not want to become slight and fantastic, abstract and unintelligible."

Whether one accepts those four adjectives as descriptive of much modern art, it is not difficult to understand why Jeffers chose them. Certainly the general drift of art in all its forms has been away from an understanding or interpretation of the world outside and toward the inner world of self. Reasons for this retreat on the part of artists are not hard to find. To begin with, science has, oddly enough, had the effect of splintering man's world rather than unifying it. While we have inherited the chilling conclusions of science we have in no way been able to keep pace, psychologically and morally, with the findings of the mind, which Jeffers described in a marvelous metaphor as "like a many-bladed machine subduing the world with deep indifference." With no intelligible end or goal in the seeming infinity of life forms, we are all in the position of E. A. Robinson's Man Against the Sky, moving alone between the darkness and the glare. The little bit we have learned about existence has taught us that we know next to nothing about nonexistence. We are interested in matter and the play of forces thereon. More and more, we are made to realize that only matter matters. The world of fauna and flora, of men and moths and the mouse in the wall, is phenomenological and may best be viewed up close—through a microscope or through a telescope. In any case, whatever we know for a certainty, we know sensually, empirically.

And the most important thing modern man has learned concerns his place in the universe. Once upon a time, as Jeffers tells us in lines from "Margrave":

The earth was the world and man was its measure, but our minds have looked
Through the little mock-dome of heaven the telescope-slotted observatory eyeball, there space and multitude came in
And the earth is a particle of dust by a sand-grain sun, lost in a nameless cove of the shores of a continent.

Galaxy on galaxy, innumerable swirls of innumerable stars, endured as it were forever and humanity
Came into being, its two or three million years are a moment, in a moment it will certainly cease out from being
And galaxy on galaxy endure after that as it were forever. . . .

A cold and forbidding truth—one that sends most men running for shelter. And if no refuge is to be found outside, where there is only the play of force, of matter in motion, then man looks for it inside amidst the constructs of the individual mind and imagination. Unable to see any unity of things and now prevented by scientific knowledge from making a priori assumptions concerning unity, the artist frequently concludes, somewhat prematurely to be sure, that there is none and further concludes that his proper mission is to reflect the unrelatedness of things—and to do so in a manner that is purely private. Modern poets, as every college sophomore knows, develop their own private symbols on the assumption that no tests may be applied to the perceiver since what is perceived is solely dependent upon the individual perceiver. Actually this is nothing more than idealism souring towards solipsism. As I shall show in the next chapter, the knowledge gained in the last century has paradoxically led to a denial of or retreat from the real—and to the triumph of romanticism, which in its late nineteenth-century and twentieth-century form is the same as escapism.

In the foreword to *The Selected Poetry* Jeffers commented again on the need for poetry to "concern itself with (relatively) permanent things"—this time adding the parenthetical adverb. Only those things in which a reader might be interested and would understand a thousand years from now should occupy the attention of the poet-at-work. One paragraph in particular is important. Here he again states his objections to the direction that modern poetry has taken. There seems to me to be no doubt that he was referring to the verse being composed by those in the Eliot-Pound school, verse he considered "thoroughly defeatist." Notably the paragraph contains scraps of what he had previously written on the subject:

> Long ago, before anything included here was written, it became evident to me that poetry—if it was to survive at all—must reclaim some of the power

> and reality that it was so hastily surrendering to prose. The modern French poetry of that time, and the most "modern" of the English poetry, seemed to me thoroughly defeatist, as if poetry were in terror of prose, and desperately trying to save its soul from the victor by giving up its body. It was becoming slight and fantastic, abstract, unreal, eccentric; and was not even saving its soul, for these are generally anti-poetic qualities. It must reclaim substance and sense, and physical and psychological reality. This feeling has been basic in my mind since then. It led me to write narrative poetry, and to draw subjects from contemporary life; to present aspects of life that modern poetry had generally avoided; and to attempt the expression of philosophic and scientific ideas in verse. It was not in my mind to open new fields for poetry, but only to reclaim old freedom.

In reclaiming that "old freedom" Jeffers set himself apart from other poets of the period, when only Masters and Robinson, among important poets, were writing narrative poetry. (Both those men, by the way, were among his earliest and most enthusiastic supporters.) Considering his view that poetry should concern itself only with those permanent aspects of life, one can understand the disavowal of any intention to open new fields in poetry; indeed, there are no new fields, only new excursions into old country, new renderings of timeworn and everpresent subjects.

From his early twenties to the end of his life, Jeffers commented in his poetry on the "affair" of the poet. Even here he seems a solitary among his contemporaries who preferred the essay or the classroom as a podium for statements concerning their craft. Since he considered poetry important enough to warrant serious concern, Jeffers felt it not just permissible but proper to discuss the aims of poetry in his verse. Given his belief that poetry is more than expression, that it is actually both facsimile of those most enduring aspects of life as well as thing-in-itself, it is logical that the poet should discuss poetry, which, as he said, is "a beautiful work of nature, like an eagle or a high sunrise." Is poetry one of the permanent things in life? If so, it is a likely subject for poetry. It is that simple.

In "Triad," Jeffers says that poetry is as important as science or government; or, rather, he implies that the three human concerns are of equal importance. Notably he criticizes modern science, which has fallen away from its proper concern; and "new Russia," which has not fulfilled its early promise; and, through implication, poetry, which has been turned into a word game. Finally he shows that all three have importance only for humanity and are thus of less importance than those things they seek to explore, direct, or describe. First published in the *Carmel Pine Cone* (19 August 1932) and then in somewhat different form in *Give Your Heart to the Hawks and Other Poems* (1933), "Triad" is a remarkable condensation of views that other writers would be forced to share years later:

Science, that makes wheels turn, cities grow,
Moribund people live on, playthings increase,
But has fallen from hope to confusion at her own business
Of understanding the nature of things;—new Russia,
That stood a moment at dreadful cost half free,
Beholding the open, all the glades of the world
On both sides of the trap, and resolutely
Walked into the trap that has Europe and America;—
The poet, who wishes not to play games with words,
His affair being to awake dangerous images
And call the hawks;—they all feed the future, they serve God,
Who is very beautiful, but hardly a friend of humanity.

In an earlier poem, published in 1925, Jeffers perfectly combined the expression (the awakening of dangerous images) with the criticism or didacticism which is overtly stated in many of the shorter lyrics and is always symbolically present in his long narratives (which are never the idle tales of violence that a few critics, notably Yvor Winters, mistook them for). No one, I daresay, would today dispute the prophetic truth of "Science":

Man, introverted man, having crossed
In passage and but a little with the nature of things this latter century
Has begot giants; but being taken up
Like a maniac with self-love and inward conflicts cannot manage his hybrids.
Being used to deal with edgeless dreams,
Now he's bred knives on nature turns them also inward: they have thirsty points though.
His mind forebodes his own destruction;
Actaeon who saw the goddess naked among the leaves and his hounds tore him.
A little knowledge, a pebble from the shingle,
A drop from the oceans: who would have dreamed this infinitely little too much?

This poem is as nearly flawless as it is possible for a poem to be: I cannot imagine changing a single word. And while it is intellectual, addressed to the mind of the reader, its somber rhythm and imagery evoke an emotional, or physical, response in the reader that is remembered long after the exact wording has been forgotten or mislaid in the vaults of memory. Art and wisdom are married in the lines.

V

In *Poetry, Gongorism, and a Thousand Years*, Jeffers commented on the hypothetical great poet. He was harsh on the symbolists and/or imagists because their poetry tended toward an almost exclusive concern with subjective states of mind. (It should be obvious that Jeffers depended on symbolism and imagery, but with a great difference from the poets of the symbolist and imagist schools.) Their poetry constituted a retreat from the larger questions and problems of life rather than a grappling with those issues. Just as science has fallen into "confusion at her own business / Of understanding the nature of things," substituting for that worthy aim the much less worthy aim of manipulating nature, so too have the symbolists substituted the symbol for the thing symbolized, shadow for substance, at the same time denying, implicitly at least, that poetry should be concerned with understanding.[9] In his strictures Jeffers might well have been thinking of Nietzsche's condemnation of the poets, which he quotes in the foreword to *The Selected Poetry:* "The poets? The poets lie too much." He might have added that people admire them for precisely that trait.

Jeffers was nineteen at the time that phrase of Nietzsche stuck in his mind, but several years would pass before it worked effectively and he decided not to tell lies in verse: "Not to feign any emotion that I did not feel; not to pretend to believe in optimism or pessimism, or unreversible progress; not to say anything because it was popular, or generally accepted, or fashionable in intellectual circles, unless I myself believed it; and not to believe easily." Having thus limited himself, he could expect only hostility from all coteries—from the proletarians, the Marxists, the New Humanists, the New Critics, all the little groups of whatever persuasion. He thus resists categorization. The least academic of all our poets, he wrote about the elemental passions which rule, and generally ruin, the lives of the characters in his long narrative poems; and in the short lyrics, he constantly passed judgment on the larger questions of his own time.

This hypothetical great poet would, Jeffers wrote, "understand that Rimbaud was a young man of startling genius, but not to be imitated; and that 'The Waste Land,' though one of the finest poems of this century and surely the most influential, marks the close of a literary dynasty, not the beginning. He would think of Gerard Hopkins as a talented eccentric, whose verse is so overloaded with self-conscious ornament and improbable emotion that it is hardly readable, except by enthusiasts, and certainly not a model to found one's work on, but a shrill note of warning." Later in this essay, Jeffers remarked that his poet "would distrust the fashionable poetic dialect of his time; but the more so if it is studiously quaint and difficult; for if a poem has to be explained and diagrammed even for contemporary readers, what will the future make of it?" And, as has been shown, Jeffers believed that the poet should write with the readers of the future always in his mind.

Putting his censures or warnings another way, Jeffers states that "our man would turn away from the self-consciousness and naive learnedness, the undergraduate irony, unnatural metaphors, hiatuses, and labored obscurity that are too prevalent in contemporary verse." Rather, he would strive to say something and say it clearly. "He would be seeking to express the spirit of his time (as well as all times), but it is not necessary, because an epoch is confused, that its poet should share its confusions." To avoid those confusions, so that he might see around as well as through his age, the poet would of necessity have to remain detached, for "detachment is necessary to understanding."

That detachment should not, however, be confused with indifference to or separation from the turbid flow of events in which it is man's fate to be caught up. Far from attempting to escape the world, Jeffers sought to live on the closest terms possible with it and to live in company with those people most nearly integrated and whole. The true escapist, Jeffers believed, was the city dweller, the man who insulated himself from the earth by surrounding himself with man-made things, with baubles and noise. Since he lived in a world that was increasingly urban and wrote poems that would be read by individuals whose lives were far more complicated by civilized complexity than was his own, he knew that he would be misunderstood by the many. And though he could write in the preface to the Modern Library edition of *Roan Stallion, Tamar and Other Poems* that he had never considered, once his period of greensickness was past, whether his verses "were original or followed a tendency, or would find a reader," he still wrote a number of apologies for, or more correctly explanations of, his poetic principles. Near the end of his life he was still explaining his attitude toward "Rhythm and Rhyme." That poem, now something of a collector's item, illustrates through its controlled accents precisely what the poem says:

The tide-flow of passionate speech, breath, blood-pulse, the sea's waves and the tide's returns
They make the meter, but rhyme seems a child's game.
Let the low-Latin languages, the lines lacking strong accents, lean on it;
Our north-sea English needs no such ornament.
Born free, and searaid-fed from far shores why would it toggle its hair
With tinkling sheep-bells like Rome's slaves' daughters? [10]

As explanation of his characters, so many of them haunted by dreams, filled with frustrations and desires, and subject to demonic drives they can neither understand nor resist, he composed, among others, "Self-Criticism in February," a kind of dialogue-with-self as well as an answer to critics who might object to his violent themes and harsh portrait of man. In answer to the final objection, "*If only you could sing / That God is love, or perhaps that social / Justice will soon prevail*," he sarcastically concludes, "I can tell lies in prose."

He was aware moreover that in striving for timelessness in his poetry he would be accused by those caught in the passions of the present of not having represented truly the features of man. He could accept and even admire the universal God, whose self-torture can be seen in the strain and tension of the atom, in the perpetual struggle of all living and nonliving things. In numerous poems he celebrated the beauty that grows from that tension. The difficulty lay in finding beauty in man, who seemed the one smear on the face of nature that deserved little praise. He confronts the problem squarely in "De

Rerum Virtute" from *Hungerfield and Other Poems* (1954). In part 4 of the poem he admits that "it is hard to see beauty / In any of the acts of man":

I believe that man too is beautiful,
But it is hard to see, and wrapped up in falsehoods. Michelangelo and the Greek sculptors—
How they flattered the race! Homer and Shakespeare—
How they flattered the race!

In the fifth and final section he resolves the problem, as always, by proposing that man find "value and virtue" in the greater beauty of the nonhuman world:

One light is left us: the beauty of things, not men;
The immense beauty of the world, not the human world.

To thus delimit man's stature has been a favorite occupation of writers and thinkers for hundreds of years, though not until Darwin did we have tangible evidence to support the naturalistic theory of our origin and our kinship to other creatures. And today we are less inclined to argue with Jeffers's view that man is "a sick microbe" than we would be with Emerson's view that he is a fallen god. Of all the witty and usually censorious definitions of man, one of Nietzsche's best expresses the modern temper: "The earth has a skin, and that skin has diseases. One of those diseases is called man."

In "Soliloquy" Jeffers spoke of the risk one runs for not flattering the race and at the same time made an important disclosure of his intentions in the narrative poems:

August and laurelled have been content to speak for an age, and the ages that follow
Respect them for that pious fidelity;
But you have disfeatured time for timelessness.
They had heroes for companions, beautiful youths to dream of, rose-marble-fingered
Women shed light down the great lines;
But you have invoked the slime in the skull,
The lymph in the vessels. They have shown men Gods like racial dreams, the woman's desire,
The man's fear, the hawk-faced prophet's; but nothing
Human seems happy at the feet of yours.
Therefore though not forgotten, not loved, in gray old years in the evening leaning
Over the gray stones of the tower-top,

You shall be called heartless and blind;
And watch new time answer old thought, not a face strange nor a pain astonishing;
But you living be laired in the rock
That sheds pleasure and pain like hailstones.

I think he overstates the penalty—of being called "heartless and blind"—that would be imposed by future readers. Certainly no intelligent reader today would call him either. It is true though that he "disfeatured time for timelessness" in drawing various of his characters, who are less individualized persons than they are vessels engraved with hieroglyphic markings of the racial past. As Radcliffe Squires wisely wrote, "To understand the characters at all, one must understand that they reflect past, present, and future historicity."[11] In contrasting the "august and laurelled" poets (or artists of any sort) who "have been content to speak for an age" with his own attempts to give his creations a timelessness, Jeffers makes an important distinction between those artists who "have shown men Gods like racial dreams" and his own invocation of "the slime in the skull, / The lymph in the vessels." Where earlier men (and one assumes he refers to classical and Renaissance artists primarily) have endeavored to create what they considered perfected or godlike forms, Jeffers assumes the role of creative God interested not only in blowing breath into the clay he molds but in showing the markings on the clay as it was slowly shaped by the evolutionary process. Rather than imitate and incarnate the dreams of perfection that men have always had, he sought to understand the forms that exist in fact.

For the most conclusive statement of his aesthetics, we must look closely at his "Apology for Bad Dreams." In part a defense of his poetic themes, the poem is more importantly an exploration of the artist's (and, by analogy, God's) relationship to his creations. The artist and his materials, the creative force (God), good and evil, and the self-torture through which both artist and God create good and evil from an inherently amoral matter—these central concerns of all Jeffers's poetry combine and coalesce in "Apology for Bad Dreams" to make it one of his most remarkable poems and one of the finest poems of our century. If Jeffers really believed that the poet's sole concern was with the beauty in the world, then, to be logical, he should have been little concerned with humanity. As he said, it takes only eyes to see that the world is beautiful. But what of man and his acts? Is there beauty there? Very little, and difficult to see, Jeffers said. Then why the concern? He tells us in his ars poetica.

Part 1 begins with a description of the beach below and then moves outward to include the ocean and, beyond that, "the fountain / And furnace of incredible light flowing up from the sunk sun." The reader observes the physical scene as if he were viewing it through the lens of a giant camera. And then the lens zooms in on a specific scene, on a phenomenon:

> *In the little clearing a woman*
> *Is punishing a horse; she had tied the halter to a sapling at the edge of the wood, but when the great whip*
> *Clung to the flanks the creature kicked so hard she feared he would snap the halter; she called from the house*
> *The young man her son; who fetched a chain tie-rope, they working together*
> *Noosed the small rusty links round the horse's tongue*
> *And tied him by the swollen tongue to the tree.*
> *Seen from this height they are shrunk to insect size.*
> *Out of all human relation. You cannot distinguish*
> *The blood dripping from where the chain is fastened,*
> *The beast shuddering; but the thrust neck and the legs*
> *Far apart. You can see the whip fall on the flanks. . .*
> *The gesture of the arm. You cannot see the face of the woman.*

At which point the short, five-stress lines of mostly monosyllables give way to longer, flowing lines descriptive of natural pheonomena in contrast to the one phenomenon:

> *The enormous light beats up out of the west across the cloud-bars of the trade-wind. The ocean*
> *Darkens, the high clouds brighten, the hills darken together. Unbridled and unbelievable beauty*
> *Covers the evening world . . . not covers, grows apparent out of it, as Venus down there grows out*
> *From the lit sky. What said the prophet? "I create good: and I create evil: I am the Lord."*

Here Jeffers sets up the polarities of good and evil, both of which emanate from the same fountain—the pool of whirling atoms which discloses the multifarious faces of God. In his listing of God as the source, Jeffers reminds us of Emerson's similar view in "Brahma."

Both the good and the evil polarities derive their particular savor from the passion which acts, here as elsewhere in his poetry, as prime mover. Indeed, one can almost say that passion and God are synonymous terms.

While Jeffers obviously does not accept or condone the act of the woman and her son, he does seem to insist that it is a part of the consistency of things. All such explosions (and that seems the proper word for it) of passion are, as the poem later shows, the transmutations of a self-torturing God just as, on a lower level, all creations of the artist are the residual remains of self-torture. It would be a mistake to see in the oppositions of the "bridled" tongue of the horse and the "unbridled" beauty of nature a mere contrast between human and nonhuman qualities. After all, the act of the woman and son is "out of all *human* relation." Moreover, seen from that height the humans involved are "shrunk to insect size"—an example of the double meaning found so often in his poetry. The literal meaning, having to do with physical distance, is obvious; the more important metaphorical meaning is perhaps less so. Quite simply, the two people are dehumanized, are shown as subhuman; they are in effect demoted from mammals to crustaceans. Like Twain, Swift, Dostoevsky, and numerous other writers, Jeffers found his darkest polarity in those actions of humanity which, paradoxically, strike us as being most inhuman. (In his later years, true enough, Jeffers would insist that such actions were peculiarly human, or all too human.) If one considers cruelty the blackest of crimes, he will perforce list man as the arch-satanic force in the world since only man can commit, in the sense of *willing*, an act of cruelty.

Having set his "poles" in part 1, he begins part 2 with the arresting line, "This coast crying out for tragedy like all beautiful places," which he repeats four lines later, adding after a colon:

and like the passionate spirit of humanity
Pain for its bread: God's, many victims', the painful deaths, the horrible transfigurements: I said in my heart,
"Better invent than suffer: imagine victims
Lest your own flesh be chosen the agonist, or you
Martyr some creature to the beauty of the place." And I said,
"Burn sacrifices once a year to magic

Horror away from the house, this little house here
You have built over the ocean with your own hands
Beside the standing boulders: for what are we,
The beast that walks upright, with speaking lips
And little hair, to think we should always be fed,
Sheltered, intact, and self-controlled? We sooner more liable
Than the other animals. Pain and terror, the insanities of desire; not accidents but essential,
And crowd up from the core:" I imagined victims for those wolves, I made them phantoms to follow,
They have hunted the phantoms and missed the house. It is not good to forget over what gulfs the spirit
Of the beauty of humanity, the petal of a lost flower blown seaward by the night-wind, floats to its quietness.

This is, to be sure, a self-defensive theory of aesthetics, one that critics have considered more Freudian than Aristotelian. By this they presumably mean that Jeffers was more concerned with the cleansing or rather the protection of himself than he was with evoking a cathartic reaction in his reader. But I see no reason to read the passage about burning sacrifices and magicking horror away from his house in so literal a fashion. It may more profitably be read as both a reduction of man and a reminder to himself (and hence to his readers who are no more or less human than the poet) that he was "liable" to the "pain and terror, the insanities of desire" which lie in the path of all our species. His explanation of the "bad dreams" is hence a warning as well. By "imagining victims" he metaphorically remembers "over what gulfs the spirit / Of the beauty of humanity" floats. The beauty of humanity, like "all beautiful places" in the opening line of this section, thus beckons tragedy—that is to say, beauty is destroyed (in the sense of undergoing change) by the very force that created it. Though change is inevitable in a dynamic universe, and thus cannot be considered evil, it is painful to see beauty decay; nor is tragedy beautiful, as some would have it, but is the transformation and even destruction of the beautiful. Such disintegration can best be seen in the cyclic patterns of nature, which Jeffers described in "Shine, Perishing Republic":

I sadly smiling remember that the flower fades to make fruit, the fruit rots to make earth.

Out of the mother; and through the spring exultances, ripeness and decadence; and home to the mother.

In part 3, the most difficult of the four sections to interpret, Jeffers goes beneath the present, which offers only experience, into the past, from which understanding might be gleaned. In contrast to the act we viewed in part 1, he invokes ghosts from the past to act as reminders of our mortality and also as our "redeemers." Here memory and creativity combine to form the understanding that Jeffers considered the most important attribute of all art, more important certainly than its entertainment value. Thus *one* of the functions of art is similar to *the* function of science. Since human nature in history (though not of course when considered biologically or in terms of evolution) is unchanging, we might find in the records of those who preceded us an unconscious guide or at least warning. In speaking of humanity, or even of individuals, Jeffers is seldom content to simply record; he invariably interprets. An eminently civilized poet in the sense that he believed man's only hope lay in his rationality, Jeffers constantly made use of the past in order to show the present was a continuum. It is necessary that "we living keep old griefs in memory," for "to forget evils calls down / Sudden reminders from the cloud: remembered deaths be our redeemers; / Imagined victims our salvation." In memory there are "redeemers"; in creativity there is "salvation." Jeffers says here that to create is to remember. He concludes part 3 with a reference to Tamar Cauldwell, through whose person atavistic voices or presences had wreaked their havoc:

white as the half moon at midnight
Someone flamelike passed me, saying, "I am Tamar Cauldwell, I have my desire,"
Then the voice of the sea returned, when she had gone by, the stars to their towers.
. . . Beautiful country burn again, Point Pinos down to the Sur Rivers
Burn as before with bitter wonders, land and ocean and the Carmel water.

In the final part of the poem Jeffers compares the conscious creations of the poet with the unconscious creations of God, showing that each expression of the creative force is necessarily self-destructive or in any case self-torturing. If God is depicted as artisan, then the poet is "only the ape of that God."

He brays humanity in a mortar to bring the savor
From the bruised root: a man having bad dreams, who invents victims, is only the ape of that God.
He washes it out with tears and many waters, calcines it with fire in the red crucible,
Deforms it, makes it horrible to itself: the spirit flies out and stands naked, he sees the spirit,
He takes it in the naked ecstasy; it breaks in his hand, the atom is broken, the power that massed it
Cries to the power that moves the stars, "I have come home to myself, behold me.
I bruised myself in the flint mortar and burnt me
In the red shell, I tortured myself, I flew forth,
Stood naked of myself and broke me in fragments,
And here am I moving the stars that are me."
I have seen these ways of God: I know of no reason
For fire and change and torture and the old returnings.
He being sufficient might be still. I think they admit no reason; they are the ways of my love.
Unmeasured power, incredible passion, enormous craft: no thought apparent but burns darkly
Smothered with its own smoke in the human brain-vault: no thought outside: a certain measure in phenomena:
The fountains of the boiling stars, the flowers on the foreland, the ever-returning roses of dawn.

In these intense lines is the essence of Jeffers's essentially amoral aesthetic. The artist does more than hold his mirror up to nature, which in any case could do no more than reflect various acts and events from out the infinite flow of matter; rather he goes behind the physical shapes and breaks the atoms, thereby releasing the spirit from its material husk and allowing it, thus momentarily dislocated, to flame. Most importantly, in the creative act there is a disintegration of the self, just as there is a fragmentation of God in all natural beauty. In other words, beauty is the final residue of God's self-torture. It flames before us in "the fountains of the boiling stars, the flowers on the foreland, the ever-returning roses of dawn." So far as the mind can perceive there is no reason for divine beauty any more than there is reason in the creative impulse of the artist.

In the last three lines, behind each of the four colons, are the ascending steps that lead from the necessary ingredients of art to the unconscious cycles of time and space. Although there is no thought outside the brain-vault, what measure there is must be found in phenomena rather than in human idea; which is to say, man imports his values from the natural world against which he struggles and from which he derives his essence. The only valid measuring stick is found outside, among the natural phenomena. When man considers himself the measure of all things, he commits the arch-crime against himself and against the world.

In his best narrative poems—*Roan Stallion*, *Tamar*, *Cawdor*, *Give Your Heart to the Hawks*, and *Thurso's Landing*—Jeffers dramatizes the terrible beauty of human agony as it darkly shines against the non-human world. In such poems the reader sees and feels and understands what Jeffers saw, felt, and understood. They are testaments to his power, passion, and craft. While we may disagree with him and be irritated by his apparent need to exhort and teach in the short poems, we can never be indifferent to his poetry. In a century when artists vie with one another to find new ways of expressing what often is not worth expressing, at a time when manner and style are considered more important than content, when the new romantics mistake their personal anguish for universal pain—in a word, in this age of the rococo—Jeffers's celebration of universal passion stands like a lonely peak. He spoke of that passion in a late poem, "The Beauty of Things":

To feel and speak the astonishing beauty of things—earth, stone and water,
Beast, man and woman, sun, moon and stars—
The blood-shot beauty of human nature, its thoughts, frenzies and passions,
And unhuman nature its towering reality—
For man's half dream; man, you might say, is nature dreaming, but rock
And water and sky are constant—to feel
Greatly, and understand greatly, and express greatly, the natural
Beauty, is the sole business of poetry.
The rest's diversion: those holy or noble sentiments, the intricate ideas,
The love, lust, longing: reasons, but not the reason.[12]

Add to that statement the last sentences from *Themes in My Poems* and you have the essence of Jeffers's views on the proper business of poetry:

> It seems to me that *great poetry* gathers and expresses the whole of things, as prose *never can*. Its business is to contain a whole world at once, the physical and sensuous, the intellectual, the spiritual, the imaginative, all in

one passionate solution. Thus it becomes a means of discovery, as well as a means of expression. Science usually takes things to pieces in order to discover them; it dissects and analyzes; poetry puts things together, producing equally valid discovery, and actual creation. Something new is found out, something that the author himself did not know before he wrote it; and something new is made.

THREE The Sickness Called Self

I call the classic healthy, the romantic sickly. —Goethe

As numerous individuals have said (so far with little effect), man needs a new measuring stick, something far greater than the various forms of humanism (or superhumanism) he has been using to his great injury. When Protagoras expressed the famous view that "man is the measure of all things," he substituted an anthropocentric fiction for the anthropomorphic fiction that had made the gods the sole arbiters of value. While Greek drama largely sides with the older view (and thereby exonerates in large part the human victims), Renaissance art tended to follow Protagoras. But since then science has effectually exploded both views—locating value in neither gods nor men, who are actually the same since the gods are metaphorical extensions of human hopes and fears. Today we are confronted by the melancholy fact that man is the measure of nothing. Even to say that he is the measure of himself is palpable nonsense since a thing cannot be its own measure.

In attempting to expose those "depths of human nature" (as Shelley worded it) and thus unearth those human qualities that have persisted throughout history, Jeffers relied, as no other modern poet, upon what history teaches and the sciences explain. Unlike other poets of renown (Eliot and Pound come to mind at once), he was little concerned with contrasting one historical period or culture with another in order to show preference for this or that period. Rather he sought only to explain and, above all, to exemplify what he called the same-colored passions that have always given man his peculiar essence. If those passions have at times caused the creature to be unbelievably ugly, the one smear on the face of nature, they have also been the source of what beauty he displays against the infinitely larger beauty of the nonhuman world, which is more beautiful than man not just because of the forms it discloses to the eye or its majesty and permanency but because its passion is more single-purposed and less grained with mere desire. We see this in the passage near the end of *Thurso's Landing*, just after Helen has (mercifully) killed Reave and then taken poison. In his interpolation Jeffers places the little tragedy of blood and death in direct relation to the natural setting, and then he makes a final comment:

The platform is like a rough plank threatre-stage
Built on the brow of the promontory: as if our blood had labored all around the earth from Asia
To play its mystery before strict judges at last, the final ocean and sky, to prove our nature
More shining than that of the other animals. It is rather ignoble in its quiet times, mean in its pleasures,
Slavish in the mass; but at stricken moments it can shine terribly against the dark magnificence of things.

It might be well to pause briefly at this point and explain Jeffers's use of the terms *desire* and *passion*. Paradoxically, in passion lies the source of both beauty and tragedy—the one thing most to be desired and the other most to be avoided. When employed as a synonym for "burning intensity," passion is generally positive—as in the case of the integrated, single-purposed passion of the hawk or in the chemical "passion" of celestial bodies. In "The Caged Eagle's Death Dream," a fragment from *Cawdor* that he included in his *Selected Poetry*, he contrasts the passion of the eagle with the desires of man:

The nerves of men after they die dream dimly
And dwindle into their peace; they are not very passionate,
And what they had was mostly spent while they lived.
They are sieves for leaking desire; they have many pleasures
And conversations; their dreams too are like that.
The unsociàl birds are a greater race;
Cold-eyed, and their blood burns. What leaped up to death,
The extension of one storm-dark wing filling its world,
Was more than the soft garment that fell. Something had flown away. Oh cage-hoarded desire,
Like the blade of a breaking wave reaped by the wind, or flame rising from fire, or cloud-coiled lightning
Suddenly unfurled in the cave of heaven: I that am stationed, and cold at heart, incapable of burning,
My blood like standing sea-water lapped in a stone pool, my desire to the rock, how can I speak of you?

Never reaching the intensity of the hawk's passion, the "leaking desire" of men is too multifarious and ephemeral to warrant praise. What Pascal called the "thinking reed," Jeffers would call the wanting animal. And the more wants he has the less passionate, in Jeffers's sense of the word, he will be. Although Jeffers is not at all consistent in his use of the word, he clearly rejects those desires which have been created by civilization while at the same time he admires the natural passion inherent in the will to survive. Having broken away somewhat from nature, man has forfeited that singleness of purpose we discern in wild animals for an increase in the number of his wants and desires. The wanting or desiring man is, of course, the selfish, or self-full, man. He wants and desires in order to feed the self, to give it identity. Naturally the man in search of self will almost invariably seek it in the eyes of his fellows. He will thus be a prisoner to fashions and fads since only through the recognition and acknowledgment of his being can his hunger be momentarily assuaged.

If Jeffers was contemptuous of most human desires, certainly the ones he considered artificial, as an atomist he believed that strain (a form of desire) lay at the heart of all life. In his poetry there is no still point in the turning world, no place of hope and quiet where the faithful may lay aside their burdens, no final release from change and the old returnings. Where T. S. Eliot found peace, Jeffers found the self-torturing God of atomic stress. In the "Prelude" to *The Women at Point Sur* he displayed that strain in earth, sky, wind, rain, man and beast—all of nature. A few lines:

Always the strain, the straining flesh, who feels what God feels
Knows the straining flesh, the aching desires,
The enormous water straining its bounds, the electric
Strain in the cloud, the strain of the oil in the oil-tanks
At Monterey, aching to burn, the strain of the spinning
Demons that make an atom, straining to fly asunder,
Straining to rest at the center,
The strain in the skull, blind strains, force and counterforce,
Nothing prevails. . . .

Jeffers in no sense deplores the fact of universal strain. In his poetry there is none of Eliot's fastidious disdain for a "burning" world, a world set on fire by lust.

II

Though I realize the risks involved in all labeling, I feel that Jeffers may better be understood if viewed against (that is, in relation to) the romantic and classical traditions. But even here some may object to saying there is a romantic tradition since romanticism is usually considered antitraditional. I readily agree that the battle between the classicists and romantics has been fought repeatedly, and always to a standstill, only to be reopened by the next commentator on the relationship between art and nature, between humanity and the nonhuman world, between tradition and individualism. During the past century it would seem that all the vital juices had been drained from the argument between the Apollonians and the Dionysians, the advocates of order and the exponents of vital force, those who seek form in the world outside and those who seek it in the unconscious (or deny its existence altogether except as mental construct), the individuals who find man in nature and those who insist that he is separate from nature. The lines between the opposing armies often become extremely obscure—so much so that the so-called classicist may find himself occupying romantic ground and vice versa. The question of man's place in nature has been answered over and over but with little effect since it keeps cropping up—even today, a century after the definitive answer was at least generally arrived at by Darwin. The modern existentialists, for example, seem at times almost medieval in their insistence that man is not in nature. Certainly Sartre says as much again and again; see *The Flies* in particular. Though it is obvious to the vast majority of literate people that man is biologically a part of nature, we nonetheless speak of man *and* nature, as if of two separate entities.

While the denotation of the words *classical* and *romantic* tends to vary (there of course is agreement concerning the broadest outlines), the connotation of the words offers no problem. To call the romantic a self-centered egotist is as tautological as to say that water is wet or that politics corrupts. No matter how it is used, the word is now a pejorative term. On the other hand, to call anything classical is to praise it, although the term also carries with it a flavor of enervation. In its crudest form, as it is used by the man on the street, romanticism describes a heart condition afflicting feckless youth, or a postadolescent recurrence of that condition. On a more mature level, the term is applied to a particular manner of calibrating experience or of relating oneself to the phenomenological world. If a person is more concerned with the act or manner of perception than with the object being perceived, he is romantically inclined. In the fiction of Joseph Conrad we probably have our most probing, incisive analysis of the romantic temperament. Lord Jim epitomizes all that is most romantic in so far as he forever confused thought and dream with action; he constantly mistook his will to act for the fait accompli.

That Jeffers has himself been considered a romantic (only his detractors make this mistake) is reason enough to reconsider the meaning of the term. To be sure, he does possess certain traits (or tastes) that superficially considered might lead one to that error. His extreme individualism, his pantheism, his central concern with the passionate intensity of nature which he contrasts with the desires that propel his character-victims, his opposition to urban life, his criticism of civilization as a source of frustration and anxiety, his periodic excursions into something not far removed from mysticism—all these aspects of his verse have been used as evidence that he belongs to the tradition of Wordsworth and Shelley, writers whom he admired and as a young man imitated. But then none of those traits is necessarily romantic; they may all be found in the Greek playwrights and philosophers, and most of them in Lucretius and Marcus Aurelius.

Moreover, the romantic poets (such as Wordsworth, Shelley, Keats, Byron, Landor and Coleridge) were not nearly as "romantic" as the fin de siècle heirs of the great upheaval in thought that took place during the middle years of the nineteenth century. Indeed the romantic poets seem quite traditional, in both form and content, when compared to the symbolists of the late nineteenth and early twentieth centuries. Gilbert Highet has even objected to their being called romantic: "The real moving force of the [romantic] period was social, political, religious, aesthetic, and moral *protest*. It was a time of revolt, and it would be better called the Revolutionary than the Romantic era."[1] Like most other classical scholars, Highet is particularly defensive about Shelley's being called romantic: "It is painful to hear such a poet as Shelley described as 'romantic,' when 'romantic' is taken to mean 'turning away from Greek and Latin literary tradition': for very few great English poets have loved Greco-Roman literature more deeply or understood it better."[2] In their objections to the sterile latinizing of eighteenth-century poetry, the romantics were not rejecting classical forms or even myths (look at the subject matter of Keats and Shelley, in particular). Rather they sought to revitalize pagan stories.

On the other hand, there is everywhere in their verse a cloying self-pity that can only be designated as romantic. When Shelley compares himself to the west wind, insisting that he too is "tameless, and swift, and proud" and then concludes the stanza: "I fall upon the thorns of life! I bleed!"—the mature reader must necessarily blanch or laugh out loud. Note that I say *mature* reader. When I was twenty I memorized that ode since it summed up my own youthful delight in despair, but what enthralls at twenty will make us uneasy at thirty and cause us to grin at forty. It is still a truly splendid poem—for young readers. Shelley's idealization of the skylark as a "blythe Spirit!"—"Bird thou never wert"—is simply embarrassing. He was much less concerned with understanding or even celebrating the worlds of mind and matter than he was with escaping into some farfetched realm of pure idea. It is difficult to sympathize with anyone who seeks escape from human bondage through an empathetic spiritualization of matter. And Shelley always attempted in his transcendental flights to flee the human condition and no less the nonhuman matrix enclosing that condition.

Reduce romanticism to one word, and that word will invariably be *egotism*. Above all else, the romantic seeks to establish or even create the self and then protect that creation from all which threatens it. (As we shall see later, Jeffers's "Fog" contains an excellent portrait of the romantic egotist.) John Fowles has remarked that all romantic and postromantic art is pervaded by fear of the "nemo," Fowles's coinage for "man's sense of his own futility and ephemerality; of his realtivity, his comparativeness; of his virtual nothingness."[3] The smaller a man feels, the more likely he will strive to develop a unique style that might give him individuality, or a semblance thereof. In the arts this fear, Fowles says, accounts for not only the proliferation of styles and techniques at the expense of content, but also explains "that only too characteristic coupling of exoticism of presentation with banality of theme. Once artists ran to a centre; now they fly to the circumference. And the result is our new rococo."

Paradoxically this rage for the unique style has had the final effect of blurring personality in art. It should be evident that the more impersonal an art becomes, the more it will tend to be abstract, and vice versa. Dadaism is a good illustration of this fact. Nothing is finally more egotistic than complete defiance of all intellectualism since in that defiance there is an implicit assumption that nothing can be known and that nothing could be worth knowing in a meaningless and chaotic world. What we have is a new kind of intellectualism, now gone abstract and much more self-conscious than ever before. The impersonality of abstract painting has its humorous side effects when an award is given to a blob of color that turns out to be the work of an industrious chimpanzee. Carried far enough, self-expression (the unique style) will ascend into abstraction; there is nothing to hold it back or keep it down. The last gesture of defiance and revolt is retreat into pure self—alone, unattached, godlike. Before looking at Jeffers's depiction of this hunger for unity in a world of multiplicity, something must be said about the possible audience of the artist.

Obviously there is nothing in the rhythms of nature which might be considered fashionable or exotic. But there is, Jeffers insisted, permanence and meaning and hence value in the nonhuman world. Any emphasis upon mere style is an admission that one writes out of need for self-assurance rather than from strength of character, which will always contain within it the desire to know the world rather than to simply express the self. When Jeffers looked beyond the fashions of the moment to the permanence of the eternally recurring rhythms of nature, he was in effect disassociating himself from that audience which rewards conformity to contemporary tastes with the accolades of transient notoriety. Indeed he never seemed to consider what possible audience might be interested in his work; rather, he was interested in only what might be of concern a thousand years from now or might have concerned sober minds a thousand years ago. As he put it in his most conclusive essay on his craft: "Permanent things, or things forever renewed, like the grass and human passions, are the material for poetry; and whoever speaks across the gap of a thousand years will understand that he has to speak of permanent things, and rather clearly too, or who would hear him?"[4] He had little patience with the man who sought fame and an audience today: "To be peered at and interviewed, to be pursued by idlers and autograph hunters and inquiring admirers, would surely be a sad nuisance. And it is destructive too, if you take it seriously; it wastes your energy into self-consciousness; it destroys spontaneity and soils the springs of the mind. Whereas posthumous reputation could do you no harm at all, and is really the only kind worth considering."[5]

Two of his posthumously published poems comment on the relationship between the artist and his audience. The first is entitled "Let Them Alone":

If God has been good enough to give you a poet
Then listen to him. But for God's sake let him alone until he is dead; no prizes, no ceremony,
They kill the man. A poet is one who listens
To nature and his own heart; and if the noise of the world grows up around him, and if he is tough enough,
He can shake off his enemies but not his friends.
That is what withered Wordsworth and muffled Tennyson, and would have killed Keats; that is what makes
Hemingway play the fool and Faulkner forget his art.

In the other poem, "Eager to Be Praised," an old man ruminates on those poets who died fulfilled (or in despair) and then comments on those who are too young to know what only experience can teach:

Goethe, they say, was a great poet, Pindar, perhaps, was a great poet, Shakespeare and Sophocles
Stand beyond question. I am thinking of the few, the fortunate,
Who died fulfilled.
I think of Christopher Marlowe, stabbed through the eye in a tavern brawl by a bawdy serving-man,
Spilling his youth and brains on the greasy planks. I think of young Keats,
Wild with his work unfinished, sobbing for air, dying in Rome. I think of Edgar Poe
And Robert Burns. I think of Lucretius leaving his poem unfinished to go and kill himself. I think of Archilochus
Grinning with crazy bitterness. I think of Virgil
In despair of his life-work, begging his friends to destroy it, coughing his lungs out. Yet the young men

Still come to me with their books and manuscripts,
Eager to be poets, eager to be praised, eager as Keats.
They are mad I think.

III

The romantic can never escape Self, with a capital letter,* or perhaps it would be more precise to spell it SELF—or even GOD. That is his agony. Doubly so since the self he clings to has been shown by science (to him the arch-villain) to be almost inconsequential when viewed against the depths of time and space. Jeffers depicts the place of man in an indifferent universe without repining—and then decries the man who clings to consciousness as a last spar between the two eternities that enclose him. Consciousness itself, though an enormous gift, cannot be considered an unalloyed good since it presupposes pain, which to Jeffers was much more real than joy.

In "Night," one of his best lyrics, Jeffers compares night, "peace-bringer, the matrix of all shining and quieter of shining," with day (or rather the sun, the source of planetary life), which he calls "A father of lights and noises, wars, weeping and laughter, / Hot labor, lust and delight and the other blemishes." Viewed largely, from an astronomical standpoint, life itself (as we consider it) is the exception rather than the norm. Metaphorically life is a flicker of light in the vast darkness of time and space—designated here as "Night":

Truly the spouting fountain of light, Antares, Arcturus,
Tire of their flow, they sing one song but they think silence.
The striding winter giant Orion shines, and dreams darkness.
And life, the flicker of men and moths and the wolf on the hill,
Though furious for continuance, passionately feeding, passionately
Remaking itself upon its mates, remembers deep inward
The calm mother, the quietness of the womb and the egg,
The primal and the latter silences: dear Night it is memory
Prophesies, prophecy that remembers, the charm of the dark.
And I and my people, we are willing to love the four-score years
Heartily; but as a sailor loves the sea, when the helm is for harbor.
Have men's minds changed,
Or the rock hidden in the deep of the waters of the soul
Broken the surface? A few centuries
Gone by, was none dared not to people

The darkness beyond the stars with harps and habitations.
But now, dear is the truth. Life is grown sweeter and lonelier,
And death is no evil.

Before and after the flicker of activity, there is the "primal silence," far more real than the active moment of life since it is far more enduring. Jeffers saw nothing absurd in the fact that man's consciousness passes while the world remains. The existentialist who considers this an absurdity—which is to say, an injustice—is himself absurd and childishly egocentric. The world of course does not remain in the sense that it never changes. Rocks undergo the same transformations found in less stable objects of nature. In the slowness of those transformations they take on an appearance of permanence, whereas the lives of men and moths pass with such rapidity that the contrast of the animate with the inanimate world is heightened until the difference in tenure seems also a difference in kind. "To perceive universal mutation, to feel the vanity of life," Santayana wrote, "has always been the beginning of seriousness." Certainly Jeffers begins with that perception and that feeling.

The knowledge (call it the serious news) which Jeffers celebrates cannot, of course, be a solace for more than a few hardy natures. And for the many the news is still meaningless; their instinct for survival, the will to longer live, annuls what the mind knows, or at least is now in a position to know. Still driven by the exigencies of life, they live sensually rather than intellectually—perhaps to their good fortune. America's greatest romantic poet put it perfectly: "Logic and sermons never convince, / The damp of the night drives deeper into the soul." As the self-proclaimed poet of the body and the soul, Whitman naturally appeals to the child in all of us, and he appeals most when the mind sleeps. In "Song of Myself," his greatest poem and one to which all his other poems are addenda, he celebrates the self which contains all things, the highest and lowest (though he is careful not to distinguish anything qualitatively). In his blanket endorsement of all things as good, he literally deprives the adjective of any meaning. Whitman describes himself as a giant sponge absorbing all sensations—and finding them indistinguishable. Possessing no discrimination whatsoever, he can profess no values beyond the hazy approval of all that is natural. And he considered whatever exists as ipso facto natural. Rejecting nothing, he accepted all on equal basis. His arrogant, almost mindless, delight in *being* certainly has an antidotal aspect to it that we can enjoy. His insistence that he was divine is pure nonsense, but the sort of nonsense which we can applaud as we applaud the simian boast of a college yell or the rabble-rousing fustian of a stump speech:

I believe in the flesh and the appetites,
Seeing, hearing, feeling, are miracles, and each part and tag of me is a miracle.

Divine am I inside and out, and I make holy whatever I touch or am touch'd from,
The scent of these arm-pits aroma finer than prayer,
This head more than churches, bibles, and all the creeds.

This kind of de-Christianized antinomianism has a surface glitter that dazzles the eye at the same time it narcotizes the cerebrum. Think of Old Walt with his head slued round so he can smell his arm-pit—a beatific picture of the obscene that has a peculiar charm certainly. Without going beyond Emerson's self-reliance (the worship of the Self-God), Whitman did transliterate the lessons of his mentor in a concrete and anatomical vulgate that made the mentor blush and vacillate and finally disavow. Confronted by the logical extension of his own ideas, Emerson, who never possessed the courage of his convictions, wrapped his mantle about him and retired to his study. It is Whitman's arrogance that appeals to us. "I find no sweeter fat than sticks to these bones"—that is the Whitman we enjoy, even though a moment's reflection will make us realize he would also have said that he found no sweeter fat than stuck to everyone else's bones. As for his prophetic poetry, his incessant glorification of men en masse, his democratic faith with the concomitant "merging" and "One Identity!," his "anatomy lessons," the flatulent yea-saying, his promiscuous approval of any and all—no sober adult, I contend, can read that Whitman, which is to say most of Whitman, without gagging or indefinitely suspending his disbelief. In his famous essay "The Poetry of Barbarism," Santayana remarked that Whitman spoke to those "minds and to those moods in which sensuality is touched with mysticism." It is only when we are weary of the real world that Whitman can please us; his poetry is thoroughly escapist. His greatest mistake, like that of other nineteenth-century transcendentalists, was in assuming that the people of the New World were somehow exempted from the laws that bind men of all nations at all times. Although there are marvelous descriptions among his "leaves," the poetry remains two-dimensional, a vast surface filled with colors but intellectually as empty as a jug.

Even those who have heard and assimilated the news concerning the proper positioning of humanity in the cosmos usually find the loss greater than the gain. E. A. Robinson, for example, derived little joy from contemplating "The Man Against the Sky," going God knows where but certainly going down. He poses a question that is still asked half a century later:

If after all we have lived and thought,
All comes to Nought,—
If there be nothing after Now,
And we be nothing anyhow,
And we know that,—why live?

Surely the man who could ask such a question must have considered the loss indeed great, in fact, unbearable. But no, not quite: after all, he bore it. In like manner Yeats in "Among School Children" could wonder that a woman would bring children into the world, knowing that they would grow old, wither and die. Yeats's anxiety over the human condition, at times reduced to the simple fear of death, helps explain, it seems to me, his withdrawal into superstition. Seeing the world tumbling into chaos, he retreated into self, or rather into a self-sustaining iconography. For the healthy animal, death poses no problem, only an annoyance that will one day occur. For Yeats and Robinson, who viewed life only intellectually, the problem was already here and so much so that it erased all other considerations. Robinson salved the hurt of mortality by employing a pragmatic argument: the fact that so many "believed" heretofore, that so many have heard "an orient Word that will not be erased," is fact enough to believe now. That is, belief in immortality is its own excuse for being. Yeats sought escape from mortal coils in a no less unsatisfactory way when he fell back on a "mysticism of superstition," as one critic worded it. He simply turned away from life ("Cast a cold eye / On Life, on death. / Horseman, pass by!") to dwell in a world of artistic image—as in "Long-Legged Fly" and the Byzantium poems, to name only three.

Jeffers's response seems to me infinitely the best in that it denies false hopes and yet leaves ample room for a full life in which values are not only possible but necessary. Jeffers considered life and death the most important polarities from which we obtain those values most necessary to our well being—the very heart, indeed, of the tension that holds man up. Without the polarities there would be no value in existence. Without death life would be savorless, a meaningless muddle of indiscriminate reiteration enlivened only by the whimpers of Struldburgs. Without strife peace would be meaningless; without time and change, value would be unthinkable.

IV

With spiritual discomfort at such a premium today, many of our best writers shudder at the thought of the future and advocate returning to a past that they feel would at least be better than the present and less forboding then the future. Yeats expressed this modern fear and trembling perfectly in "The Second Coming." The frenetic present has turned out to be vastly different from the visions of Emerson and Whitman. Eliot sought to salve his spiritual discomfort by retreating into "a mysticism of the past, a slow ritualistic dance among the symbols of medieval Catholicism."[6] While Jeffers believed that he lived in a period of decaying Christianity and misapplied science, he neither turned his eyes to the past nor sought to escape through the portals of mysticism. Eliot's pessimism, once thought so black (and hence appealing to readers weaned on the despair which followed World War One), was derived from a fastidious disgust at all things modern. In his view that modern man was more revolting than man a thousand years ago, he was as romantic as Miniver Cheevy. Nothing in human history would indicate that man is now worse, in the sense of being more cruel or stupid, than he was during the ages of faith, nor that faith is in itself necessarily positive. Eliot's use of Sweeney as a symbol for modern degeneration is finally as sentimental and unrealistic as Lawrence's worship of the savage or Whitman's deification of the common man. Like most other symbolists, Eliot fails the final test that all great literature must pass: that is, his poetry provides the reader with no understanding of the world outside the self; and it offers no insight into the human condition but gives us, instead of that insight, a vivid account of his own personal anguish and revulsion. Temperamentally opposed to Whitman's "barbaric yawp" (which showed no regard for tradition), Eliot mistook the forms of our literary heritage for the reflection of life those forms were meant to convey. He used the past only to comment on what he disliked in the present without enlivening either the past or the present. His failure, it seems to me, is analogous to that of Whitman. Whitman, the yea-sayer, gives us quantitative pictures of the teeming life around him, but little understanding of that life. He offered nothing more cogent than the trite view that we should all love one another and live in a great fleshpot of camaraderie—touching, seeing, feeling, smelling, tasting, hearing each other and all objects and finding everyone and everything good. Whitman asks us to stop with him awhile and admire things. Eliot asks us to go with him through dirty streets and see our hollow selves silhouetted against the gorgeous backdrop of ancient literary works.

It is nevertheless true that Eliot's "medieval Catholicism" has been better understood than Jeffers's Stoicism, for the simple reason that Eliot chose a standard which lies within the immediate past and which has a lingering residue of symbolic meaning to citizens of the Western world, and which, moreover, flatters the ego of man. A reader need not agree with Eliot that the way out of despair is the way of Christ in order to understand the causes, effects, and antidotes of the dilemma he describes. Moreover our understanding is not intellectual alone but has what is far more convincing—an emotional acknowledgement of the terms of his argument. For example, the reader has no difficulty in comprehending such terms as *love* and *mercy* and *humility*; Christian texts depend on that nomenclature for their existence. Furthermore, we are all partially Christianized whether we are believers or not. It is of little importance to the majority of men that such concepts have been impotent in the face of man's self-destructive bent and are probably even less effectual today than at any time in the past five hundred years, since Christianity has not been a moving force since the Renaissance. From the hearts of men of good faith comes the old refrain, as if from a broken record endlessly repeating the now forlorn message—faith, hope, and charity.

The three beams in the eye of mankind, Jeffers would say. Could man but extract the beams from his eye and look beyond the self-love that threatens to destroy him, he would see that man's place in nature is not separate from but rather a part of all phenomena. As for hope: "Hope is not for the wise," Jeffers tells us, "fear is for fools; / Change and the world, we think, are racing to a fall, / Open-eyed and helpless." Faith, in its least harmful use, serves as a crutch for the weak; at its worst, it offers an outlet for fanatical cruelty. In "Thebaid" he wrote of those who were "delirious with fevers of faith":

How many turn back toward dreams and magic, how many children
Run home to Mother Church, Father State,
To find in their arms the delicious warmth and folding of souls.
The age weakens and settles home toward old ways.
An age of renascent faith: Christ said, Marx wrote, Hitler says,
And though it seems absurd we believe.
Sad children, yes. It is lonely to be adult, you need a father.
With a little practise you'll believe anything.

Faith returns, beautiful, terrible, ridiculous,
And men are willing to die and kill for their faith.
Soon come the wars of religion; centuries have passed
Since the air so trembled with intense faith and hatred.
Soon, perhaps, whoever wants to live harmlessly
Must find a cave in the mountain or build a cell
Of the red desert rock under dry junipers,
And avoid men, live with more kindly wolves
And luckier ravens, waiting for the end of the age.

When faith does not cause men to become "curiously ignoble," it turns them into unwitting pawns of Caesars (or Christ-figures), hungry for power. The people become "Blind Horses," turning the mill to generate power for the shepherds:

The proletariat for your Messiah, the poor and many are to seize power and make the world new.
They cannot even conduct a strike without cunning leaders: if they make a revolution their leaders
Must take the power. The first duty of men in power: to defend their power.

Nor are the masses, the "ants," the only ones who cry out for a leader, that is, an abstraction embodied in the person of a leader willing, and usually eager, to accept the power that comes with mass followers. Unable to cultivate their gardens in the self-reliant manner of a Voltaire or a Thoreau, intellectuals also "flock into fold." Having fallen in love outward, with the "unkindly all but inhuman God," Jeffers had no need to align himself with one of man's subjective, egocentric creeds, as he notes in "Intellectuals":

It is so hard for men to stand by themselves,
They must hang on Marx or Christ, or mere Progress?
Clearly it is hard. But these ought to be leaders . . .
Sheep leading sheep, "The fold, the fold.
Night comes, and the wolves of doubt." Clearly it is hard.

Yourself, if you had not encountered and loved
Our unkindly all but inhuman God,
Who is very beautiful and too secure to want worshippers,
And includes indeed the sheep with the wolves,
You too might have been looking about for a church.

He includes the flaming stars and pitiable flesh,
And what we call things and what we call nothing.
He is very beautiful. But when these lonely have travelled
Through long thoughts to redeeming despair,
They are tired and cover their eyes; they flock into fold.

It would be simple enough to list a number of other prophets (Jeffers obviously assumes the role of prophet here, as in many other of his short poems) who illustrate Jeffers's point. Think of those who have passed from the Marxian stage onto the Christian (circumstances the last thirty years have not been favorable to passing the other way round). Many of the intellectuals had also gone through a Freudian period before embracing Marx and then Christ—always moving from one dogmatism to another, and always revealing an ardent desire for belief, for release from the loneliness that accompanies doubt. For them the little truths always take the place of Truth. Mencken remarked in the 1930s that the people who most ardently and dexteriously performed the mental acrobatics necessary to good standing in the Marxist school were precisely those who had advocated the wilder theories of sexology in the 1920s, and were the ones most likely to return to Christian theology at a later date—those, in brief, who were happily blessed with believing minds.

The Hebraic-Christian worship of a personalized God, a God of human feeling, acts, and form, carries with it and even makes necessary the anthropocentricism to which Jeffers attributed the major shortcomings of our species. Unable to rely on a God outside, one capable of rewarding or punishing, Jeffers advocated a self-reliance similar to that of Emerson and Nietzsche, but with a major difference. Both Emerson and Nietzsche felt that belief in a personal God was childish superstition, but when Emerson replaced the Christian God with self-reliance (and thereby reliance on the God outside through the over-soul) he actually reintroduced the belief that man was subject and the world object, a belief that eighteenth-century skepticism had challenged in all areas, and which nineteenth-century biology exploded once and for all. Could man, whom Emerson called "a god in ruins," but fully awake, he would realize that the world was indeed his special oyster. Nietzsche went a step further. In offering a way out of the nihilism that modern man inherited from the scientific discoveries since the Renaissance, Nietzsche developed his philosophy of the *Übermensch*—and thereby compounded Emersonian self-reliance with a divine ego. They rejected religious dogmatism for a dogmatic faith in the self.

For anyone who separates man from nature dogmatic belief will be a constant temptation. Indeed, the intelligent romantic—that is, the man who gets outside the self long enough to describe the relations of that self to the universe—divides the world, as did the young Emerson, into only two parts, the "me" and the "not-me." Subject and object. The object necessarily existing for the sake of the subject. Viewed through Emerson's anthropocentric lens, the "not-me" ran errands for the "me": "Nature is thoroughly mediate," he wrote. "It is made to serve. It receives the dominion of man as meekly as the ass on which the Savior rode." Before we smile and cough behind our hand we must remember that the majority still gives credence to that heady nonsense. The many still consider the world an oyster to be eaten by its "owners," never dreaming that they are the ones being slowly devoured. In partial defense of Emerson, it must be pointed out that he later had misgivings about his early idealism. Though never quite able to rid himself of the childish notion that mind is a thing-in-itself, he nonetheless admitted later in such essays as "Experience" and "Fate" that mind was responsive to matter. Of course he could never adopt the materialist position which holds that mind is to matter what cutting is to the knife—that is, a function or process. His wit and wisdom were simply powerless in the face of his will to believe, his need to exalt man, to locate the conscious "I" above and beyond fate or circumstance.

After the Darwinian revolution, which knocked man off his stilts and set him to searching for his origin in the mud below rather than the ether above, the romantic considered the "not-me" a good deal less benevolent than he had before. In fact he began to consider it as antagonistic to his being, as downright hostile. It was no longer "me" *and* "not-me," but now "me" *versus* "not-me" with all the odds on the world's side. Though he was no less anthropocentric than before, the Victorian romantic (Tennyson, Swinburne, et al.) found the earth cold and dark rather than warmly bathed in light. Imagine the inordinate conceit inherent in this new choosing up of sides: puny man pitted against the malignant forces of nature, or, in Swinburnean terms, man versus "the supreme evil, God." As foreordained loser in the contest, man is the sentimental favorite whose glory lies in his going down fighting, his boots on and spurs ajingle. A kind of cosmic melodrama, played to the tune of rattling sabers and defiant yells, full of "tears and laughter," as Swinburne would say in one of his verses. Always implicit in the defiance and posturing is self-pity. It now permeates much existential thought, which endeavors to erect a humanistic structure on a nihilistic foundation. In the work of a Celine the self-pity becomes self-hatred. In Hemingway it parades as bravado. At times in his work the man-versus-world conflict descends to sentimentality. For example, in *A Farewell to Arms* (chapter 34) Frederic Henry–Ernest Hemingway summarizes man's destiny: "If people bring so much courage to this world the world has to kill them to break them, so of course it kills them. The world breaks every one and afterward many are strong at the broken places. But those that will not break it kills. It kills the very good and the very gentle and the very brave impartially. If you are none of these you can be sure it will kill you too but there will be no special hurry."

It would be difficult to imagine anything more adolescent than this personification of the world as the killer of man. Such egocentric division of all phenomena into victimizer "not-me" and victim "me" would be comic were it not so widespread a view and hence so injurious to the delicate balance of nature. Like most nihilists, Hemingway was by turns sentimental, self-pitying, and cruel. Unable to accept death as a necessary condition for life—obviously neither could *be* without the other—Hemingway delighted in killing animals as a symbolic gesture in defiance of his own mortality. In the first pages of *Death in the Afternoon* he attempts to elevate man's fondness for destruction into a philosophy of salvation. Considering how silly is his logic and how sophomoric his thought, we need never wonder that he should have been popular with the young a generation ago. Here is the kernel of his "philosophy": "Once you accept the rule of death thou shalt not kill is an easily and naturally obeyed commandment. But when a man is still in rebellion against death he has pleasure in taking to himself one of the Godlike attributes; that of giving it." Though the first sentence reaches a false conclusion from a vague premise, the second sentence summarizes the nihilist position perfectly: man gains pleasure from killing, an act that enables him to become God, or at least godlike.

That we reside in the most nihilistic of centuries is, I think, obvious. In our time we have also seen romanticism triumph as never before in the world of art. And that triumph is nowhere more evident than in the excessive emphasis placed on self-expression, which in turn has led to self-worship. While it is generally believed that the death of God (by which I mean the loss of faith in anthropomorphic gods) should lead to nihilism, it is perhaps less apparent that symbolism should breed nihilism. The moment man considers nature a symbol, he moves toward nihilism. That is, he takes the first step toward becoming God. The man-god is by nature pure nihilist in the sense that he is self-contained; any values must be self-induced by the divinity. In "Self-Reliance" Emerson propounds a theory of value that still has weight, indeed has even more today than before. "No law," he wrote, "can be sacred to me but that of my nature. Good and bad are but names very readily transferable to that or this, the only right is what is after my constitution; the only wrong what is against it." Right and wrong thus become matters of taste, of personal whim. Here, as Yeats put it, "Mere anarchy is loosed upon the world." In arguing the morality of bullfighting, Hemingway echoes Emerson: "So far, about morals, I know only that what is moral is what you feel good after and what is immoral is what you feel bad after and judged by these moral standards, which I do not defend, the bullfight is very moral to me because I feel very fine while it is going on and have a feeling of life and death and mortality and immortality, and after it is over I feel very sad but very fine." The existentialist glorifies this moral relativism by actually arguing that it is an absolute. In his famous lecture delivered at the Club Maintenant in 1945, Sartre expresses the same view that reliance on self, or rather the mere cognizance of self, is both source and end of all absolute truth: "There cannot be any other truth than this, *I think, therefore I am*, which is the absolute truth of consciousness as it attains to itself. Every theory which begins with man, outside this moment of self-attainment, is a theory which thereby suppresses the truth. . . . Before there can be any truth whatever, then, there must be an absolute truth, and there is such a truth which is simple, easily attained and within the reach of everybody; it consists in one's immediate sense of one's self."[7] Sartre can even logically prove that there is no human nature: "Thus, there is no human nature, since there is no God to conceive it." The implication is clear: unlike all other creatures in the world, man belongs to no species; rather, every individual man is a species unto himself, who can and indeed must through the use of his freedom and will *be* God. What travesties of human reason hath Nietzsche's superman wrought! It is no wonder that various intellectuals, like Malcolm Muggeridge, appalled by the emptiness and absurdity of such nihilism turn their backs on the modern world and affiliate themselves with the Christian myth.

Finding no order or meaning in the world, which he has given up hope of understanding, the nihilist takes revenge, as it were, on its meaninglessness and indifference by attempting to destroy it. This he does by bringing it into the self. (Jeffers perfectly describes that process in "Fog.") The symbolist does much the same thing when he reduces the world to images. Jeffers came dangerously close to saying the same thing when he spoke of "The poet, who wishes not to play games with words, / His affair being to awake dangerous images / And call the hawks." But then he never made the symbolist error of mistaking the symbol for its referent. In "Love the Wild Swan" he lamented his inability ever to capture the world in words:

"I hate my verses, every line, every word.
Oh pale and brittle pencils ever to try
One grass-blade's curve, or the throat of one bird
That clings to twig, ruffled against white sky.
Oh cracked and twilight mirrors ever to catch
One color, one glinting flash, of the splendor of things.
Unlucky hunter, Oh bullets of wax,
The lion beauty, the wild-swan wings, the storm of the wings."
—This wild swan of a world is no hunter's game.
Better bullets than yours would miss the white breast,
Better mirrors than yours would crack in the flame.
Does it matter whether you hate your . . . self? At least
Love your eyes that can see, your mind that can
Hear the music, the thunder of the wings. Love the wild swan.

In this self-criticism, Jeffers clearly admits the inferiority of the artist's copy to the thing itself. And though the perceiver cannot hope to capture the intrinsic beauty of the perceived, he does not make the idealist error of thinking the world as object can be overcome by reducing it to symbol. In a better poem, "Boats in a Fog," he expressed a Platonic view of art—a view that comes with being "adult."

Sports and gallantries, the stage, the arts, the antics of dancers,
The exuberant voices of music,
Have charm for children but lack nobility; it is bitter earnestness
That makes beauty; the mind
Knows, grown adult.

After describing the fishing boats,

trailing each other
Following the cliff for guidance,
Holding a difficult path between the peril of the sea-fog
And the foam on the shore granite,

he praises the hard reality of the scene, in no way discouraged that he cannot reveal its essence, but only filled with a sense of his good fortune in having been allowed to perceive it:

A flight of pelicans
Is nothing lovelier to look at;
The flight of the planets is nothing nobler; all the arts lose virtue
Against the essential reality
Of creatures going about their business among the equally
Earnest elements of nature.

Jeffers employs symbols, of course, but he does so in order to bring the world of phenomena closer to the observer, to aid him in ordering some aspect of the world which, unless taken in its totality (an impossible task for any human mind), will lack order and meaning. Although every thing is capable of being used as symbol, as Emerson wrote, when we employ symbols we run the constant risk of slipping into the solipsistic error of assuming that the symbol possesses an essence, that it exists apart from what it symbolizes. Whereas metaphors describe and relate, the symbol becomes (in the mind of the symbolist though certainly not in fact) what it stands for. We have no better definition of the metaphor than Aristotle's: "A good metaphor implies an intuitive perception of the similarity in dissimilars." Whereas the metaphor is a means, the symbol is too often an end. Metaphors increase our awareness of everpresent tensions in life, sharpen our responses to phenomena, and thus enable us to understand better our relative position in nature. Symbols do none of this. They readily become absolutes, thereby offering no opportunity for evaluation. Metaphoric language keeps the object at a distance where it may be examined by the perceiver. The symbol bleeds the object of its lifeblood and bottles its essence for storage in some corner of the cerebral cortex. Symbols are hence the greatest enemy of tolerance, and, no less, of understanding. When they become, as they often do, icons to be worshipped, symbols are the greatest inciters of hatred and the chief causes of ignorance, or at least the chief means of protecting and prolonging ignorance. Moreover, worship of symbols is the same as worship of self since they are creatures of the mind. In a world of constant flux, where there are no ends, the icon is static—palpable evidence of the human wish to escape change. The icon, rigid and lifeless, is often used as a club to belabor those poor souls who fail to see that it is necessary to salvation or to the social body or to whatever belief it has come to represent as absolute. Far from injuring mankind, the iconoclast by attacking idolatry engages in the most useful of all human enterprises. By removing the bung from the symbolic cask he allows the wine to flow again and be judged on its own merits according to the individual tastes of those seated at the banquet. The most amusing piece of such iconoclasm to me is that contained in Swift's "A Tale of a Tub," when Peter lambasts Jack and Martin for not seeing the crust of bread he gives them at dinner is really "excellent good mutton." Swift recalls here, through implication, the numerous people who had been hanged or otherwise executed for denying transubstantiation—an offspring of man's symbol-making faculty that is truly marvelous.

That the tremendous increase in our knowledge of nature and man's place in it during the last century has been paralleled by a like increase in the number of nihilists and symbolists might seem at first blush a paradox. But there is actually little here that is not comprehensible and perfectly consistent with human nature. Both symbolism and nihilism are defensive responses to the threat that scientific knowledge poses to human individuality. Knowledge disturbs, uncenters, and often wrecks the hopes and aspirations of man; on the other hand, nothing pleases and comforts more than self-delusion. Begin with the truism that knowledge increaseth sorrow, and you are half way home to understanding man's fondness for abstractions.

If the knowledge which we can at least tentatively call exact has deflated the ego, it has at the same time had the unwitting effect of causing the egotist to become all the more rabid in his defense of self. In its debunking of moral absolutism, science has opened the gates to all the more loony forms of individualism. By denying the validity of all moral postulates, the nihilist moves about (he assumes) in a world without underpinnings. Nothing is tied down; everything is collapsible. The only restraint comes from weakness of will. Since all phenomena are equally meaningless, the nihilist refuses to discriminate; he is preeminently the nondiscriminatory man. Brute nature appeals to him only for the sensations it provides. And since the nihilist is usually only one generation from moral absolutism, he loathes the sensual mistress while insisting at the same time that she is all he has. In effect, nihilism occupies the void left by disillusion; it is the colorless residue of dissolved faith. Genealogically the nihilist is the misshapen offspring of a bad marriage between desire for absolutes and realization that all is relative. He is Camus' "absurd" man whose only possession is an "absurd freedom" that enables him to rebel against meaninglessness through the accumulation of experience. "Belief in the meaning of life," Camus wrote, "always implies a scale of values, a choice, our preferences. Belief in the absurd, according to our definitions, teaches the contrary."[8]

Pascal wrote that when man becomes separate from God, only two courses of action are left: he may seek to become God, or he may give himself up to the transitory joys of the flesh. The statement is fatuous, of course, since there are obviously more alternatives than Pascal offers. Moreover his famous "wager" entails a leap into blind faith which few thinking individuals are willing or able to make today. As a therapist he is no better than any other since his cure simply will not take, but as a pathologist examining man's spiritual needs he deserves high marks since the alternatives he offers have been most popular. With the death of the anthropomorphic gods, many have mistakenly assumed that the only arbiter of values left was the self. Certainly Emerson made that error, as did Nietzsche later in the century. Their existential descendants make the same error today. Actually man's freedom from the gods is really meaningless when we realize that his struggle has always been with nature and its fiats, though at times man translates the terms of natural existence (man as the result of biological and psychological forces) into terms of supernatural dependence (man as the result of divine laws or intelligent design outside the natural order).

E. A. Robinson expressed the modern dilemma when he referred to the world as "a kind of spiritual kindergarten, where millions of bewildered infants are trying to spell God with the wrong blocks." If Robinson never succeeded in spelling the word to his own satisfaction, he did not, like the nihilist, give up the task as utterly hopeless. Like the philosophical idealist from whom he derives, the nihilist reasons deductively. Beginning with the existence of God, the assumed first premise, the idealist deduces order and meaning in the world. Since the nihilist cannot accept the first premise, he denies that order and meaning exist.

The naturalist reasons inductively: he finds empirical evidence of order and from that evidence moves to a tentative belief in God, which he spells *process.* While naturalism explains much, it promises little, and that in turn explains why naturalism has never been as popular as supernaturalism, which explains little and promises much. Even though all certain knowledge depends upon natural laws, man still finds it difficult to see in nature a higher being. In *The Life of Reason*, perhaps the greatest of all statements of philosophical naturalism, Santayana explained man's preference for idealistic theory over naturalistic fact:

> Aversion to an empirical or naturalistic philosophy accordingly expresses a sort of logical patriotism and attachment to homespun ideas. The actual is too remote and unfriendly to the dreamer; to understand it he has to learn a foreign tongue, which his native prejudice imagines to be unmeaning and unpoetical. The truth is, however, that nature's language is too rich for man; and the discomfort he feels when he is compelled to use it merely marks his lack of education. There is nothing cheaper than idealism. It can be had by merely not observing the ineptitude of our chance prejudices, and by declaring that the first rhymes that have struck our ear are the eternal and necessary harmonies of the world.[9]

It would be well to pause a moment and recapitulate. The paths men have traveled in the last two hundred years keep crossing each other. We keep finding in our intellectual baggage items that clearly belonged to the man who left us the bag and which we now reject as outmoded. In the most violent rejection there is generally some assimilation of that which has been rejected. Naturalism rejected the romantic emphasis upon self but approved romantic pantheism—although for reasons different from those given by the romantic. Appalled by the "emptiness of naturalism," the symbolist or postromantic sought to restore self to its primary position, but at the same time he adopted, somewhat sadly, the view that man was a part of nature. Moreover he could not believe in a personal God, no matter how hard he might have wanted to believe. Norman Mailer expressed the forlorn wish in a *Life* magazine article (28 July 1972) when he wrote, "The world's more coherent if God exists. And twice coherent if He exists like us." Mailer has written much else that is equally as absurd, but nothing better illustrates Santayana's remarks about dreamers and their lack of education.

In his separation from God, the absurdly reasoning man of Camus (who spoke for many postromantics) becomes, as Pascal predicted, both God and sensualist. He is sensualist in his belief that quantity of experience delineates his being: "A man's rule of conduct and his scale of values have no meaning except through the quantity and variety of experiences he has been in a position to accumulate"—an assertion that recalls Nietzsche's profound remark that a man has no ears except for that which he has experienced. But then Nietzsche did not imply, as Camus does, that only quantity of experience matters. It should be obvious moreover that the mere preference for quantity, in so far as that preference implies judgment and choice, is qualitative. Camus says then that quantity is quality—which is palpable nonsense. When one reasons absurdly, it is only to be expected that one will be absurd (in the nonexistential sense of the word). Awareness of self becomes the supreme test of the man in search of character or being: "Being aware of one's life, one's revolt, one's freedom, and to the maximum, is living, and to the maximum." From the absurd he draws "three consequences, which are my revolt, my freedom, and my passion."[10] Which is to say, out of my own self I draw God; I create myself. Readers of *The Stranger* will recall that not until too late does Meursault become aware of self, when he is in prison awaiting his execution—just as each of us awaits his execution, the death sentence having been passed at the moment of our conception. As long as we are unaware of the self, so Camus says, we must remain strangers in the world.

And yet what could be more childish, even infantile, than this constant preoccupation with self, this fondling of the ego? And what could be more unhealthy? The only ones who gain at all from such narcissism are the psychiatrists. In numerous poems, Jeffers depicts the agony attendant upon this particular perversion. Though he considered consciousness a gift which enabled man to bring "the world to focus in a feeling brain" and in a net of nerves catch the splendor of things, he bitterly decried self-consciousness. If anything, man's great interest in self blinded him to the splendors outside the brain-vault. When he commented on the poet's proper business, he was also commenting on an ideal for human response to the world: "to feel /

Greatly, and understand greatly, and express greatly, the natural, / Beauty, is the sole business of poetry."

In "The Poet" Emerson called the poet the representative man who expresses what others merely feel. Jeffers would agree but insist also on the need for understanding the world. Emerson's idealism placed the world in a subservient relation to man and hence made understanding relatively unimportant—relative, that is, to understanding of self, from which the world, according to idealistic thought, derived its being. All the poet needed to do was express the self, which contained all. "Things admit of being used as symbols," Emerson notes, "because nature is a symbol, in the whole, and in every part. . . . The Universe is the externization of the soul. Wherever the life is, that bursts into appearance around it. Our science is sensual, and therefore superficial. The earth and the heavenly bodies, physics and chemistry, we sensually treat, as if they were self-existent; but these are the retinue of that Being we have." In confusing perception with creation and in thinking the part (man) is larger than the whole (nature), Emerson makes the arch romantic error. I certainly do not deny that many poets, who are by nature egotistic, have fallen into this solipsistic delusion; I insist only that when they make that error their poetry can provide no understanding and will at best warrant praise for the manner in which it tells mellifluous lies.

Needless to say, Jeffers indulged in partial contradiction when he attacked self-consciousness since man makes up part of that world of which man is conscious. In "Margrave," for example, his hatred of self-consciousness seriously flaws a poem that contains many beautiful lines. The story of Margrave, the young medical student who murdered a child in an attempt to get money for his education, depicts with a vengeance the results of extreme self-consciousness. Though certainly a memorable poem, one no reader is likely to forget, "Margrave" is philosophically top-heavy. The story simply cannot bear the weight of the message which Jeffers thrusts upon it. When he says the stars would be wise to flee the infection of consciousness, the beauty of the lines cannot prevent our dismay over his exaggeration—not of human perversity but of the human capacity for infecting the nonhuman world. Even though the creature may succeed in destroying much of his habitat, the earth in cosmic terms, as Jeffers would admit, is of little consequence.

Nor does Jeffers's confession of personal guilt in spreading the contagion of consciousness do much to restore an equilibrium to the poem, but in themselves the lines are important:

I also am not innocent
Of contagion, but have spread my spirit on the deep world.
I have gotten sons and sent the fire wider.
I have planted trees, they also feel while they live.
I have humanized the ancient sea-sculptured cliff
And the ocean's wreckage of rock
Into a house and a tower,
Hastening the sure decay of granite with my hammer,
Its hard dust will make soft flesh;
And have widened in my idleness
The disastrous personality of life with poems,
That are pleasant enough in the breeding but go bitterly at last
To envy oblivion and the early deaths of nobler
Verse, and much nobler flesh;
And I have projected my spirit
Behind the superb sufficient forehead of nature
To gift the inhuman God with this rankling consciousness.

After a pause the poet then questions his guilt. In all his poems of meditation, Jeffers employed this strophe-antistrophe structure, usually (as in this case) to fit his individual response into the infinitely larger nonhuman frame of reference:

But who is our judge? It is likely the enormous
Beauty of the world requires for completion our ghostly increment,
It has to dream, and dream badly, a moment of its night.

V

The greatest difference between Jeffers and the romantic (or nihilist or symbolist or existentialist) lies in their variant attitudes toward essence and the manner of (for Jeffers) discovering or (for the romantic) creating that essence. Primary essence for Jeffers resides in the beauty of physical nature, a beauty which is given permanence through the cyclic rhythms of molecular growth and decay. In this view he is thoroughly Grecian. Man discovers, or rather discerns, through his sense organs the essential beauty of the world and derives health and strength therefrom. Jeffers has been criticized, as might be expected, for his assumption that the world possesses a beauty which exists apart from any human perceiver. Joseph Warren Beach has commented on this problem, or perhaps contradiction:

> One would like to know how this poet justifies in his own mind his constant judgment that the world is beautiful. He is a trained and subtle thinker; and I fancy that, if he were challenged, he would admit that he cannot support this judgment on strictly philosophic grounds—that it is, in the last analysis, an anthropomorphic view. He tries to rise above the plane of man's judgments, and has rid himself of many purely human assumptions—emotional, ethical, religious. But in the end he must fall back on his own instruments of perception, and his purely esthetic appraisal of the universe is put in terms of man's physical vision and his intellectual craving for order.[13]

That Jeffers was aware of the problem is clear from his various attempts to resolve it. For example, in the second part of *The Double Axe*, "The Inhumanist," the old man begins by trying to answer the question, "What does God want?" That He is an amoral force seems clear enough, but He is also an ordering agent, always seeking harmonies. The old man speaks of this God:

> *"I see he despises happiness; and as for goodness, he says, What is it? and of evil, What is it?*
> *And of love and hate, They are equal; they are two spurs,*
> *For the horse has two flanks.—What does God want? I see here what he wants: he wants what man's*
> *Feeling for beauty wants—if it were fierce as hunger or hate and deep as the grave."*

And though that beauty is in the beholder's brain, it is reflected there from God's body. How does Jeffers know this? Only in the sense, I suppose, that one knows of one's existence—through animal faith:

> *"The beauty of things—*
> *Is in the beholder's brain—the human mind's translation of their transhuman*
> *Intrinsic value. It is their color in our eyes: as we say blood is red and blood is the life:*
> *It is the life. Which is* like *beauty. It is* like *nobility. It has no name—and that's lucky, for names*
> *Foul in the mouthing."*

Whereas Jeffers works from the outside in, the romantic moves from the self outward; he considers nature only in its relation to self, and is concerned above all else with *his* essence. The Sartrean existentialist even goes so far as to insist that existence precedes essence; which is to say, there is no essence until I exist. In other words, essence is a peculiarly human possession that the individual must create. In that creation man becomes God—a view the Christian considers blasphemous, and one that Jeffers considered ridiculous. The symbolist makes the same error when he reduces matter to symbol (after the fashion of Emerson), a process which then enables him to read the world as he wishes. As I remarked before, Jeffers never confused symbol with the thing being symbolized. Moreover, the symbols he used were those which the human race has been using since the development of language. Indeed all forms of knowledge are to some degree symbolic. Man no longer resides in a merely physical universe, and as our knowledge increases so too does the extent of our dependence upon symbols, as Ernst Cassirer has pointed out:

> Language, myth, art, and religion are parts of this [symbolic] universe. They are the varied threads which weave the symbolic net, the tangled web of human experience. All human progress in thought and experience refines upon and strengthens this net. No longer can man confront reality immediately; he cannot see it, as it were, face to face. Physical reality seems to recede in proportion as man's symbolic activity advances. Instead of dealing with the things themselves man is in a sense constantly conversing with himself. He has so enveloped himself in linguistic forms, in artistic images, in mythical symbols or religious rites that he cannot see or know anything except by the interposition of this artificial medium. His situation is the same in the theoretical as in the practical sphere. Even here man does not live in a world of hard facts, or according to his immediate needs and desires. He lives rather in the midst of imaginary emotions, in hopes and fears, in illusions and disillusions, in his fantasies and dreams. "What disturbs and alarms men," said Epictetus, "are not the things, but his opinions and fancies about the things."[13]

Jeffers was intensely aware of this and was thus all the more careful to avoid employing private symbols in order to create a private world, which would wall him out of the real world that exists symbol-free. His concern is clearly apparent in his "Credo"; there he comments on the manner in which individuals have turned the material world into symbols in order to escape multiplicity and become pure "subjects"—that is, gods—leaning silently on the dream of an all-inclusive self.

My friend from Asia has powers and magic, he plucks a blue leaf from the young blue-gum
And gazing upon it, gathering and quieting
The God in his mind, creates an ocean more real than the ocean, the salt, the actual
Appalling presence, the power of the waters.
He believes that nothing is real except as we make it. I humbler have found in my blood
Bred west of Caucasus a harder mysticism.
Multitude stands in my mind but I think that the ocean in the bone vault is only
The bone vault's ocean: out there is the ocean's;
The water is the water, the cliff is the rock, come shocks and flashes of reality. The mind
Passes, the eye closes, the spirit is a passage;
The beauty of things was born before eyes and sufficient to itself; the heart-breaking beauty
Will remain when there is no heart to break for it.

In "Boats in a Fog," Jeffers spoke of the "essential reality / Of creatures going about their business among the equally / Earnest elements of nature." The picture of the fishing boats "Following the cliff for guidance, / Holding a difficult path between the peril of the sea-fog / And the foam on the shore granite" is a portrait of a shared reality, of that "bitter earnestness" that makes beauty. The poem recalls Emerson's "Each and All" in its insistence that beauty (and for Jeffers, beauty gives meaning as for Emerson it reflected truth) depends upon the relatedness of things. To remove an object from its proper setting is to deprive it of its natural beauty, and hence of its meaning. In poem after poem he comes back to the view that man separated from nature is ugly; directly and unequivocally he employs the polarities of beauty and ugliness, of meaning and meaninglessness, of health and sickness. In "The Answer," for example, he denies that there is any escape from relatedness or that the props of civilization can prevent the periodic breakings-down, the violent upheavals. Any attempt man makes to remove himself from the fabric of the phenomenological world causes him to appear to be monstrous.

A severed hand
Is an ugly thing, and man dissevered from the earth and stars and his history . . . for contemplation or in fact . . .
Often appears atrociously ugly. Integrity is wholeness, the greatest beauty is
Organic wholeness, the wholeness of life and things, the divine beauty of the universe. Love that, not man
Apart from that, or else you will share man's pitiful confusions, or drown in despair when his days darken.

Published on the page next to "Boats in a Fog" (in *Roan Stallion, Tamar and Other Poems* and then later in *The Selected Poetry*) is a complementary poem entitled "Fog," which analyzes the human hunger to reside outside the natural environment. The two poems complement each other as do opposite polarities. Much less well known than "Boats in a Fog" (one of the most widely anthologized American poems), "Fog" is also one of Jeffers's most difficult poems. An explication should help to clarify his attitude toward idealism and the saviors it spawns. The poem follows:

Invisible gulls with human voices cry in the sea-cloud
"There is room, wild minds,
Up high in the cloud; the web and the feather remember
Three elements, but here
Is but one, and the webs and the feathers
Subduing but the one
Are the greater, with strength and to spare." You dream, wild criers,
The peace that all life
Dreams gluttonously, the infinite self that has eaten
Environment, and lives
Alone, unencroached on, perfectly gorged, one God.
Caesar and Napoleon
Visibly acting their dreams of that solitude, Christ and Gautama,
Being God, devouring
The world with atonement for God's sake . . . ah sacred hungers,
The conqueror's, the prophet's,
The lover's, the hunger of the sea-beaks, slaves of the last peace,
Worshippers of oneness.

In the opening line the "invisible gulls with human voices" cry to us from the fog, that is, from the realm of illusion and, as we shall see, from self-delusion and egocentric vanity. The gulls are both the scavengers of earth and the deceived ones, the "gulled" humans, the "worshippers of oneness." From the sea-cloud (fog) comes the cry, addressed to the "wild minds" (minds made wild by the desire to escape the confines, or rather the indifference, of Nature and her multitude), that in the ethereal realm may be found strength or power unattainable in the phenomenological world. The "web and the feather" constitute the natural or physical aspect of the "voices." They "remember" the three elements of nature (earth, air and water); which is to say, they empirically remember multiplicity. The voices, which seem to be nothing more than the articulated imaginations of men, inform us, however, that the subduing of "but the one" element is greater than remaining a part of the plural elements of life. In other words, the contraction of all phenomena into one essence will satisfy the desire of man to look upon himself as not just one of the parts of the natural world, but as the crown and source of all the parts—hence, the god of phenomena. Such reasoning will satisfy man's ancient urge to unify, to make all things One Thing—in effect, to find a shelter against the world, against every thing outside the "brain vault." It placates man's fear of being separate from the universe he inhabits by placing him in the godlike position of having created his habitat. Ironically it separates him even further; gods are obviously distant from their subjects, just as the subject is removed from the object. It is, in brief, solipsism—the most ludicrous, as well as most injurious, outgrowth of philosophical idealism.

After the speech of the gulls has ended in "Fog," the poet answers sarcastically: "You dream, wild criers, / The peace that all life / Dreams gluttonously, the infinite self that has eaten / Environment, and lives / Alone, unencroached on, perfectly gorged, one God." That is, the gulls imagine the oneness, "the peace," that all creatures desire, since all are captives of their own being, especially man, whose active imagination aids in the building of his illusions. Furthermore, since man cannot escape his being, since he cannot climb outside his microcosm, he takes revenge on nature by attempting to drag the world of phenomena into his self, thereby quieting his uneasy sense of separateness. The "infinite self" expresses perfectly the concept of man as subject only, as solipsistic creator who has devoured the world. As creator he lives alone, unencroached on, containing multitudes (as Whitman might say)—in brief, the source and end of all things—more briefly, "one God."

The last seven lines of "Fog" illustrate by the examples of two conquerors and two prophets the process by which men create their gods through dreams and gluttony. Unable to believe that all men are gods, which would deprive the elected gods of their uniqueness in any case, man delegates divinity to certain individuals who are, needless to say, most desirous of wearing the divine plumage. Some of these gods or saviors visibly act "their dream of . . . solitude"—the solitude being the oneness that the gulls (and gulled) crave. Such minor gods are embodiments of power, one of the attributes of God. Then there are those who desire more than just the active power of the dictator, or, more realistically, who see that such power is beyond their grasp. Like Christ and Gautama, they desire power over the minds of men, as contrasted to the Caesarian power over the bodies of men. To gain such power, they strive to become God in the eyes of men. To maintain posthumous power over the mind of posterity, they demand atonement from the world, which they in fact rejected when they rejected naturalism for idealism or supernaturalism. Which is to say, in order to possess men's minds, they must reject the physical world, and the more memorably vivid that rejection the better—by hanging from the cross, for example. As long as the mind of man retains an image of the dead god and feels responsible for his death, the god will be mistaken by some for God. The metamorphosing of flesh into image (or symbol) is at the heart of all theogonies. Since nothing in nature may reside at the still point of the turning world, the man seeking escape from time's flow must denaturize his god and thus place him outside time. Having once placed his god outside time, the worshiper then joins him there through the simple act of devouring his flesh. In nearly all religions, ancient and modern, there is some element of theophagy, or god-eating.

In "Fog" the "sacred hungers" of the conqueror, the prophet, and the lover (who obviously wishes to possess the mind and body of his loved one) are similar to the hunger of the scavenger sea-beaks. They are slaves of the "last peace," which could be the final peace of extinction as it is in many Jeffers poems; but in this case, it is more likely

"The peace that all life / Dreams gluttonously," the oneness that the fogbound dreamers find when removed from the earth, that "materiality" which makes possible and which precedes the mind and its imaginings of grandeur. "Worshippers of oneness" stands in apposition to "slaves of the last peace"—the only two phrases in the last lines that are not possessive case, that are not possessive of the sacred hungers.

While those hungers may be sacred, they nonetheless cause man to be the most destructive of all the beasts. It was the hunger of the crucified Jew, as Jeffers tells us in "Theory of Truth," that has "stained an age; nearly two thousand years are one vast poem drunk with the wine of his blood." In that poem Jeffers muses over those rare individuals who seek answers to the "large time-worn questions." He mentions specifically Lao-tze, Jesus, Buddha, and the main character in his long narrative *The Women at Point Sur*, the Reverend Arthur Barclay. Though each man found truth, he then muddled his finding by mixing with it his private impurity—Lao-tze's envy of Confucius and the Chinese princes, the bastardy of Jesus (which he attempted to deny by claiming God for his father), and the immense pity of Buddha and his need to annul suffering.

In his inability to discern any essence in matter and his attempt then to find essence in abstraction, the nihilist is the perfect innocent, intent solely on creation of self. The extent or compass of that self depends on awareness, both the awareness one has of his own self and the awareness others might have. To find self, to locate it temporally and spatially, one must "revolt," which is to say, one must dare to "disturb the universe." It is no wonder that nihilists have been known to shake the earth since what being they possess is determined by the amount of noise they make in a hollow world. (The man who finds himself at home in the world obviously will have no need to revolt against the conditions of existence though he can, like a Copernicus, or a Darwin, or an Einstein, have great influence on mankind through his discovery of natural truths.) The most romantic of all the romantics, the nihilist is most convinced that he possesses the power of creativity, which takes the place of discovery. In order to create, one must of course destroy. The artist who hacks at marble to find in stone the portrait of self is romantic; the sculptor seeking forms of perfection that have always existed does something quite different. He creates nothing new; rather he seeks those physical embodiments outside self that might coincide with forms that have always resided, however latently, in that brain compartment that houses our racial dreams of perfection. His is not an attempt at self-expression so much as it is a search for beauty of line and texture, of harmonies and relationships. He does not actually create; rather he finds or discovers. He is, as Jeffers put it, "only the ape of that God" who "brays humanity in a mortar to bring the savor / From the bruised root."

The true artist then (that rare individual unresponsive to fad or fashion) shares with the scientist a common quest: they both seek truth. In a late poem ("The Great Wound" from *The Beginning and the End*), Jeffers commented on the similar methods, the one employing equations and the other using metaphors, of science and poetry:

The mathematicians and physics men
Have their mythology; they work alongside the truth,
Never touching it; their equations are false
But the things work. *Or, when gross error appears,*
They invent new ones; they drop the theory of waves
In universal ether and imagine curved space.
Nevertheless their equations bombed Hiroshima.
The terrible things worked.
The poet also
Has his mythology. He tells you the moon arose
Out of the Pacific basin. He tells you that Troy was burnt for a vagrant
Beautiful woman, whose face launched a thousand ships.
It is unlikely: it might be true: but church and state
Depend on more peculiarly impossible myths:
That all men are born free and equal: consider that!
And that a wandering Hebrew poet named Jesus
Is the God of the universe. Consider that!

Forty years ago, long before the division between the "two cultures" was popularized by C. P. Snow, Hans Zinsser commented on the scientist-artist conflict in his classic *Rats, Lice and History*. His observations still possess an amazing immediacy:

> To most of the literary critics—probably because of their almost incredible ignorance of scientific thought—the so-called scientist is a "mere rationalist," and science is held, in respect to art, as photography is to painting. This separation on the basis of precision is utterly untenable.

Science is not a whit more photographic than is art. Measurements and formulations are, even in the so-called exact—the physical—sciences, not much more than reasonably accurate approximations. Scientific method is again and again forced to employ abstract conceptions, irrational numbers like $\sqrt{2}$ and $\sqrt{3}$, the line without breadth, the point without volume, zero, the negative quality, or the idea of infinity. And scientific thought continually sets sail from ports of hypothesis and fiction, advance bases of the exploring intellect. Matter becomes molecules, molecules become atoms; atoms, ions; ions, electrons; and these, in turn, become uncomprehended sources of energy—not more clear as seizable reality than the poet's conception of the "soul," which he knows only from its "energy"—the yearnings, delights, and sorrows which he feels. The history of science is full of examples of what, in art, would be spoken of as inspiration, but for which Whitehead's definition, "speculative reason," seems much more appropriate.[14]

Zinsser then looks briefly at the misuse of the word *creative*, concluding that both scientist and artist are really observers. Jeffers would doubtless have agreed completely with what the bacteriologist says here:

It is only too painfully obvious, moreover, that neither the scientist nor the artist is ever a "creator." The word "creative," so incessantly misused by our younger critical schools, is a fiction of that optimism about human achievement which—it has been said—thrives most vigorously in lunatic asylums. Nature, as Goethe puts it, runs its course by such eternal and necessary principles that even the gods themselves cannot alter them. The most that the scientist and the artist accomplish is new understanding of things that have always been. They "create" a clearer perception. They are both, in this sense, observers, the obvious differences being that the scientist impersonally describes the external world, whereas the artist expresses the effects which external things exert upon his own mind and heart. In both cases, the more generally applicable the observations, the greater is the science or art.

Would it not be fair to say that an achievement of observations becomes science or art according to the degree to which its comprehension calls upon perception by the reason or by the emotions, respectively? The capacities of intelligence form a sort of spectrum which extends from what we may call an infra-emotional to an ultrareason range. At the infra-emotional extreme lie the perceptions set in motion by music and by lyrical poetry. At the opposite end—that of pure reason—is placed the perceptional capacity for mathematics. Between the two there is a wide range of overlapping where art is scientific and science artistic. Literature in the

> sense of prose may be taken to hold a middle ground, shading on the left into epic and narrative poetry, and on the right through psychology, biology, and so forth, toward mathematics.
>
> "What happens when you go off the deep end of either side?" asked my friend.
>
> "Well, beyond the 10^{-10} range experience seems to show that the end organs give out and the physicist joins the church; whereas on the other side, as I should judge from Joyce, Gertrude Stein, and their imitators, the spinal cord begins to horn in on the brain. In either case it ceases to be science or art."[15]

All of this will no doubt be considered blasphemous by the self-delegated defenders of the literary domain. Zinsser realized this himself: "This chapter," he wrote, "will be received with contemptuous shrugs by the professionally literary." Moreover, his belief that "the greatest poetry is communication and is clear" will not be popular among the explicators. Indeed, the obscurantism which makes respectable that which is incomprehensible has, ironically (since a major responsibility of the critic is the clarification of the obscure), afflicted the contemporary critic more than the artist. I wish Zinsser's merry assault on certain passages of Eliot, the later Joyce, and the nonsense of Stein could be made required reading for all graduate students of modern literature.

As I remarked above, the cause for the frenzied search for a unique style, so apparent in much contemporary art, is probably attributable to the fact that at no other time has man's individuality been more diminished. Shorn of anything remotely resembling significance when viewed against the vast rhythms of evolution, the species stands shivering before a crossroads. One way leads man outward, away from self into nature and its eternal flow and endless being. The other leads him back into the self, a journey possible to those who can close their minds to empirical evidence or who can transform that evidence into symbols that take the place of reality. The smaller he is made to feel by scientific thought, the more man retreats from objective consideration of the world into subjective manipulation of all that seems to oppress him. A Shelley or a Wordsworth could draw from nature analogues to fit his own moods without doing violence to those objects in nature from which he drew his comparisons. But the latter-day romantic can no longer take comfort in the knowledge that he is a part of nature. Having been apprised of its heartless impersonality, he retreats even further from his natural home into the artificiality of imagery and symbol, which are no longer mere vehicles to the expression of his weltansicht but have become ends in themselves. It would be little exaggeration to say that art has ceased to be an effort to understand and describe the world and has become a haven for those in need of escape. One of the best ways of escaping into self, of walling out the world, is to devise a separate language that might be comprehended at least vaguely by the select few who are willing to spend their lives studying your life. Joyce said as much in his famous remark about how long it would take for the reader to plumb his depths. One hopes we might be forgiven if Joyce seems to us somewhat less important than the world we inhabit. The artist engaged in creating his self, on whatever anvil of the soul, is analogous to the infant in the crib playing with his toes. The picture might delight, but it can be instructive only in the narrowest sense. What seems precious in the infant readily becomes preciosity in the adult.

In "Signpost" Jeffers proposed that the only way civilized man might become human again was to "climb the great ladder out of the pit of yourself and man":

> *At length*
> *You will look back along the stars' rays and see that even*
> *The poor doll humanity has a place under heaven.*
> *Its qualities repair their mosaic around you, the chips of strength*
> *And sickness; but now you are free, even to become human,*
> *But born of the rock and the air, not of a woman.*

That the "ladder" exists should be obvious, but all civilization in general and the corporate state in particular inveigh against our employing it to climb out of the pit of self; moreover, that ascent is far too arduous for all but the rare spirits who can bear the loneliness of the journey that leads outward from humanity, or more precisely humanity as it is in an increasingly urbanized and interdependent social setting. So outraged by human conceit (or self-consciousness) and cruelty was he that Jeffers recommended cutting humanity from out our natures—as did for that matter Nietzsche, the patron saint of so much contemporary thought. It was Nietzsche who said that man must be overcome, that he was a going-under, a bridge spanning the gulf between the protozoa and the *Übermensch*. He depicted our species as dangling forlornly between two worlds—one of pure instinct, now dead; the other of pure reason, powerless to be born. Jeffers asked man to lean on the silent rock and admire the noble hawk rather than share in the contagions of humanity. In contrast to Nietzsche, he asked that we defuse the ego and uncenter our lives by loving the physical world rather than man; after all, we share the qualities of what we love.

FOUR Breaking Out of Humanity

There is a great deal of human nature in man. —Charles Kingsley

In a letter to Rudolph Gilbert, written from England in November 1929, Jeffers sought to answer Gilbert's query concerning the meaning of the phrase "breaking out of humanity." After first admitting that poetry cannot be translated into prose "without seeming exaggerated and mystical, or else flattened down to mere common sense," he suggested a number of things that were meant by the phrase. His comments, which have been quoted in nearly all the important studies of his work, explain his intentions better than anything else ever written:

> (1) We have learned within the past century or so that humanity is only a temporary and infinitesimal phenomenon in a large universe. The knowledge involves a readjustment of values that can only be managed by looking at humanity objectively, from the outside.
>
> (2) The phrase refers also to those moments of visionary enlightenment that I should hate to call "cosmic consciousness" because so much foolishness has been written about them under that name.
>
> (3) It seems to me wasteful that almost the whole of human energy is expended inward, on itself, in loving, hating, governing, cajoling, amusing, its own members. It is like a new born babe, conscious almost exclusively of its own processes and where its food comes from. As the child grows up its attention must be drawn from itself to the more important world outside it.
>
> (4) In a civilization like ours, metropolitanism intensified by machinery, human nature (which was developed under very different conditions) becomes an anachronism. We can't turn back the civilization, not at least until it collapses, and our descendents will have to develop a new sort of nature—will have to "break out of humanity"—or suffer considerably—probably both.[1]

It is not difficult to see why the phrase, and the adjacent lines, should have been widely misunderstood forty years ago. Events of the past few decades have forced even the average man to see, however dimly, what Jeffers meant. The great concern for ecology has led many commentators to reassess our values and take up with renewed vigor the question of human nature and possible ways of reprogramming that nature. But at the time Jeffers seemed almost to have regretted writing the passage that led to all the misinterpretation. In any case, he saw fit, for the first and only time in his career, to write poetry that would clarify his meaning, or at least correct the misconceptions. In an often quoted letter to James Rorty, he remarked that one of the primary intentions of *The Women at Point Sur*, published two years after *Roan Stallion*, "was to show in action the danger of that 'Roan Stallion' idea of 'Breaking out of humanity,' misinterpreted in the mind of a fool or a lunatic." He added that "Just as Ibsen in the Wild Duck made a warning against his own idea in the hands of a fool, so Point Sur was meant to be a warning; but at the same time a reassertion."[2] As it turned out, his explanation needed explaining. *The Women at Point Sur* is considered at greater length in the following chapter. Here I shall concentrate on the idea as it is first enunciated in *Roan Stallion*, then as it is embodied, in a negative sense, throughout *Tamar*, and finally as it is given a positive statement in *The Tower Beyond Tragedy*.

These lines from *Roan Stallion*, including the important passage on tragedy, are at the heart of most of Jeffers's narrative poems.

Humanity is the start of the race; I say
Humanity is the mould to break away from, the crust to break through, the coal to break into fire,
The atom to be split.
Tragedy that breaks man's face and a white fire flies out of it; vision that fools him
Out of his limits, desire that fools him out of his limits, unnatural crime, inhuman science,
Slit eyes in the mask; wild loves that leap over the walls of nature, the wild fence-vaulter science,
Useless intelligence of far stars, dim knowledge of the spinning demons that make an atom,
These break, these pierce, these deify, praising their God shrilly with fierce voices: not in a man's shape
He approves the praise, he that walks lightning-naked on the Pacific, that laces the suns with planets,

The heart of the atom with electrons: what is humanity in this cosmos? For him, the last
Least taint of a trace in the dregs of the solution; for itself, the mould to break away from, the coal
To break into fire, the atom to be split.

Out of context the lines naturally lack the cogency they have in the poem where they complement events in the narrative. Immediately following the passage, California goes to the corral for the stallion and then rides it to the top of the hill—"the great arch and pride of the hill, the silent calvary." Before discussing the event that takes place there I must comment on the lines above. Obviously they express a decided criticism of the present state of humanity, depicted here as being in a perilous stage of half-development. Man has moved just far enough away from nature (in which the stallion is a fitting part and in which man, too, was more or less at home before his imaginative grasp of things enabled him to move beyond his former place) to be out of his depth. He is, as Robert Frost once put it, neither out far nor in deep, but still far enough from his original moorings to be an alien in nature. No longer able to depend entirely on his instincts, he must employ intelligence as a guide. And yet paradoxically his intelligence and imagination are responsible for his tragic dilemma; his intellectual growth, accompanied by and to some extent the result of his loss of instinct, has created his tragic condition. Were choice denied man, he could never of course be tragic. Hence various writers, D. H. Lawrence for example, have advocated a return to pure instinct and thus an escape from tragedy. Since he knew that such a return was flatly impossible to man, Jeffers insisted that he must break through the crust of humanity to a new awareness based upon knowledge, which cannot in any case be annulled or forgotten. The thoroughly rational being, Jeffers implies, will be able to avoid tragedy. But having arrived at the half-baked stage of humanity, man lives in a world of calvaries. The visions, desires, unnatural crimes, inhuman science, wild loves—these are the leading attributes of humanity, no matter how much man may wish to deny their existence.

California's half-formed desire to break the bounds of nature and become part of the roan beauty and strength illustrates the extent to which humanity has moved away from the natural or unreasoning world. Though capable of recognizing beauty and of imagining a kind of transcendence, she is only partially a reasoning animal. In the absence of reason man can imagine anything; in other words, his visions can "fool him out of his limits." California does possess imagination, which makes her certainly superior to her clod of a husband, but at the same time her imaginative faculty makes her an alien. In a sense her unnatural desire reminds us of the romantic perversities of the Marquis de Sade, who derived the greatest joy from whatever seems (to most of us anyhow) most unnatural. (Needless to say, many people, particularly psychologists, today refuse to believe that the words *natural* and *unnatural* are definable terms.) A moral absolutist, de Sade considered all of nature evil. As much an absolutist in his view that all of nature is evil as was Rousseau in his view that all of nature is good, de Sade could insist, quite logically (logic, after all, has always been the handmaiden of absolutists), that to practice vice was to conform to the laws of nature.

California's perverse wish for transcendence never gets beyond vision of course. Moreover we consider her, as did Jeffers, a thoroughly pathetic figure, more deserving of pity than censure. In a penciled draft of a letter written on 5 November 1944, Jeffers remarked that though the writer's interpretation of a poem had no particular authority, he personally believed she fell in love with the stallion because there was no one else she could fall in love with. Also, since her love was physically impractical "and the stallion seemed infinitely superior to any man she had known she identified him half-consciously with God. First with the God she had heard religious stories about, the Conception and so forth; and then with a more real God—not a human invention but the energy that is the universe. She was glad to sacrifice her husband to him—for whatever the man was worth. But at the end she slipped back into ordinary life, 'obscure human fidelity'—an animal had killed a man—she must kill the animal. Though the animal was also God."[3]

Considering her human environment, we must commend California for seeing in the stallion an object of adoration. She differs radically from Tamar in that she does not actually will herself beyond good and evil. In her unmoral innocence she seeks union with the beauty of nature; that is, she for the first time in her life finds an object worthy of adoration and then unconsciously and irrationally attempts to lose herself in that object. In brief, she loves outward rather than inward. Indeed she wished to do literally what Jeffers advocated figuratively. It is humanity she gropingly seeks to leave behind—something that in any literal fashion is, as Jeffers pointed out, impossible to do. Certainly she makes no attempt to overcome nature or go beyond good and evil, which are, at least in the circumscribed view of humanity, inherent in most human relations.

On the other hand, Tamar will seek to place humanity above nature and at the same time sever all relations with the human past. She will strive for an absolute freedom that will abrogate all morality and thus allow her to become the sole arbiter of moral value. In her total dedication to the abstraction *freedom* Tamar becomes monstrous. Hence she embodies the Nietzschean-Zarathustrian ideal of leaving humanity in order to become God. Unlike California, whose acts reveal a worship of God's beauty, Tamar attempts to draw that beauty into her ego. She finally insists that only in her consciousness can there exist quality; this assertion is of course the same thing as saying that she is God. She is the perfect romantic in that she wills the self into the position of the divine. That she is self-destructive as well as destructive of all around her is made clear in the poem. Nor should we wonder that modern readers find in Tamar's revolt much to praise. She would make a fitting heroine for today's counterculture. Jeffers succeeded all too well, as he was appalled to learn, in his portraiture. But before turning to *Tamar*, a final passage from *Roan Stallion* will help reveal the ever-widening gulf between human visions and desires, and the natural world against which those visions and desires are contrasted and belittled.

In the lines describing her location on calvary (a calvary in the sense that a kind of immolation takes place there), California dreams of breaking out of humanity, as we all do at times.[4]

Here is solitude, here on the calvary, nothing conscious
But the possible God and the cropped grass, no witness, no eye but that misformed one, the moon's past fullness.
Two figures on the shining hill, woman and stallion, she kneeling to him, brokenly adoring.

He cropping the grass, shifting his hooves, or lifting the long head to gaze over the world,
Tranquil and powerful. She prayed aloud, "O God, I am not good enough, O fear, O strength, I am draggled.
Johnny and other men have had me, and O clean power! Here am I," she said, falling before him,
And crawled to his hooves. She lay a long while, as if asleep, in reach of the fore-hooves, weeping. He avoided
Her head and the prone body. He backed at first; but later plucked the grass that grew by her shoulder.
The small dark head under his nostrils: a small round stone, that smelt human, black hair growing from it:
The skull shut the light in: it was not possible for any eyes
To know what throbbed and shone under the sutures of the skull, or a shell full of lightning
Had scared the roan strength, and he'd have broken tether, screaming, and run for the valley.

The "light" glowing in the skull of California does not find release. When such light is released, havoc and destruction pour forth on the world. That is to say, when humans are most responsive to the hallmarks of humanity (the visions, desires, unnatural crimes, inhuman science, wild loves) they are at their most outrageous.

Breaking away from humanity is tantamount to cleansing oneself of unnatural desires—the most monstrous and terrible (albeit at times "terribly beautiful") of which is the desire to transcend one's biological nature at the behest of some metaphysical or supernatural fantasy. It is obviously the all-too-human desire to become superhuman that Jeffers attacks. Compare this kind of overcoming (abjuring unnatural desires) with the Nietzschean variety, and you will begin to comprehend the great dichotomy between their respective exhortations. Jeffers believed that man had already gone too far in the direction of romantic excess; Nietzsche asked that he go even further. Nietzsche's violent attacks on Darwinian thought are thus in perfect accord with his philosophy of the superman. Darwin's "bulldog," T. H. Huxley, who was as great an opponent of the Christian myth as Nietzsche, was a far saner and wiser man than the German prophet. That the latter has had a greater influence on modern thought is a sad commentary on our age and on men of letters in particular, but it is not very difficult to understand: Huxley's appeal is to the intellect; Nietzsche's, as often as not, is to the emotions. Above all, Nietzsche's denunciations of the canaille are ipso facto flattering to the ego of his readers, none of whom is likely to lose much love for the herd.

In praising the will to power as a means of elevating humanity beyond itself, Nietzsche apparently did not realize that he was in the process isolating man from nature as well as from anthropomorphic gods. This is ironic since his war on Christianity was really an attack on the nihilism to which Christianity inevitably led in its denaturizing of man; it is ironic in that his superman was as far removed from nature and as nihilistic as any Christian ever was. All gods—whether they reside in the sky or on earth—are by their very nature nihilistic in that they are deprived of anything outside themselves that might give meaning and order to existence. The nature of a god is that he is self-subsistent, that all values come from within. Obviously, an inborn value cannot be measured against anything; indeed, such inner values are the creatures of individual whim. To such men the outer world is nothing, the individual soul everything.

It is a matter of simple fact that Jeffers believed the exact opposite of this. For him it is the outer world that is "real and divine," whereas "one's own soul might be called an illusion, it is so slight and so transitory."[5] In *The Women at Point Sur* he would draw his most complete portrait of the Nietzschean hero. Literature offers no more frightening picture than that of the Reverend Arthur Barclay, whose search for truth, noble in its inception, conveys him into the dark recesses of sadistic self-indulgence and finally total insanity. Having lost faith in the Christian god, he seeks him elsewhere until he finds him in the self. The greatest human perversion, to which all other perversions are mere footnotes, is the belief that one is god.

II

It is interesting to note how similar are the wellsprings of Tamar's actions and the philosophical exhortations of Nietzsche. Like most great discoverers (and I consider him second to none in the area of morals or values), Nietzsche opened our eyes so we might see precisely what our moral values do for us and how much they cost. In *Beyond Good and Evil* he wrote that not until the present did modern

Europeans know for certain the precise nature of morality. That is, they had answered the one question that Socrates admitted he could not. (Nietzsche probably refers here to modern philosophers, not the common man since the commoner or herd-man has always been sure that he knew the difference between good and evil.) A quotation from that inspired attack on all the self-deluded ones, the "sleepy ones," as Nietzsche called them, is useful in showing the sort of moral monism or absolutism which Tamar rejects. We need to remember of course that Tamar acts out her rejection in dramatic fashion, as a character in a narrative poem, whereas Nietzsche's rejection is one of statement. Philosophy and art may reach the same destination, but they will invariably arrive by different routes.

> We have found that in all major moral judgments Europe is now of one mind, including even the countries dominated by the influence of Europe: plainly, one now *knows* in Europe what Socrates thought he did not know and what that famous old serpent once promised to teach—today one "knows" what is good and evil.
>
> Now it must sound harsh and cannot be heard easily when we keep insisting: that which here believes it knows, that which here glorifies itself with its praises and reproaches, calling itself good, that is the instinct of the herd animal, man, which has scored a breakthrough and attained prevalence and predominance over other instincts—and this development is continuing in accordance with the growing physiological approximation and assimilation of which it is the symptom. *Morality in Europe today is herd animal morality*—in other words, as we understand it, merely *one* type of human morality beside which, before which, and after which many other types, above all *higher* moralities, are, or ought to be, possible. But this morality resists such a "possibility," such an "ought" with all its power: it says stubbornly and inexorably, "I am morality itself, and nothing besides is morality." Indeed, with the help of a religion which indulged and flattered the most sublime herd-animal desires, we have reached the point where we find even in political and social institutions an ever more visible expression of this morality: the *democratic* movement is the heir of the Christian movement.[6]

I quote the passage at length, including the remark about democracy being an offshoot of the *Sklavenmoral*, because most of Jeffers's poetry, early and late, will in its moral implications begin right there. It would be presumptuous, however, to say that Jeffers necessarily followed from Nietzsche since we can find thinkers all the way back to Greece

(Heraclitus, for example) who professed much the same views. But Nietzsche described herd morality better than most other moderns, and he is everywhere credited with having influenced Jeffers.

Though he agreed with Nietzsche's description of modern man's peculiar plight, Jeffers veered sharply away from the Nietzschean solution. Like all other romantics, Nietzsche could never escape the anthropocentricism or even the anthropomorphism that he objected to in the Christian myth. For all their differences in manner, the romantic and the Christian are really quite similar in that they both elevate man beyond his natural origins when they place him in a position above the phenomenological world. What could be more egotistic than the Christian view that man is fallen, that he is of such cosmic importance that God should have him fall so that He might send His son to lift him up again? Well, the romantic goes the Christian one better: man *is* the god who fell and can, through the use of his will, lift himself up again.

When Tamar, who is described as "half innocent" before she entices her brother Lee to commit incest with her, rejects all authority, even that of "custom," which Jeffers says creates human nature, she makes the arch mistake of thinking herself free. Moreover she thinks she has gone beyond nature, until the scene on the beach when she is visited by the phantom presences called up by her aunt Stella, the medium who is obviously the mouthpiece for our racial past; through Stella's lips the dead Helen, in particular, speaks. And Tamar is no more able to deny the atavistic demands of that past than was Kurtz in *Heart of Darkness*. The origins of her being are not in the skies but in the earth beneath, or more precisely at the water's edge where man first began his journey.

It seemed to her that all her body
Was touched and troubled with polluting presences
Invisible, and whatever had happened to her from her two lovers
She had been until that hour inviolately a virgin,
Whom now the desires of dead men and dead Gods and a dead tribe
Used for their common prey . . . dancing and weeping,
Slender and maidenly . . . The chant was changed,
And Tamar's body responded to the change, her spirit
Wailing within her. She heard the brutal voice
And hated it, she heard old Jinny mimic it

In the cracked childish quaver, but all her body
Obeyed it, wakening into wantonness,
Kindling with lust and wilder
Coarseness of insolent gestures,
The senses cold and averse, but the frantic too-governable flesh
Inviting the assaults of whatever desired it, of dead men
Or Gods walking the tide-marks,
The beautiful girlish body as gracile as a maiden's
Gone beastlike, crouching and widening,
Agape to be entered, as the earth
Gapes with harsh heat-cracks, the inland adobe of sun-worn valleys
At the end of summer
Opening sick mouths for its hope of the rain,
So her body gone mad
Invited the spirits of the night, her belly and her breasts
Twisting, her feet dashed with blood where the granite had bruised them,
And she fell, and lay gasping on the sand, on the tide-line.

On reawakening from the trance, with the visitors departed, Tamar implores Stella to call up her dead aunt Helen, her father's sister and partner in incest. The ensuing dialogue between Tamar and Helen, whose symbolic meaning is quite important to our understanding of Jeffers's view of human history as enmeshed in eternal recurrence, clearly shows, for one thing, that Tamar was given free choice in the direction she would take. The choice she makes is the romantic one—the Nietzschean way whereby man seeks to leave humanity behind by becoming superhuman, a choice that is neither more nor less intelligent than the dipsomaniac's attempt to cure his alcoholism by drinking everything in the liquor store. In her first remarks to Tamar, Helen says,

"We dead have traded power for wisdom, yet it is hard for us to wait on the maniac living
Patiently, the desires of you wild beasts. You have the power."

In the next lines Tamar repudiates Helen and thereby racial knowledge. It is not wisdom that she wants, but only the power that comes with possession, or with fulfillment of desires. It is also noteworthy that Tamar tells Helen that God has set their house on fire, when in fact, as Helen knows, it was Tamar who tried to burn the house. In other words, Tamar blames God for the actions of men, whereas

Helen knows that only man is culpable. Thus rebuked by Helen, Tamar vents her hatred on the dead:

"O believe me I hate you dead people
More than you dead hate me. Listen to me, Helen.
There is no voice as horrible to me as yours,
And the breasts the worms have worked in. A vicious berry
Grown up out of the graveyard for my poison.
But there is no one in the world as lonely as I,
Betrayed by life and death."

Tamar's hatred of death is clearly perverse in that it causes her to disassociate herself from the human condition and seek to go beyond nature. It is noteworthy, however, that Jeffers insists that God accepts Tamar as a part of things; only *human* gods would be capable of hating, or of loving, or of expressing any emotion.

God who makes beauty
Disdains no creature, nor despised that wounded
Tired and betrayed body. She in the starlight
And little noises of the rising tide
Naked and not ashamed bore a third part
With the ocean and keen stars in the consistence
And dignity of the world. She was white stone,
Passion and despair and grief had stripped away
Whatever is rounded and approachable
In the body of woman, hers looked hard, long lines
Narrowing down from the shoulder-bones, no appeal,
A weapon and no sheath, fire without fuel . . .

The implication here is that God is so far removed from, so indifferent to, such individual catastrophes as to make all the more ridiculous the human belief that what man does is of universal importance. Certainly Jeffers's God does not love humanity; to say that He does would be to impugn the divine force. But to believe, as Jeffers did, that the universe is well made makes mandatory the acceptance of finite humanity by the infinite nonhuman universe.

More importantly, Jeffers is thus able to contrast his naturalistic conception of God with the romantic conception. In conceiving of God in a Judeo-Christian sense, Tamar is thoroughly anthropocentric. She is arrogantly wrong in her romantic insistence that she bears a one-to-one relation with God and nature. Having been despoiled by human desires, which is to say having despoiled herself, she seeks revenge through defiance of God—the last infirmity of romantic minds.

> *"I have so passed nature*
> *That God himself, who's dead or all these devils*
> *Would never have broken hell, might speak out of you*
> *Last season thunder and not scare me."*

Henceforth all her efforts will be bent on destruction. With her god now dead she falls into the emptiness of nihilism and seeks to destroy all those around her. When the farmbell rings notification that the house is burning (she had started the blaze some time before), she prays that the house will be destroyed, which would, she believes, be evidence that her god, the god of retribution and revenge, did still exist:

> *"O strong and clean and terrible*
> *Spirit and not father punish the hateful house.*
> *Fire eat the walls and roofs, drive the red beast*
> *Through every wormhole of the rotting timbers*
> *And into the woods and into the stable, show them,*
> *These liars, that you are alive."*

The house does not burn. Only later will Jinny, the idiot, succeed in destroying it and all the inhabitants in one great rush of flame.

After learning that her sin with Lee was but the repetition of an act that had been performed over and over since the beginning of human history, Tamar attempts to "purify" her sin and thus elevate it beyond the self-limiting estate of eternal recurrence. She now hates Lee, partly because he plans to leave home for the war in Europe, but more because of his remorse and pity, which she correctly interprets as an outcropping of moralism and weakness. The confrontation between Tamar and her father, David, is obviously a meeting between the moral emptiness of the present and the outmoded religious props of the recent past. Notably in several of Jeffers's narrative poems—this is particularly important in *Give Your Heart to the Hawks*—the parents are depicted as nominal Christians whereas their children are non-believers trying to find some substitute for the religion in which they can no longer believe but from whose ethical values they cannot quite escape. In other words, Jeffers places modern man in a valueless state, able neither to sustain belief in the Christian myth nor develop new values to replace the myth. Though Tamar rejects Christian repentence, forgiveness, and salvation, she clings desperately to the view that she is a sinner. Indeed, as all such "believers" do, she glories in her sin. As she tells her father from whom she has wrested "power" in the house, which represents the modern world:

"Poor old man I have earned authority." "You have gone mad," he answered.
And she: "I'll show you our trouble, you sinned, your old book calls it, and repented: that was foolish.
I was unluckier, I had no chance to repent, so I learned something, we must keep sin pure
Or it will poison us, the grain of goodness in a sin is poison. Old man, you have no conception
Of the freedom of purity. Lock the door, old man, I am telling you a secret." But he trembling,
"O God thou hast judged her guiltless, the Book of thy word spake it, thou hast the life of the young man
My son . . ." and Tamar said, "Tell God we have revoked relationship in the house, he is not
Your son nor you my father." "Dear God, blot out her words, she has gone mad. Tamar, I will lock it,
Lest anyone should come and hear you, and I will wrestle for you with God, I will not go out
Until you are His." He went and turned the key and Tamar said, "I told you I have authority.
You obey me like the others, we pure have power. Perhaps there are other ways, but I was plunged
In the dirt of the world to win it, and, O father, so I will call you this last time, dear father
You cannot think what freedom and what pleasure live in having abjured laws, in having
Annulled hope, I am now at peace."

David insists that peace may be found only in God, and further insists that God never really forgives but rather allows evil to punish evil "with the horrible mockery of an echo"—that is, his incestuous relation with Helen receives punishment through the incest of his children. This line of causality Tamar necessarily rejects since it would make her a mere link in a chain rather than a free agent and hence a source of power. The thought that she might be nothing more than a factor in a causal sequence, rather than the mover of events, is as galling to her as it is to the Sartrean existentialist.

"Is the echo louder than the voice, I have surpassed her,
Yours was the echo, time stands still old man, you'll learn when you have lived at the muddy root
Under the rock of things; all times are now, to-day plays on last year and the inch of our future
Made the first morning of the world. You named me for the monument in a desolate graveyard,
Fool, and I say you were deceived, it was out of me that fire lit you and your Helen, your body
Joined with your sister's
Only because I was to be named Tamar and to love my brother and my father.
I am the fountain."

A few lines later, Tamar clarifies her remark that she is "the fountain" when she proposes that her father might recapture the past only by repeating in the present his past crime—his sin of incest. If all things are determined, as Tamar says, then a repeated action is, in a world of eternal recurrence, the same thing as an initial action. In a world in which all things are related and are circular, returning upon themselves, it is impossible to say just where the circle begins. In other words, there is no way to distinguish cause from effect.

It is a mistake to think that Tamar really offers herself to her father with the intention of possessing him. Rather she wishes power over the past which she can have only by convincing her father that she is the antecedent mover rather than the conditioned effect of forces outside her individual will. In effect she wishes to annul causality and thereby gain complete freedom. In brief, she desires to become God, and to become God she must gain absolute power. That power can be hers, she believes, only when she has enticed her father to "spit on" the dead Helen whom he has come to consider the cause of his sin and the sins of his children. In her attitude toward the dead, Tamar resembles very closely other romantics, particularly transcendentalists like Emerson who demanded above all else the "freedom" to be one's own god. Her hatred of Helen and her desire for power over the dead are clearly portrayed in the passage describing her humiliation of her father. She tells him that she has talked with the dead, with his "pitiful Helen," at which point he approaches her bed:

And he blindly
Clutching at her, she left the coverlet in his hands and slipping free at the other side
Saw in a mirror on the wall her own bright throat and shoulder and just beyond them the haggard
Open-mouthed mask, the irreverend beard and blind red eyes. She caught the mirror from its fastening
And held it to him, reverse. "Here is her picture, Helen's picture, look at her, why is she always
Crying and crying?" When he turned the frame and looked, then Tamar: "See that is her lover's.
The hairy and horrible lips to kiss her, the drizzling eyes to eat her beauty, happiest of women
If only he were faithful; he is too young and wild and lovely, and the lusts of his youth
Lead him to paw strange beds." The old man turned the glass and gazed at the blank side, and turned it
Again face toward him, he seemed drinking all the vision in it, and Tamar: "Helen, Helen,
I know you are here present; was I humbled in the night lately and you exulted?
See here your lover. I think my mother will not envy you now, your lover, Helen, your lover,
The mouth to kiss you, the hands to fondle secret places." Then the old man sobbing, "It is not easy
To be old, mocked, and a fool." And Tamar, "What, not yet, you have not gone mad yet? Look, old fellow.
These rags drop off, the bandages hid something but I'm done with them. See . . . I am the fire
Burning the house." "What do you want, what do you want?" he said, and stumbled toward her, weeping.
"Only to strangle a ghost and to destroy the house. Spit on the memory of that Helen
You might have anything of me."

When he says that he does hate Helen, then Tamar tells him "gently" that he may "unlock the door, old father, and go, and go." When he reminds her of her promise to commit incest with him, Tamar tells him that she has "no feeling of revolt against it," but wonders why she should let him be mocked by his God—a sarcasm that he does not miss.

And he, the stumpage of his teeth knocking together, "You think, you think
I'll go to the stables and a rope from a rafter
Finish it for you?" "Dear, I am still sick," she answered, "you don't want to kill me?
A man
Can wait three days: men have lived years and years on the mere hope."

It is obvious that Tamar does learn certain naturalistic truths from her experience—that is, from the ancestral voices that speak to her through Stella. She is far from being a mere stalking-horse for Jeffers's anti-romantic views; for all its gothic outlines, the story is convincingly real. Most importantly she learns that the moral dogmas of her father are simply empty words. Man's natural impulses—some of which have been necessarily deemed unnatural by social custom—can in no way be turned aside by Christian taboos. At the end of the narrative, with the house burning down upon the helpless captives of Tamar's hatred, old David Cauldwell is still forlornly praying to his god:

"Fierce, fierce light,
Have pity, Christ have pity, Christ have pity, Christ have pity,
Christ have pity,
Christ have pity . . ."
And Tamar with her back to the window embraced
Her brother, who struggled toward it, but the floor
Turned like a wheel.

The final four lines of the poem place the tragedy in natural perspective, showing that no matter how horrible the events may have been to the persons involved, the wound inflicted on nature was but slight and transitory:

Grass grows where the flame flowered;
A hollowed lawn strewn with a few black stones
And the brick of broken chimneys; all about there
The old trees, some of them scarred with fire, endure the sea wind.

In rejecting all moral guides or ideals outside the self, Tamar effectually cut herself off from the world of which she was a finite part. Ironically it was a naturalistic truth that caused her to reject the nonhuman world and attempt to live by the will to power. She was one of those for whom a little knowledge was infinitely too much. For instance, she got far enough out of humanity to view man's place in nature with naturalistic objectivity, as evidenced in her remark that suffering is universal and hence, in the largest view, meaningless:

> *"But I was thinking*
> *Last night, that people all over the world*
> *Are doing much worse and suffering much more than we*
> *This wartime, and the stars don't wink, and the ocean*
> *Storms perhaps less than usual."*

Far from being humbled by such knowledge (as were the men in Crane's "The Open Boat"), Tamar uses it as justification for what she has done and plans to do. Like many of those residing in the post-Darwinian period, she saw in that cosmic indifference reason for believing that God is dead. And from that assumption she moves to the romantic conclusion that all is permissible. Stripped of all but her ego, she wanders the middleground between values outlived and values unborn—in the transition stage between the anthropomorphic Christianity of her father and the new values now forming, whatever they may be. With no higher value than the self, she is both pathetic and dangerous. Leaving the rapidly failing light of her father's morality behind her, she steps into the moral darkness that covered the Victorian age and covers our own. She saw clearly enough that his moralism was composed of equal parts of hypocrisy and ignorance, but beyond that she could not see. From an imperfect knowledge of naturalistic tenets, she moves inevitably into nihilism. This, in the final analysis, is what Nietzsche did. She simply substitutes the self for the "dead god" created in the image of the self, thus compounding the anthropomorphic folly. Tamar in no sense breaks out of humanity. Rather she plunges, as do all romantics, into humanity. And this she does in the name of freedom.

If Tamar is caught in the net of self and perishes there, along with her three "lovers"—brother, father, and dupe (Will Andrews)—she at least does not extend that self to include disciples. Unlike Jesus in *Dear Judas* and Barclay in *The Women at Point Sur*, she does not use love to lead others into the abyss. She is not, in short, a savior. Tamar loves only physically, not at all abstractly as does the savior—although both Tamar and the savior love incestuously, one literally, the other symbolically. Between the two kinds of incest, Jeffers seems to say, there is no difference in kind but a vast difference in degree of degradation. In "Meditation on Saviors," he described the process of the will to power more completely than anywhere else. In two lines he catches the inevitable movement in any purely human salvation:

Out of incestuous love power and then ruin. A man forcing the imaginations of men,
Possessing with love and power the people; a man defiling his own household with impious desire.

The savior's desire for power, as we shall see in the next chapter, is engendered by some private inpurity, by his hatred for his station in society or even for the total human condition. Tamar's incest began in half innocence; in the beginning she possessed no desire for power over Lee or anyone else, nor was she particularly discontent with her world. And when her love for Lee sours to jealousy and then hatred, she possesses no more power than can be engendered by that hatred and expressed in single acts.

And here Jeffers expresses a view that his readers have too often misunderstood, and one that he would say is too little known by mankind. That is, hatred is much less powerful and hence, in the final analysis, much less destructive (which is to say, inimical to happiness) than its counterpart. Love, so we are told, can conquer the world; and to some extent that is true. What agonies have grown out of love of Caesar, love of Christ, love of Napoleon, love of Hitler, and their multitudinous copies. Are not the great loves of massed humanity always attached to those historical figures responsible for the greatest injury to the species? Hatred tends to burn itself out quickly; it is, moreover, less contagious than love. Of course the two emotions, one a repellent and the other an attractive force, are often difficult to distinguish. Still, it is unthinkable that masses of men would engage in wholesale slaughter because they hated their leaders or their country. A devotion to the abstraction of love can cause even the most contented of men to hate and seek to destroy the presumed enemies of that abstraction. More evil was done during the Middle Ages out of love for the Cross than has resulted from all the combined antipathies since Cain and Abel. It should be obvious that those leaders most adroit at employing love as a shibboleth have been the most destructive not only of the enemies of their faith but of its adherents as well. All of which makes more comprehensible Jeffers's insistence that a love of life precluded a devotion to leaders. He insisted that the man who loves life cannot at the same time either love or hate mankind. As early as 1928, he was exhorting man to deny the saviors who demanded his worship to satisfy their passion for power, saviors who baited their traps with love, a carrot dangling before the noses of herd animals.

But while he lives let each man make his health in his mind, to love the coast opposite humanity
And so be freed of love, laying it like bread on the waters; it is worst turned inward, it is best shot farthest.

Love, the mad wine of good and evil, the saint's and murderer's, the mote in the eye that makes its object
Shine the sun black; the trap in which it is better to catch the inhuman God than the hunter's own image.

III

In only one of Jeffers's narrative poems does a character succeed in breaking out of humanity—that is, in loving "the coast opposite humanity" and thus being "freed of love." This Orestes does near the end of *The Tower Beyond Tragedy.* If in that breaking away Orestes seems somewhat less than human—and not very believable as a character in the drama—that is only to be expected. I believe also that the sudden conversion of the character to Jeffers's philosophy diminishes the poem as a work of art. Jeffers is at his best when his characters act out *their* lives, when they are defeated by their humanity and by circumstances beyond their control. Orestes is thus less important as a figure in a work of art than he is as spokesman for Jeffers's inhumanism. I am here, needless to say, interested primarily in what Orestes' final act means rather than in the quality of the play.

Before looking at Orestes' casting of humanity, something must be said about Jeffers's blanket rejection of love for humanity. His rejection is actually no more than a shifting of emphasis from the self to the world, from the part to the whole. It involves a new scale of values, or at least of priorities, when it substitutes an appreciation of and delight in the outer world for the will to power and the extension of the self. It is much less a rejection than it is an affirmation. In *Themes in My Poems* Jeffers spoke of the feeling, or rather the "certitude . . . that the world, the universe, is one being, a single organism, one great life that includes all life and all things; and is so beautiful that it must be loved and reverenced; and in moments of mystical vision we identify ourselves with it." It is thus not love which Jeffers rejects but only the piecemeal love of humanity which warps and perverts the greater and necessary love for the world. He clearly distinguishes that love for the universe, in which man is a small part, from the idealistic love which pulls all phenomena into the self: "This is, in a way, the exact opposite of Oriental pantheism. The Hindu mystic finds God in his own soul, and all the outer world is illusion. To this other way of feeling, the outer world is real and divine; one's own soul might be called an illusion, it is so slight and transitory."

When Orestes rejects his sister's incestuous offer, the symbolic extreme of human love, adding that he has "found a fairer object," Electra can only assume, as Tamar did, that her brother refers to another human, "some nymph of the field." When she asks what "madness / Met you in the night and sticks to you?," he makes clear his (and Jeffers's) attitude toward the forms love might take—the one destructive, the other salubrious. The following passage contains both a rejection of solipsism and an acceptance of the greater love that frees man from the sickness of the self.

ORESTES: *Here is the last labor*
To spend on humanity. I saw a vision of us move in the dark: all that we did or dreamed of
Regarded each other, the man pursued the woman, the woman clung to the man, warriors and kings
Strained at each other in the darkness, all loved or fought inward, each one of the lost people
Sought the eyes of another that another should praise him; sought never his own but another's; the net of desire
Had every nerve drawn to the center, so that they writhed like a full draught of fishes, all matted
In the one mesh; when they look backward they see only a man standing at the beginning,

Or forward, a man at the end; or if upward, men in the shining bitter sky striding and feasting,
Whom you call Gods . . .
It is all turned inward, all your desires incestuous, the woman the serpent, the man the rose-red cavern,
Both human, worship forever . . .

ELECTRA: *You have dreamed wretchedly.*

ORESTES: *I have seen the dreams of the people and not dreamed them.*
As for me, I have slain my mother.

ELECTRA: *No more?*

ORESTES: *And the gate's open, the gray boils over the mountain, I have greater*
Kindred than dwell under a roof. Didn't I say this would be dark to you? I have cut the meshes
And fly like a freëd falcon. To-night, lying on the hillside, sick with those visions, I remembered
The knife in the stalk of my humanity; I drew and it broke; I entered the life of the brown forest
And the great life of the ancient peaks, the patience of stone, I felt the changes in the veins
In the throat of the mountain, a grain in many centuries, we have our own time, not yours; and I was the stream
Draining the mountain wood; and I the stag drinking; and I was the stars,
Boiling with light, wandering alone, each one the lord of his own summit; and I was the darkness
Outside the stars, I included them, they were a part of me. I was mankind also, a moving lichen
On the cheek of the round stone . . . they have not made words for it, to go behind things, beyond hours and ages,
And be all things in all time, in their returns and passages, in the motionless and timeless center,
In the white of the fire . . . how can I express the excellence I have found, that has no color but clearness;
No honey but ecstasy; nothing wrought nor remembered; no undertone nor silver second murmur
That rings in love's voice, I and my loved are one; no desire but fulfilled; no passion but peace,
The pure flame and the white, fierier than any passion; no time but spheral eternity.

Appalled by what she considers his desertion of honor, Electra turns from Orestes to enter "the ancient house." She remains, one might say, a humanist, incapable of envisioning the inhumanism of Orestes, who was saved not by the intervention of a Greek goddess, as in the Aeschylus play, but rather by the intervention of the outer world. After his awakening, he was saved from humanity; his visionary experience enabled him to see man in relation to the world. Rather than attempt to move beyond good and evil, Orestes moved beyond humanity, as the last lines of the play indicate:

Orestes walked in the clear dawn; men say that a serpent
Killed him in high Arcadia. But young or old, few years or many, signified less than nothing
To him who had climbed the tower beyond time, consciously, and cast humanity, entered the earlier fountain.

It is a mistake to interpret this casting of humanity as a rejection of man, something Jeffers never did, no matter how violent his denunciation of the species. Rather, he asks us to look outward beyond humanity, to break out of the narcissism that, as is now frighteningly obvious, threatens to destroy us and perhaps even the other life of our natural habitat. After quoting Orestes' speech in *Themes in My Poems* Jeffers informed his audience of his intention:

> These verses express a mystical experience; they also express a protest against human narcissism. Narcissus, you know, fell in love with himself. If a person spends all his emotion on his own body and states of mind, he is mentally diseased, and the disease is called narcissism. It seems to me, analogously, that the whole human race spends too much emotion on itself. The happiest and freest man is the scientist investigating nature, or the artist admiring it; the person who is interested in things that are not human. Or if he is interested in human things, let him regard them objectively, as a small part of the great music. Certainly humanity has claims, on all of us; we can best fulfill them by keeping our emotional sanity; and this by seeing beyond and around the human race.

While this is far from humanism, as Jeffers went on to remark, it is certainly conducive to the health of humanity. Put bluntly, humanism injures what it ostensibly strives to protect. Jeffers claimed that his view was the same as the Christian's: "to love God with all one's heart and soul, and one's neighbor as one's self—as much as that, but as little as that."

While Jeffers doubtless intended us to weight the final qualifying phrase ("but as little as that") so as to place man in proper perspective with the more important nonhuman aspect of God, it is nonetheless a fact that he never ceased barking at his fellows, lecturing them on their egotistic behavior (which he considered simply irrational), and even pointing his finger in the direction they must take to avoid catastrophe. One of his most unwittingly amusing lines comes at the end of "Birth-Dues" when he protests that having paid his birth-dues he is now "quits with the people." The one thing he wished for, invulnerability, he was never to possess for a moment. Indeed he admits as much in "Crumbs or the Loaf." Though he saw more clearly than any other modern poet the necessity of upheaval, the risings and fallings of cultures as of ocean tides, the constant movement from strophe to antistrophe, he never watched change without being torn himself. In "Still the Mind Smiles," an excellent illustration of his cyclic view of history, his admiration of the "whole fabric" is qualified by his sympathy for the necessary parts:

Still the mind smiles at its own rebellions,
Knowing all the while that civilization and the other evils
That make humanity ridiculous, remain
Beautiful in the whole fabric, excesses that balance each other
Like the paired wings of a flying bird.
Misery and riches, civilization and squalid savagery,
Mass war and the odor of unmanly peace:
Tragic flourishes above and below the normal of life.
In order to value this fretful time
It is necessary to remember our norm, the unaltered passions,
The same-colored wings of imagination,
That the crowd clips, in lonely places new-grown; the unchanged
Lives of herdsmen and the mountain farms,
Where men are few, and few tools, a few weapons, and their dawns are beautiful.
From here for normal one sees both ways,
And listens to the splendor of God, the exact poet, the sonorous
Antistrophe of desolation to the strophe multitude.

While it is obvious that the poetry written in the 1930s and during the war years is often closely attached to current events, it should also be clear, more so now than when the poetry was written, that the verse maintained an intellectual distance and objectivity even when the poet's emotions were most engaged. Near the end of "The Purse-Seine," one of his most striking commentaries on the inevitability of the disasters that must follow the separation of man from the earth, Jeffers wrote a rather typical (for him) conclusion:

These things are Progress;
Do you marvel our verse is troubled or frowning, while it keeps its reason? Or it lets go, lets the mood flow
In the manner of the recent young men into mere hysteria, splintered gleams, crackled laughter. But they are quite wrong.
There is no reason for amazement: surely one always knew that cultures decay, and life's end is death.

The movement from dark prophecy to stoical resolution is found again and again in poems written during this period. If we dislike the Cassandra element in the verse, we must still praise Jeffers for having seen clearly what the vast majority of others could view only existentially—and then praise him again for saying what he knew must be denied and attacked by his fellows. Actually he was, if anything, overly cautious in that poem about how long the disasters might be held in abeyance. After describing the beauty inherent in the netting of the fish, he then makes the analogy:

Lately I was looking from a night mountain-top
On a wide city, the colored splendor, galaxies of light: how could I help but recall the seine-net
Gathering the luminous fish? I cannot tell you how beautiful the city appeared, and a little terrible.
I thought, We have geared the machines and locked all together into interdependence; we have built the great cities; now
There is no escape. We have gathered vast populations incapable of free survival, insulated
From the strong earth, each person in himself helpless, on all dependent. The circle is closed, and the net
Is being hauled in. They hardly feel the cords drawing, yet they shine already. The inevitable mass-disasters
Will not come in our time nor in our children's, but we and our children
Must watch the net draw narrower, government take all powers—or revolution, and the new government
Take more than all, add to kept bodies kept souls—or anarchy, the mass-disasters.

Though few people today would dispute the fact that the net has indeed been drawn nearer in the thirty-five years since Jeffers wrote these lines, his contemporaries during the depression and war years often objected to what seemed to them mere hopelessness in his poetry. Certainly the Marxist critics, who formed the most optimistic of all the critical schools, attacked Jeffers for not seeing that in "kept bodies" and "kept souls" lay man's only hope. Like Aldous Huxley, Jeffers considered *that* brave new world but little better than the barbarism from which our civilization had only recently emerged, and into which it threatened to return. At precisely the time when most writers and leaders were imploring men to have faith in this or that nostrum so they might escape the ills of economic depression or the terrors of political tyranny, Jeffers condemned all faiths for aiding and abetting those ills. In "Decaying Lambskins" he asked, "What is noble in us, to kindle / The imagination of a future age?" and then answered:

We shall seem a race of cheap Fausts, vulgar magicians.
What men have we to show them? but inventions and appliances. Not men but populations, mass-men; not life
But amusements; not health but medicines. And the odor: what is that odor? Decaying lambskins: the Christian
Ideals that for protection and warmth our naked ancestors . . . but naturally, after nineteen centuries. . . .

Jeffers believed that as Christianity decays, civilization would increase until it, too, had spent itself in the mass-disasters. The discoveries of the mind show the supernaturalism of Christianity to be superstition; on the other hand, civilizations, which are the enemies of superstition, finally decline when they become overly introspective.

Two poems in *Solstice and Other Poems* (1935) clearly reveal Jeffers's inability to remain at the same time intellectually detached from humanity and emotionally involved in human concerns. The tension between that detachment and involvement is everywhere apparent in his verse, particularly during the Great Depression and Second World War. In the first poem, "Life from the Lifeless," he shows that the loss of illusion enables man, even forces him, to live more closely with the naked beauty of things than had before been possible.

Spirits and illusions have died,
The naked mind lives
In the beauty of inanimate things.

Flowers wither, grass fades, trees wilt,
The forest is burnt;
The rock is not burnt.

The deer starve, the winter birds
Die on their twigs and lie
In the blue dawns in the snow.

Men suffer want and become
Curiously ignoble; as prosperity
Made them curiously vile.

But look how noble the world is,
The lonely-flowing waters, the secret-
Keeping stones, the flowing sky.

In the other poem, "Rearmament," written (according to *Themes in My Poems*) in 1934, the involvement makes detachment impossible, though a kind of "beauty" may be discerned, he insists, in the "disastrous rhythm" of the "dream-led masses."

These grand and fatal movements toward death: the grandeur of the mass
Makes pity a fool, the tearing pity
For the atoms of the mass, the persons, the victims, makes it seem monstrous
To admire the tragic beauty they build.
It is beautiful as a river flowing or a slowly gathering
Glacier on a high mountain rock-face,
Bound to plow down a forest, or as frost in November,
The gold and flaming death-dance for leaves,
Or a girl in the night of her spent maindenhood, bleeding and kissing.
I would burn my right hand in a slow fire
To change the future . . . I should do foolishly. The beauty of modern
Man is not in the persons but in the
Disastrous rhythm, the heavy and mobile masses, the dance of the
Dream-led masses down the dark mountain.

In "Shine, Republic," from the same volume, he even allows a note of hope, which he normally depicts as foolish, to glimmer briefly through the exhortation to keep America free rather than try to make her prosperous: "You [America] were not born to prosperity, you were born to love freedom." It was not Whitman's "en masse," but rather "independence" that was important. He concludes (strangely for Jeffers) that "the states of the next age will no doubt remember you, and edge their love of freedom with contempt of luxury." There is even "a kind of desperate optimism" (Jeffers called it) in "The Bloody Sire," which was written in the summer of 1940, "after the great attacks." None of his poems better illustrates his attempt to place the war in historical perspective, or to show that violence has a natural usefulness:

It is not bad. Let them play.
Let the guns bark and the bombing-plane
Speak his prodigious blasphemies.
It is not bad, it is high time,
Stark violence is still the sire of all the world's values.

What but the wolf's tooth whittled so fine
The fleet limbs of the antelope?
What but fear winged the birds, and hunger
Jeweled with such eyes the great goshawk's head?
Violence has been the sire of all the world's values.

Who would remember Helen's face
Lacking the terrible halo of spears?
Who formed Christ but Herod and Caesar,
The cruel and bloody victories of Caesar?
Violence, the bloody sire of all the world's values.

Never weep, let them play,
Old violence is not too old to beget new values.[7]

Nearly all the poems of *Be Angry at the Sun* (1941) are filled with the painful knowledge of man's helplessness before the gathering forces of another world war.[8] Refusing to subscribe to the comfortable lies on which moral indignation feeds, he viewed the sorry spectacle from a distance, from his tower, at the same time realizing that "the present is always a crisis; people want a partisan cry, not judgment." Lacking faith in any of the multifarious "causes," the poet judged the passing scene with an objectivity that only the faithless can show.

That is not to say that objectivity in any way innured him to the suffering implicit in historical change. As conceived by the whole mind, the world was filled with a "Divinely Superfluous Beauty"; in the love poem of that name from *Tamar and Other Poems* he celebrated the beauty that "Rules the games, presides over destinies, makes trees grow / And hills tower, waves fall." Returning, seventeen years later, to the theme of that justly famous lyric, Jeffers wrote "The Excesses of

God," one of the few poems in *Be Angry at the Sun* which does not reveal his preoccupation with current events:

Is it not by his high superfluousness we know
Our God? For to equal a need
Is natural, animal, mineral: but to fling
Rainbows over the rain
And beauty above the moon, and secret rainbows
On the domes of deep sea-shells,
And make the necessary embrace of breeding
Beautiful also as fire,
Not even the weeds to multiply without blossom
Nor the birds without music:
There is the great humaneness at the heart of things,
The extravagant kindness, the fountain
Humanity can understand, and would flow likewise
If power and desire were perch-mates.

Notably that "humaneness" had all but disappeared from human affairs, making it difficult for Jeffers to praise God. He reveals as much in "Contemplation of the Sword":

Dear God, who are the whole splendor of things and the sacred stars, but also the cruelty and greed, the treacheries
And vileness, insanities and filth and anguish: now that this thing comes near us again I am finding it hard
To praise you with a whole heart.
I know what pain is, but pain can shine. I know what death is, I have sometimes
Longed for it. But cruelty and slavery and degradation, pestilence, filth, the pitifulness
Of men like little hurt birds and animals . . . if you were only
Waves beating rock, the wind and the iron-cored earth, the flaming insolent wildness of sun and stars,
With what a heart I could praise your beauty.

In that poem he repeats three times the line "Reason will not decide at last; the sword will decide." A lament, to be sure, since Jeffers believed that *only* reason should decide. But critics thirty years ago were wrong in labeling such views as pessimistic; he was simply being realistic in his assessment of the times.

In place of "Shine, Republic," published in 1935, he wrote "Shine, Empire," from which all hope of freedom has drained. Although he believed "all Europe was hardly worth the precarious freedom of one of our states," he saw that the nation must become involved in the conflict: "We must put freedom away and stiffen into bitter empire." Although neither "Shine, Republic" nor "Shine, Empire" is a bad poem, both pale in comparison with "Shine, Perishing Republic." "Shine, Republic" is interesting, however, since it expresses a view not often even implied by Jeffers:

The quality of these trees, green height; of the sky, shining, of water, a clear flow; of the rock, hardness
And reticence: each is noble in its quality. The love of freedom has been the quality of Western man.

There is a stubborn torch that flames from Marathon to Concord, its dangerous beauty binding three ages
Into one time; the waves of barbarism and civilization have eclipsed but have never quenched it.

For the Greeks the love of beauty, for Rome of ruling; for the present age the passionate love of discovery;
But in one noble passion we are one; and Washington, Luther, Tacitus, Aeschylus, one kind of man.

And you, America, that passion made you. You were not born to prosperity, you were born to love freedom.
You did not say "en masse," you said "independence." But we cannot have all the luxuries and freedom also.

Freedom is poor and laborious; that torch is not safe but hungry, and often requires blood for its fuel.
You will tame it against it burn too clearly, you will hood it like a kept hawk, you will perch it on the wrist of Caesar.

But keep the tradition, conserve the forms, the observances, keep the spot sore. Be great, carve deep your heel-marks.
The states of the next age will no doubt remember you, and edge their love of freedom with contempt of luxury.

If there is rather too much lecturing on history in this poem, Jeffers does at least maintain a balance in both imagery and theme. But in "Shine, Empire," written five years later, he allows his bitterness to destroy that balance. Even his attempt to gain a distance between himself and his subject is altogether too obvious, as when he remarks condescendingly that "Roosevelt's intentions were good, and Hitler is a patriot." (Though not yet in the war at the time he wrote the poem, we had long since given up all appearance of neutrality and were in fact making war in all but name.) As a matter of fact, he is much too close to his subject matter to gain anything resembling objectivity. His revulsion is understandable; indeed decency demanded it; but emotion is better recollected in tranquility than exploited at white heat.

In "Shine, Perishing Republic," Jeffers maintains that necessary distance between himself and his subject. Here there is no crying-up or -down, no false emotions, no opinions even, nor any judgments until the last two stanzas, and those are so nearly apodictic as to make argument inadmissible. Moreover, the images from astronomy and botany perfectly mesh, and the somber rhythms accord with the theme. The concluding advice to his children has the same appropriateness as the closing couplet of a Shakespearean sonnet: it concludes all that the first six lines have implied.

While this America settles in the mould of its vulgarity, heavily thickening to empire,
And protest, only a bubble in the molten mass, pops and sighs out, and the mass hardens,

I sadly smiling remember that the flower fades to make fruit, the fruit rots to make earth.
Out of the mother; and through the spring exultances, ripeness and decadence; and home to the mother.

You making haste haste on decay: not blameworthy; life is good, be it stubbornly long or suddenly
A mortal splendor: meteors are not needed less than mountains: shine, perishing republic.

But for my children, I would have them keep their distance from the thickening center; corruption
Never has been compulsory, when the cities lie at the monster's feet there are left the mountains.

And boys, be in nothing so moderate as in love of man, a clever servant, insufferable master.
There is the trap that catches noblest spirits, that caught—they say—God, when he walked on earth.

If "Shine, Perishing Republic" remarks a specific process that belongs to a certain time and place, it also bears the dateless stamp of a natural process. On the other hand, many of the poems in *Be Angry at the Sun* are literally dated, either through mention of date in the poem or in its title. For example, the rather frequently anthologized "The Soul's Desert (August 30, 1939)" can hardly be read with understanding unless one knows something of the events taking place in Europe at the time. Such poems could have only historical significance for future readers; they are important to us for what they reveal about the mind of Jeffers—a mind that had, as I have indicated, become divided in the years just before the Second World War. Nor is it difficult to understand why a poem like "The Soul's Desert" should have galled the professional patriots:

They are warming up the old horrors; and all that they say is echoes of echoes.
Beware of taking sides; only watch.
These are not criminals, nor hucksters and little journalists, but the governments
Of the great nations; men favorably
Representative of massed humanity. Observe them. Wrath and laughter
Are quite irrelevant. Clearly it is time
To become disillusioned, each person to enter his own soul's desert
And look for God—having seen man.

As one might expect, Jeffers's refusal to take sides in the contemporary issues caused people to assume that he was simply heartless or even fascist. His refusal to believe that Marxism or Christianity or fascism might save mankind, that science might cure our ills, that Hitler (or Stalin) was somehow responsible for the troubles in Europe, that the defeat of Germany and Japan would usher in a world of peace—in effect, his refusal to ascribe eternal significance to temporal circumstances caused people to call him a hater of his own kind, and a blind one at that. Such of course is the fate of all men who are not readily susceptible to the lures of illusion. Such was the fate of Cassandra, a favorite figure of both Jeffers and E. A. Robinson. It was not so much any of Jeffers's beliefs as it was his lack of belief that caused various writers to censure him. For any man of vision, the man who views history from outside, events become part of a gigantic fabric rather than the personal clothing one wears next his skin.

Moreover Jeffers is not so much contemptuous of man as he is knowing of the ways of men (in reading him I am often reminded of Swift). That the mass of men are led by lies to self-destruction may be pitiful but nonetheless a matter of eternal recurrence, and therefore necessary to accept as one accepts or anyway expects violent changes in weather. Jeffers did not converse with the mass in his poetry—unlike Whitman, who thought (mistakenly) that he wrote for that large common denominator—but only with the individuals who possessed "the cold passion for truth [which] / Hunts in no pack." His warning, itself an expression of love or at least concern, was always addressed to Tom and Bill, never to manunkind:

Let boys want pleasure, and men
Struggle for power, and women perhaps for fame,
And the servile to serve a Leader and the dupes to be duped.
Yours is not theirs.[9]

If in the 1930s Jeffers still felt it possible for man to avoid the mass disasters by choosing rational alternatives (see particularly "Signpost" and "The Answer") he had, by the war's end, nearly given up hope that actual choice was possible. Not in the foreseeable future, at any rate, would there be any breaking out of humanity. His worst fears having been fully realized during the late thirties and early forties, he attempted to remove himself even further from the wallow of the "political animals." In "Fourth Act," written in January 1942 and published in *The Double Axe*, he again equated power with ruin. The play, apparently of five acts, is neither tragic nor comic and, so far at least, has had no cathartic effect on the audience. The second half of the poem:

It is scene two, act four, of the tragic farce The Political Animal. *Its hero reaches his apogee*
And ravages the whole planet; not even the insects, only perhaps bacteria, were ever so powerful.
Not a good play, but you can see the author's intention: to disgust and shock. The tragic theme
Is patriotism; the clowning is massacre. He wishes to turn humanity outward from its obsession
In humanity, a riveder le stelle. *He will have to pile on horrors; he will not convince you*
In a thousand years: but the whole affair is only a hare-brained episode in the life of the planet.

In "Historical Choice," written in 1943 and also printed in *The Double Axe*, Jeffers wrote that we "could have forced peace, even when

France fell," but had chosen instead to "make alliance and feed war." Having thus chosen we have no alternative but to reap the harvest of our choice. I quote the second half of the poem.

Actum est. There is no returning now.
Two bloody summers from now (I suppose) we shall have to take up the corrupting burden and curse of victory.
We shall have to hold half the earth; we shall be sick with self-disgust,
And hated by friend and foe, and hold half the earth—or let it go, and go down with it. Here is a burden
We are not fit for. We are not like Romans and Britons—natural world-rulers,
Bullies by instinct—but we have to bear it. Who has kissed Fate on the mouth, and blown out the lamp—must lie with her.

In all that collection (*The Double Axe and Other Poems*) of extraordinarily bitter indictments of modern man and his hopes and fears, no poem states more conclusively the idea that all nations were losers in the war than the one entitled "Greater Grandeur." It is noteworthy that Jeffers realizes and admits that he is observing events from a level far removed from the one at which our daily lives are played out. He views the risings and fallings from a distance, as some future historian might view them; which is to say, his judgments are aesthetic rather than moral.

Half a year after war's end, Roosevelt and Hitler dead, Stalin tired, Churchill rejected—here is the
Triumph of the little men. Democracy—shall we say?—has triumphed. They are hastily preparing again
More flaming horrors, but now it is fate, not will; not power-lust, caprice, personal vanity—fate
Has them in hand. Watch and be quiet then; there is greater grandeur here than there was before,
As God is greater than man: God is doing it. Sadly, impersonally, irreversibly,
The tall world turns toward death, like a flower to the sun. It is very beautiful. Observe it. Pity and terror
Are not appropriate for events on this scale watched from this level; admiration is all.

If in that volume Jeffers no longer exhorts man to choose this or that course of action in order to avoid catastrophe, he is more concerned than ever with individual freedom. While he clearly believed in historical necessity, he at the same time allowed for at least some freedom in the individual. If this seems at first a flat contradiction of his determinism, one should note that he did not believe freedom could be shared; indeed, what free choice was possible depended upon the individual's reducing to a minimum all outside influences, and at the same time closing one's ears to wish or fear which, when present, check free choice. In reading his "Advice to Pilgrims," one should recall Jeffers's early decision "not to feign any emotion that I did not feel; not to pretend to believe in optimism or pessimism, or unreversible progress; not to say anything because it was popular, or generally accepted, or fashionable in intellectual circles, unless I myself believed it; and not to believe easily." He might as well have said that the will to believe, which may be found in all of us, is the greatest enemy of rationality. Above all, one must guard against being misled by wish and fear, and one must never believe the politician:

That our senses lie and our minds trick us is true, but in general
They are honest rustics; trust them a little;
The senses more than the mind, and your own mind more than another man's.
As to the mind's pilot, intuition—
Catch him clean and stark naked, he is first of truth-tellers; dream-clothed, or dirty
With fears and wishes, he is prince of liars.
The first fear is of death: trust no immortalist. The first desire
Is to be loved: trust no mother's son.
Finally I say let demagogues and world-redeemers babble their emptiness
To empty ears; twice duped is too much.
Walk on gaunt shores and avoid the people; rock and wave are good prophets;
Wise are the wings of the gull, pleasant her song.

Here, as in numerous other poems ("Shine, Perishing Republic," "Signpost," "The Answer," and "Meditation on Saviors" are notable examples), Jeffers clearly indicates that man must turn away from humanity to find a trustworthy guide. It is noteworthy that he incites the individual to break away from humanity rather than from God or nature. Though Jeffers at times expressed the deterministic view that man's being was as much fixed as any other of the objects in nature, he constantly spoke of our need for trustworthy guides and hence, through implication, assumed a freedom of choice. (I think it obvious, by the way, that the whole question of free choice is purely academic: we choose, freely or not, and we are responsible for our choices.) In seeking that guide, Jeffers never makes the solipsistic mistake of assuming that a product or an effect might be its own maker or cause. Rather he goes to the source for his guide. The difficulty of course lies in how one gets back to that nonhuman source. If he places a (limited) trust in intuition, he always qualifies that trust in such a way as to transform the self into a kind of sensory organ of the transhuman world and hardly related to humanity. This difference is important. Jeffers is not concerned here with the nature of man but rather with finding a guide. On the other hand, when the romantic like Emerson abjures reason for intuition he does so in order to realize the infinitude of man. When in "The Poet" he speaks of releasing his intellect to nature—"As the traveler who has lost his way throws his reins on his horse's neck and trusts to the instinct of the animal to find his road, so must we do with the divine animal who carries us through the world"—Emerson not only returns to the source of life (God) but actually becomes that source. Thus Emerson's love of nature is really an expression of his love of man—of his view that man is actually anterior to nature and indeed to all matter. Jeffers believed no such thing. When he contrasts the world (the macrocosm) with man, the fragile, disturbed child of indifferent nature, he invariably displays the finitude of the species. More importantly he contrasts the inherently ordered whole with one of its parts, the one part which must find order or make it himself.

Even when Jeffers does not satisfactorily, either for himself or his reader, resolve the question of whom or what to trust, there is an admirable integrity in the lines. For example, in "New Year's Dawn, 1947" from *The Double Axe*:

Two morning stars, Venus and Jupiter,
Walk in the pale and liquid light
Above the color of these dawns; and as the tide of light
Rises higher the great planet vanishes
While the nearer still shines. The yellow wave of light
In the east and south reddens, the opaque ocean
Becomes pale purple: O delicate
Earnestness of dawn, the fervor and pallor.
—Stubbornly I think again: The state is a blackmailer,
Honest or not, with whom we make (within reason)

Our accommodations. There is no valid authority
In church or state, custom, scripture nor creed,
But only in one's own conscience and the beauty of things.
Doggedly I think again: One's conscience is a trick oracle,
Worked by parents and nurse-maids, the pressure of the people,
And the delusions of dead prophets: trust it not.
Wash it clean to receive the transhuman beauty: then trust it.

The first eight lines describe the mindless and lovely order that exists outside the brain vault. No thought is apparent out there; indeed thought would be an intrusion on the natural divinity of that atomic consistency. Only the "I" thinks. If one assumes that thinking is an end in itself, one will have no need to go beyond humanity or human institutions. Which is to say, one will assume that humanity is above and beyond nature. Jeffers rejects that view for the more naturalistic (and classical) view that thought is an instrument, a kind of divining rod, to enable humanity to find the path leading back to original source.

In 1933 Jeffers had written of the need to cleanse oneself of "thoughts" and so be restored to the passionate source of life: "A little too abstract, a little too wise, / It is time for us to kiss the earth again." In "Return" Jeffers in no sense advocates irrationality, nor does he "depreciate the intellect," as Sara Bard Field accused him of doing in her review of *Solstice and Other Poems*.[10] Rather he simply notes the "temporary need," as Una Jeffers wrote Field and her husband, Erskine Scott Wood, to evade thought for a time and thus restore a proper balance between thought and things.[11] "Return" is a plea for sanity, for the undivided self, and it is a warning against becoming overly abstract. What is injurious to the individual organism is doubly destructive of the social or cultural body. When a man or a culture becomes addicted to introspection, he or it is in a dying way. In *The Life of Greece*, Will Durant states this view perfectly:

> The life of thought endangers every civilization that it adorns. In the earlier stages of a nation's history there is little thought; action flourishes; men are direct, uninhibited, frankly pugnacious and sexual. As civilization develops, as customs, institutions, laws, and morals more and more restrict the operation of natural impulses, action gives way to thought, achieve-

> ment to imagination, directness to subtlety, expression to concealment, cruelty to sympathy, belief to doubt; the unity of character common to animals and primitive men passes away; behavior becomes fragmentary and hesitant, conscious and calculating; the willingness to fight subsides into a disposition to infinite argument. Few nations have been able to reach intellectual refinement and esthetic sensitivity without sacrificing so much in virility and unity that their wealth presents an irresistible temptation to impecunious barbarians. Around every Rome hover the Gauls; around every Athens some Macedon.[12]

Jeffers not only agreed with that view but had written narrative poems which display all the contradictions and frustrations that Durant mentions. The character of Gudrun in *At the Birth of an Age* (1935) is a particular case in point. In his prefatory note to that work, which is included in *The Selected Poetry*, Jeffers said that the self-contradiction and self-frustration in Gudrun's character were intended to express "a characteristic quality" of our own culture-age, which he called "the Christian age, for it is conditioned by Christianity, and—except a few centuries' lag—concurrent with it." He went on to characterize our age again in a way that still causes some readers to set him down mistakenly as a pessimist; as a matter of fact, his historical view is no more pessimistic than were the similar views of Giovanni Battista Vico, or Santayana, or Durant, or any other proponent of the cyclic, rather than progressive, theory of history. As Christian faith becomes extinct as an influence, Jeffers remarked, "compensatorily the Christian ethic becomes more powerful and conscious, manifesting itself as generalized philanthropy, liberalism, socialism, communism, and so forth. But the tension is relaxed, the age prepares for its long decline. The racial pole is weakened by the physical and especially the spiritual hybridization that civilized life always brings with it; the Christian pole is undergoing constant attrition, steadily losing a little more than it gains." If all this is true, then obviously new values—or rather values different from those of the dying culture—must be given the forthcoming generations. Needless to say, the values that Jeffers proposed for adoption are by no means the ones that we have been adopting and will probably continue to adopt at least until this civilization has run its course.

IV

Near the end of "The Inhumanist" (part 2 of *The Double Axe*), a young man—fleeing "'The fire, the blast and the rays. The whiffs of poisoned smoke that were cities.'"—stumbles up the hill to encounter the old man with the double axe and demand self-righteously: "Are you utterly merciless?" The old man's answer is also Jeffers's.

> *"No,"*
> *He answered, "carefree. I did warn you." "I know you,"* [*the young man*] *screamed,*
> *"You have betrayed us, you have betrayed humanity. You are one of those that killed hope and faith,*
> *And sneered at Progress; you have killed the lies that men live by, and the earth*
> *Is one huge tomb." "A beautiful one," he answered. "Look. Only look. Even in this bad light*
> *What a beautiful one." Then the youth flashed a knife and stabbed at him,*
> *But failed through weakness. The old man laughed and said, "How they love to be comforted.*
> *Yet," he said, "it is more than comfort: it is deep peace and final joy*
> *To know that the great world lives, whether man dies or not. The beauty of things is not harnessed to human*
> *Eyes and the little active minds: it is absolute.*
> *It is not for human titillation, though it serves that. It is the life of things,*
> *And the nature of God. But those unhappy creatures will have to shrug off*
> *Their human God and their human godlessness*
> *To endure this time."*

That is to say, the people will have to abandon not only the faith in their human God, something they have already done in large part, but will have to abandon the self-centered values that they inherited with that (now moribund) faith; and they will be forced, for the sake of survival, to give up the godless worship of luxuries as well.

In the following final section of that most remarkable poem, the old man, standing in the very center of death and humanity, waves aside what to all appearances is flatly inevitable and chooses life and sanity. This final affirmation grows out of animal faith perhaps but certainly not from a human creed. Before it is possible to affirm life, one must, Jeffers insists, be free from human bondage; only by overcoming one's humanity can life be affirmed. Whoever begins by affirming humanity must end by choosing death, an assertion that is the same as saying that to side with humanity in its present state is to affirm death. This Jeffers refuses to do:

The day like a burning brazen wheel heavily revolved, and in the evening
A tribe of panting fugitives ran through the place: the old man caught one of them,
Who was too sick to flee. He crouched and vomited some green bile and gasped, "God curse the Army,
That got us in, and the air-force that can't protect us. They've done it now." "Done," he said, "what?" "Rammed their bull-heads
Into the fire-death. This is the end of the world." "Yea?" he said. "Of yours, perhaps.
The mountains appear to be on their feet still. And down there the dark ocean nosing his bays and tide-breaks
Like a bear in a pit. As for the human race, we could do without it; but it won't die. Oh: slightly scorched. It will slough its skin and crawl forth
Like a serpent in spring." He moaned and cried out and answered, "What is that to me?
I *am dying." "Come to the house," he answered, "poor man, and rest. You will not certainly die." But the man*
Coughed blood and died.
The old man sat down beside his body in the blood-brown day's end
On the dark mountain, and more deeply gave himself
To contemplation of men's fouled lives and miserable deaths. "There is," he said, "no remedy.—There are two *remedies.*
This man has got his remedy, and I have one. There is no third."
About midnight he slept, and arose refreshed
In the red dawn.

"The Inhumanist" is like nothing else in the Jeffers canon. I suppose we must call it one of his narratives since it has story elements in it, but we are more interested in the old man's interpretations of the events that transpire before him than we are in the events themselves. For the first time Jeffers gives us a spokesman of his views. If the central characters in his other narratives displayed in act and thought those human weaknesses which lead to destruction, both of the individual and the species, they remained, even in the supernatural poems, peculiarly human. The old man with the double-bladed axe is an inhumanist. He is nevertheless made to see the limits of the inhumanist position and, in the end, is drawn back to humanity, though not to humanism. In the course of events he learns things; which is to say, he undergoes change. He thus resembles Nietzsche's old serpent, Zarathustra, who found it necessary to slough off old skin and put on new. On the other hand, he differs vastly from Whitman's persona in "Song of Myself," who merges with both good and evil rather than differentiate or interpret experience.

At the beginning of the poem, the old man lives alone as caretaker of the Gore place, where the events described in "The Love and the Hate" had recently occurred. In an early prose passage the old man considers the double-bladed axe, which in Crete, long before the Greeks came, was a god. An obvious phallic symbol, the axe "was a symbol of generation: the two lobes and the stiff helve: so was the Cross before they christened it. But this one can clip heads too. Grimly, grimly. A blade for the flesh, a blade for the spirit: and truth from lies." He cannot, however, escape intrusions from the outside world, which range from a sheet of newspaper blown across the road to a hungry bitch hound that stays with him for a time to a girl, who is his daughter. The fact that he does not at first remember the girl illustrates, and softly mocks, his inhumanism:

> *"I am the Spanish woman's little girl.*
> *You called me Gaviota, Father." He sighed and answered:*
> *"My eagles did not tell me that. I thought I could live alone and enjoy old age. First a dog: now a daughter:*
> *And tomorrow a canary!"*

There are other passages of grim humor in which the old man is pulled up short and forced to reconsider his premises. For example, in section 35 (in the sixty-two-page poem there are 52 numbered sections, several of them concerned with a "love" story in which Gaviota plays a central part), the old man, gazing on the gray eye of the ocean below, is suddenly stricken by the natural beauty:

> *Suddenly he knelt, and tears ran down the gullied leather*
> *Of his old cheeks. "Dear love. You are so beautiful.*
> *Even this side the stars and below the moon. How can you be . . . all this . . . and me also?*
> *Be human also? The yellow puma, the flighty mourning-dove and flecked hawk, yes, and the rattlesnake*
> *Are in the nature of things; they are noble and beautiful*
> *As the rocks and the grass—not this grim ape,*
> *Although it loves you.—Yet two or three times in my life my walls have fallen—beyond love—no room for love—*

I have been you."
His dog Snapper
Pitied him and came and licked his loose hand. He pushed her off:
"I have been you, *and you stink a little."*

In the next section, the longest in the poem, the old man encounters a German scientist, who is now fleeing the Americans whom he joined after the war rather than be taken and used by the Russians. The German fled from the Americans after he realized that they, too, were bent on destruction. He now believes that

"Science is not to serve but to know. Science is for itself its own value, it is not for man,
His little good and big evil: it is a noble thing, which to use
Is to degrade," "I see *you are not American," the old man answered, "nor German either." And the other:*
"Therefore astronomy is the most noble science: is the most useless." "You are probably mad,"
He answered, "but you think nobly."

But a few lines later the old man remarks that science "is an adoration; a kind of worship," and finally that it is "a contemplation of God," which is too much for the German, who snorts,

"Das fehlte noch! *I am a man who thought that even old peasants and leather cowboys after this war*
Had learned something."

He misunderstands the old man of course; he mistakes the Inhumanist's God for the anthropomorphic God, the one, who, as Nietzsche told us, is now dead. The old man probably refers to Nietzsche's famous news when he tells the scientist that he has "perhaps heard some false reports / On the subject of God," adding that He is neither dead nor a fable.

"He is not mocked nor forgotten—
Successfully. God is a lion that comes in the night. God is a hawk gliding among the stars—
If all the stars and the earth, and the living flesh of the night that flows in between them, and whatever is beyond them,
Were that one bird. He has a bloody beak and harsh talons, he pounces and tears—
And where is the German Reich? There also

Will be prodigious America and world-owning Russia. I say that all hopes and empires will die like yours;
Mankind will die; there will be no more fools; wisdom will die; the very stars will die;
One fierce life lasts."
While he spoke, his axe
Barked like a hunting eagle but incessantly; the old man lifted his voice to be heard above it;
The German, stunned by their double clamor, flung up his hands to his head and returned away from them
Down the dark silent hill.

Left alone, the old man wonders why he should care whether the German heard him, since God certainly did not care. He even has a moment of doubt and wonders if God has really died, but in the moment he sees again the "endless succession, the shining towers of the universe" that leap "back and forth like goats / Between existence and annihilation."

The old man laughed and said,
"Skin beyond skin, there is always something beyond: it comes in and stirs them. I think that poor fellow
Should have let in the mad old serpent infinity, the double zero that confounds reckoning,
In his equation."

After stripping off his coat and huddling the still screaming axe-head in it, he rides down the hill to the German:

"Brother:
Because you have chosen nobly between free science and servile science: come up with me—
If you are hungry or have to hide from pursuers—
I know every crack of the mountain." But the man would not.

The old man's final transformation results from his meeting the man of fears, who is a part of himself. These sections (39–42) also illustrate Jeffers's undiminished skill as a storyteller. He relates the tale with the utmost economy, and the reader knows without being told that the story is his as well as the old man's. Here is section 39, which can no more be adequately paraphrased than can a good sonnet:

He was on the fish-wharf
Buying a boat: a man with white lips and the long eyes of terror tiptoed behind him whispering,
"Are you going to escape?" The old man turned and made him a sign for silence and whispered,
"I have *escaped." "Oh," he said, "take me with you, take me with you." "But," the old man said, "it is likely*
I have escaped the things you want, and am seeking
The things you fear. What do you fear?" "The war, the war," he said, "the death-rays, the fire-hail,
The horrible bombs." "Certainly," the old man said, "there will be a war—
After while. There will be a new ice-age—
After while." "Oh, God," he answered, "more terror!"
It chanced that a load of ice for the fish-stalls
Had lately passed, and some lumps fallen lay melting: the man saw them and shouted, "Oh, God, more terror.
An ice-age comes!" He ran and leaped from the wharf and cast himself
Into the sea's cold throat. The old man leaped after him,
And wrestled with him in the choking water,
And saved his life.
"Why have I done so insanely?" the old man said. "It would be better
That twenty million should die than one be saved. One man in ten miles is more
Than the earth wants: and clearly this man's life's worthless, being full of fears. I have acted against reason
And against instinct." He laughed and said: "But that's the condition of being human: to betray reason
And deny instinct. Did I tell this poor fellow
I had escaped?"
The man clung to him, as a pilot-fish
Clings to a shark. The old shark groaned and said, "The crime and the punishment: because I saved you
I must endure you." But when the boat was boughten and they sailed it south, and were off Point Sur,
The man screamed, "I fear shipwreck!" and flung himself
Over the side into the sea's cold throat. The old man watched him, and said, "Who am I, that I should come
Between man and man's need?" But in a moment he kicked the tiller and swung back: "By God," he said,
"I have been in error again; I am full of errors. It is not death they desire, but the dear pleasure
Of being saved." He caught the drowner by the hair and dragged him
Inboard; who, after he had breathed and vomited,

"Beware," he gasped, "beware, old man, the dear pleasure
Of being Savior." "I am well warned," he answered.

When the old man brings the man of terrors to his house, they discover that it is full of refugees who have fled the cities. Since there are too many for even his axe to drive away, he decides to sleep on the hill but asks the people to take the man of terrors into the house. He then goes and sits on the hill, where he is joined by his dog. After remarking that "terror is more contagious than typhoid, and fear than diphtheria," he and his dog watch the house until three hours later the doors burst open and the people flee into the mountains.

Not long after this, three robbers come to the house while the old man sleeps. His axe kills two of them, but the old man awakens in time to save the third, the man of terrors, who now admits that he is the old man's other self. Together they tie the bodies of the two thieves onto the horses and descend from the mountain. After placing the bodies in his boat, the Inhumanist performs the final act of overcoming his humanity when he cuts off the head of his alter ego and, in a scene paralleling the crucifixion of Christ, places the body between the two thieves before setting the boat afire and adrift. Thus the Inhumanist accomplishes at last what Orestes had done through negation in *The Tower Beyond Tragedy.* Though inordinately painful, the "operation," Jeffers says, is finally necessary:

"It was not easy. Fortunate, Snapper, are all the beasts of the mountain: they live their natures: but man
Is outrageous. No man has ever known himself nor surpassed himself until he has killed
Half of himself." He leaned on the boat stern-strake and turned his dead man face upward, and the dead face
Was his own in his youth.

Is Jeffers saying then that he has at last destroyed that didactic side of himself, that tendency in his verse that became more and more prominent in the 1930s until some of his poems were little more than homilies? To an extent, yes. But more importantly, I think, he is dramatizing the need for man to develop a new nature. He is, in other words, being didactic without apology.

In the concluding sections he foretells the rioting in our cities and the looting of "the liquor shops and the haberdasher's: happy America: the luxuries and the vanities, / Whiskey and silk." When the law-and-order people asked the old man for advice on the solution of America's problems at home, he answers with uncanny insight:

"Mine?" he said. "It is not new: all the rulers know it.
If there's a flea in the water, swallow a toad. If you have trouble at home,
Try foreign war." "You are very foolish," they answered, "or very wicked." "Both," he said. "But look
How wealthy and how victorious you are. You will not labor to avert fate. Fate is your need."

After returning to his mountain home, the Inhumanist addresses the future generations, and in so doing summarizes Jeffers's central beliefs. The last lines of his sermon on the mount:

"O future children:
Cruelty is dirt and ignorance, a muddy peasant
Beating his horse. Ambition and power-lust
Are for adolescents and defective persons. Moderate kindness
Is oil on a crying wheel; use it. Mutual help
Is necessary: use it when it is necessary.
And as to love: make love when need drives.
And as to love: love God. He is rock, earth and water, and the beasts and stars; and the night that contains them.
And as to love: whoever loves or hates man is fooled in a mirror." He grinned and said:
"From experience I speak. But truly, if you love man, swallow him in wine: love man in God.
Man and nothing but man is a sorry mouthful."

Reading the short poems of *The Double Axe* volume today we can understand why critics twenty-five years ago were appalled by his "pessimism" (a word that must be set off since he no longer seems at all pessimistic). In the years immediately following the war, most people, in any case those who were on the "winning" side, saw reason to hope that the war effort had been beneficial to mankind. In any event the victory brought enormous wealth to America. What obviously irritated many readers was the simple fact that Jeffers refused to believe the war to be a conclusion of horrific events that would have no repercussions. Those events he saw as a prelude to even more flaming horrors. The monsters unleashed by the holocaust were still loose in the world and refused, once the war was over, to return to their kennels. As one of the mountainous creatures in "The Inquisitors" (obviously symbols for nature) remarked, after puzzling over the little creatures they poured from the sacks onto the huge rock:

> *"It is not likely they can destroy all life: the planet is capacious. Life would surely grow up again*
> *From grubs in the soil, or the newt and toad level, and be beautiful again. And again perhaps break its legs*
> *On its own cleverness: who can forecast the future?"*

And in "What of It?" the poet, after stating that "life's norm is lost," predicts that "after due time" that norm would probably be found again. What does it matter to life if man is not well today? the poet asks, and then concludes: "He has had too many doctors, leaders and saviors: let him alone. It may be that bitter nature will cure him." If the hope seems flimsy, too much of a *perhaps* to offer comfort, we can at least be sure that a cure will not come from within.

FIVE Meditation on Saviors

The moment one inquires about the sense or value of life, one is sick.

—Freud

Look not back to the past for measuring-rods. Still less sideways for some system or other! There are times, like our own present and the Gracchan age, in which there are two most deadly kinds of idealism, the reactionary and the democratic. The one believes in the reversibility of history, the other in a teleology of history. It makes no difference, to the inevitable failure with which both burden a nation over whose destiny they have power, whether it is to a memory or to a concept that they sacrifice it.

—Spengler

Near the end (in section 47) of "The Inhumanist," a youth comes to the old man and expresses the wish to be his disciple. (Since Jeffers believed poetry should concern itself with serious things, he appropriately wrote the section in prose.) The youth first asks the name of the old man, "so that my friends may know it and listen, when I speak wisely." The old man puts him off with the remark that his name is but a word, adding that it is false to believe that the word was in the beginning. "And those," he adds, "to whom the word is God: their God is a word." When the youth insists he will still be a disciple, the old man informs him that his conditions are not easy: "My disciples must never sleep, except the nights when a full moon sets at midnight." At which point the youth realizes that disciples are the last thing the old man wants or needs. Considering the old man's remarks about leaders and humanity in general, one must admire his restraint.

If he was contemptuous of disciples or followers (human gulls he calls them), Jeffers was fascinated with human saviors much as the pathologist is fascinated with bacterial toxins. Both saviors and toxins fill us with awe, with fear and trembling, and not infrequently (to borrow again from Kierkegaard) with sickness unto death. Put bluntly, saviors are themselves sick and can only contaminate. With the hawkers of salvation so loud in the land today, Jeffers's analysis of the savior complex has particular immediacy.

While the Reverend Arthur Barclay in *The Women at Point Sur* and Jesus in *Dear Judas* are his most memorable portraits of the savior, there are other characters who would fall under that heading—in particular, Clare Walker in *The Loving Shepherdess* and Hitler in "The Bowl of Blood." While all his saviors are driven in varying degrees by a lust for power, it is also apparent that each is finally victimized by his attachment to an absolutist concept of truth. Man is most monstrous when he attempts to become the truth, when he believes that he is a word, a concept, a symbol. Though Barclay, Jesus, Clare, and Hitler differ vastly in personality—and hence in our estimation of their moral worth—each is monstrous in that each is so unnatural. Without ever breaking away from humanity, each exaggerates his humanity until he becomes either superhuman or subhuman. All Jeffers's saviors act against reason; all are blindly committed to one ideal; all seek escape from the naturalistic world of causal relations. Finally, all act out of a love for self which they misinterpret as love for mankind. I might almost say that in their inordinate love for mankind they commit the folly of loving the self excessively. In the eyes of their votaries they claim the rank of savior by the excessive degree of their love.

To understand Jeffers's attitude toward saviors and toward the truth they seek to embody (they are uninterested in knowing the truth; they wish to become it), the reader needs to examine closely two poems—"Meditation on Saviors" and "Theory of Truth." In the latter poem, written some ten years after "Meditation on Saviors," Jeffers listed three saviors who had sought to answer the "large time-worn questions" that Arthur Barclay had proposed to himself (the poem is written as a "reference" to chapter 2 of *The Women at Point Sur*):

I stand near Soberanes Creek, on the knoll over the sea, west of the road. I remember
This is the very place where Arthur Barclay, a priest in revolt, proposed three questions to himself:
First, is there a God and of what nature? Second, whether there's anything after we die but worm's meat?
Third, how should men live? Large time-worn questions no doubt; yet he touched his answers, they are not unattainable;
But presently lost them again in the glimmer of insanity.

How many minds have worn these questions; old coins

Rubbed faceless, dateless. The most have despaired and accepted doctrine; the greatest have achieved answers, but always
With aching strands of insanity in them.

I think of Lao-tze; and the dear beauty of the Jew whom they crucified but he lived, he was greater than Rome;
And godless Buddha under the boh-tree, straining through his mind the delusions and miseries of human life.

Why does insanity always twist the great answers?
Because only tormented persons want truth.
Man is an animal like other animals, wants food and success and women, not truth. Only if the mind
Tortured by some interior tension has despaired of happiness: then it hates its life-cage and seeks further,
And finds, if it is powerful enough. But instantly the private agony that made the search
Muddles the finding.

What the tormented person eventually finds, as Jeffers points out in the poem, is an answer (in the form of a rationalization) to the "private agony" that fathered the search in the beginning. That is to say, in the answer will be reflected the agony. The young Jew's solution, for example, has had the unwitting effect of injuring untold numbers of innocent bystanders.

Here was a man who was born a bastard, and among the people
That more than any in the world valued race-purity, chastity, the prophetic splendors of the race of David.
Oh intolerable wound, dimly perceived. Too loving to curse his mother, desert-driven, devil-haunted,
The beautiful young poet found truth in the desert, but found also
Fantastic solution of hopeless anguish. The carpenter was not his father? Because God was his father,
Not a man sinning, but the pure holiness and power of God. His personal anguish and insane solution
Have stained an age; nearly two thousand years are one vast poem drunk with the wine of his blood.

To Jeffers the savior is a tragic figure, a man who is both victim and victimizer. It is true, of course, that in that willful victimization which grows out of the search for self there is a shocking beauty, a painful and torturous beauty that heightens and intensifies the viewer's understanding and love of life even as it lowers his respect for the human species. Or perhaps I should say that tragedy has the salubrious effect of encouraging us to look beyond humanity for sources of order and meaning.

In his "Meditation on Saviors," published in 1928, Jeffers described the predicament of a man (in this case Jeffers) who had pledged himself "not to seek refuge, neither in death nor in a walled garden, / In lies nor gated loyalties, nor in the gates of contempt, that easily lock the world out of doors." His solution, if that is the word, for the problem took the form of a rejection of humanity, though not of individuals. Jeffers repeatedly said, in effect, that love of man implies a concern for his welfare, which in turn begets a desire for power without which the concern is impotent and the love hollow. (In defense of Jeffers, one need only point to the fact that power-hungry individuals are without exception inordinately selfish, and those who profess a love for mankind rarely can so much as abide individuals. If there are exceptions to the rule, I have yet to hear of them.) His fascination with the psychology of the savior has, it is true, caused certain shallow critics to assume that he actually approved the acts of his savior-figures. (Yvor Winters, one of the least perceptive of his critics, thought that the Reverend Barclay was the mouthpiece of Jeffers's philosophy and that Jesus was his "mouthpiece and hero" of *Dear Judas.* There are doubtless readers of "A Modest Proposal" who believe that Swift actually advocated cannibalism as a solution to the Irish problem.) And his contempt for the followers of such saviors has led other critics, particularly the Marxist and Christian apologists, to attack his moral integrity. That he was more contemptuous of followers than of leaders is clearly revealed in these lines from the first part of "Meditation on Saviors":

Here on the rock it is great and beautiful, here on the foam-wet granite sea-fang it is easy to praise
Life and water and the shining stones: but whose cattle are the herds of the people that one should love them?

If they were yours, then you might take a cattle-breeder's delight in the herds of the future. Not yours.
Where the power ends let love, before it sours to jealousy. Leave the joys of government to Caesar.

Who is born when the world wanes, when the brave soul of the world falls on decay in the flesh increasing
Comes one with a great level mind, sufficient vision, sufficient blindness, and clemency for love.

This is the breath of rottenness I smelt; from the world waiting, stalled between storms, decaying a little,
Bitterly afraid to be hurt, but knowing it cannot draw the savior Caesar but out of the blood-bath.

The apes of Christ lift up their hands to praise love: but wisdom without love is the present savior,
Power without hatred, mind like a many-bladed machine subduing the world with deep indifference.

To which he adds an additional stanza mocking the Christians who fatuously presume to imitate the tragic figure whose self-sacrifice, so Jeffers believed, was far more complicated than any mere act of love:

The apes of Christ itch for a sickness they have never known; words and the little envies will hardly
Measure against that blinding fire behind the tragic eyes they have never dared to confront.

There may be light here but without any hint of sweetness.

Part 2 of "Meditation on Saviors" opens with the following stanzas:

Point Lobos lies over the hollowed water like a humped whale swimming to shoal; Point Lobos
Was wounded with that fire; the hills at Point Sur endured it; the palace at Thebes; the hill Calvary.

Out of incestuous love power and then ruin. A man forcing the imaginations of men,
Possessing with love and power the people: a man defiling his own household with impious desire.

King Oedipus reeling blinded from the palace doorway, red tears pouring from the torn pits
Under the forehead; and the young Jew writhing on the domed hill in the earthquake, against the eclipse

Frightfully uplifted for having turned inward to love the people:—that root was so sweet Oh, dreadful agonist?—
I saw the same pierced feet, that walked in the same crime to its expiation; I heard the same cry.

The acts, crimes against nature Jeffers would call them, of Tamar (at Point Lobos) and Barclay (at Point Sur) are thus considered identical with the incestuous crimes of Oedipus and Jesus, the former having done literally what the latter did figuratively. As I have said before, however, Tamar should not be classified as a savior since she sought to save no one. Her incest is almost as unwitting as that of Oedipus, and neither falls because of an abstract love of mankind.

Jeffers's rejection of the abstraction love probably grew from his extreme denial of saviors, who invariably employed that abstraction in order to, wittingly or not, injure others. In effect, his kindness caused him to deny the savior. As we shall see in a moment, Jeffers believed that man needed no savior since salvation is assured all living creatures in any case. Moreover the savior is a sort of supernatural do-gooder, a celestial insurance man who peddles his policies at a premium too high for reason to pay. Jeffers and Thoreau are similar in their disgust for the creature. "If I knew for a certainty," Thoreau wrote, "that a man was coming to my house with the conscious design of doing me good, I should run for my life, as from the dry and parching wind of the African deserts called the simoom, which fills the mouth and nose and ears and eyes with dust till you are suffocated, for fear that I should get some of his good done to me,—some of its virus mingled with my blood."

That Jeffers believed that "virus" was more a death potion than a life preservative is everywhere evident in his writing. While he apparently accepted the historical Jesus, he believed Christianity had grown out of an attempt to deny death, to abolish it forever. And before that could be done in a world of constant flux it was necessary also to abolish life; to deny the one is to deny the other. It should be obvious that Jeffers's intense love of life is the root cause for his hatred of all organized religions, and Christianity probably more than all the others. Again, Jeffers had no complaint with the conditions of life—of birth, growth, death, decay, and change. His poetry is remarkably free from any lament over a natural process. He constantly marveled that any intelligent man could complain about what he called cosmic harmony. Here also is a major reason for his rejection of saviors, who invariably try either to escape or to change man's fate.

In the last section of "Meditation on Saviors" he resolves the dilemma of man in search of salvation much as the elegist resolves his loss at the end of an elegy:

Yet look: are they [the people] not pitiable? No: if they lived forever they would be pitiable:
But a huge gift reserved quite overwhelms them at the end; they are able then to be still and not cry.

And having touched a little of the beauty and seen a little of the beauty of things, magically grow
Across the funeral fire or the hidden stench of burial themselves into the beauty they admired,

Themselves into the God, themselves into the sacred steep unconsciousness they used to mimic
Asleep between lamp's death and dawn, while the last drunkard stumbled homeward down the dark street.

They are not to be pitied but very fortunate; they need no savior, salvation comes and takes them by force,
It gathers them into the great kingdoms of dust and stone, the blown storms, the stream's-end ocean.

With this advantage over their granite grave-marks, of having realized the petulant human consciousness
Before, and then the greatness, the peace: drunk from both pitchers: these to be pitied? These not fortunate?

And then the final two stanzas, which I have quoted before, adjuring man to free himself from human love in order that he might love the tall world while he can. He offers, as it were, a new twist to the gather-ye-rosebuds-while-ye-may importunity of Herrick. The carpe diem of Jeffers always entails a looking beyond humanity and its pitiful, molelike concerns. In place of the closed world of human solipsism, he proposes the open world of physical beauty:

But while he lives let each man make his health in his mind, to love the coast opposite humanity
And so be freed of love, laying it like bread on the waters; it is worst turned inward, it is best shot farthest.

Love, the mad wine of good and evil, the saint's and murderer's, the mote in the eye that makes its object
Shine the sun black; the trap in which it is better to catch the inhuman God than the hunter's own image.

II

First of all, the savior must not be confused with the revolutionary or rebel. The romantic rebel, like Tamar, wars against the nonhuman world and the conditions that world imposes on matter. On the other hand, there are rebels like Orestes who seek to free themselves from human weakness, specifically from the egotistic self that keeps them in a state of pain. Usually, however, the rebel attempts to correct social conditions that he finds intolerable. That revolutions are invariably betrayed once they are successful is attributable to the fact that though an end may at times temporarily justify a means, the end can never be made static. Living in a world of constant change, of time passing, we can never achieve a goal without its melting in our hands and, in effect, ceasing to exist even as abstraction. A goal or an end is an abstraction, a flickering light that leads us through existence, the one thing, by its very nomenclature, that possesses existence. I do not intend paradox and certainly not mere play on words. All I mean to say is that only in a kind of illusion can an end possess existence. Only the means exist; from them and not from any end do we receive our essence. We are precisely what we do—no matter what reasons we may give for our actions, no matter that our actions may have been performed in the name of this or that lofty end. Only the means is active and concrete; the end is passive and abstract. The best that can be hoped for an accomplished end is that it will metamorphose into a means for something else.

When in the heat of the battle to obtain his goal the revolutionary forgets this elementary fact, he begins to think not in terms of political or social change in his life and the lives of his followers but rather in terms of an all-encompassing change that will then be changeless. He succumbs to the view that salvation is not only possible but is at hand, that the achievement of his goal will in effect place him in a timeless world. The discontent that propelled the rebel has a subtle way of warping the mind of the individual and transforming him into a savior, who differs primarily from the revolutionary in that he is less interested in the world outside than he is in discovering the self amidst the tensions of his mind and then relocating that self outside temporal affairs. The savior lives inwardly, incestuously. If Prometheus was the first revolutionary, then Narcissus was the first savior. It is finally not the redemption of others he hopes to realize but only the salvation of his single self—a self that includes all the world, or, as Jeffers put it, "the infinite self that has eaten / Environment, and lives / Alone, unencroached on, perfectly gorged, one God."

In the Reverend Barclay, Jeffers drew his most complete portrait of the savior. The longest of his narratives, *The Women at Point Sur* is also his most complex and diffuse study, one that has been generally misunderstood.[1] Nor is it difficult to understand why that bloodstained epic of madness and depravity should have shocked and mystified readers at the time of publication. Dwight MacDonald did not exaggerate much when he wrote in the *Miscellany* (September 1930) that "not since the later Elizabethans has there been such a witches' dance of incest, suicide, madness, adultery and Lesbianism." (His article, by the way, praises Jeffers highly.) Jeffers's defense of the poem, or more precisely his explanation of its intentions, does much to dispel the obscurities; but then execution is always of more importance, in any judicial sense, than intention. Keys to the meaning of James Joyce's later canon, for example, are quite useful to our appreciation but can never take the place of the work of art as an artifact. Nor for that matter will clarification of the obscure necessarily increase our admiration of the work; it might just as likely have the opposite effect.

Oddly enough, *The Women at Point Sur* is by far the most symbolic of all Jeffers's narratives and, at the same time, is his most severe indictment of the human penchant for reducing phenomena to symbols. A frontal assault on idealism, it stacks meaning on meaning until the mind boggles in an attempt to sort them out for proper identification. I do not mean that the story is incredible, or in any way Kafkaesque, but simply that we know each incident was intended by the author to be read as representative of something (or some things) in human nature. Jeffers is less concerned with specific humans and their dilemmas than he is with archetypal patterns. And yet he displays the noxious effect of an individual consciously acting in a symbolic fashion. Certainly Barclay's actions are symbolic not only as we interpret them but also as he intended them. His most outrageous act, the violation of his daughter, April, he thinks of as a symbolic gesture by which he moves beyond good and evil. He is thus closely related to such romantics as de Sade. After concluding that there is no moral order inherent in things—in the cosmic flow—he finally makes, quite consciously, a leap into nihilism when he presumes to act in defiance of all moral restraint. Only by this, he assumes, can he actually become his freedom. In effect, Barclay acts in such a way as to prove that he is outside causal relations, outside the web of necessity, free in a godless universe—or rather as free as the God who *is* the universe and who moves through all things. Thus, as I have pointed out before in looking at "Theory of Truth," Barclay does perceive a glimmer of the truth, only to muddle the finding in his private impurity. In a word, Barclay becomes God. He thus does what Nietzsche's Zarathustra did. He fills the moral vacuum with the nearest thing at hand—his self. He is mad.

In his "Prelude," Jeffers sets the scene by locating his characters in a dynamic world of stress and strain that work always to transform or reshape phenomena, and he further locates them at a time in human history when great cultural upheaval has become inevitable. The precise date is 1919, but more importantly it is at that trembling time when Yeats's "rough beast, its hour come round at last, / Slouches towards Bethlehem to be born." This need for a new transvaluation of values has not resulted from anything man has done, certainly no blame is assignable, but has come from what the mind knows. The growth in human knowledge (the "wine" in the lines below) has made obsolete the man-centered values of the past:

Culture's outlived, art's root-cut, discovery's
The way to walk in. Only remains to invent the language to tell it. Match-ends of burnt experience
Human enough to be understood,
Scraps and metaphors will serve. The wine was a little too strong for the new wine-skins . . .

Clearly Jeffers does not credit the just-ended war, which looms always in the background, as cause for the breaking down of Western culture, but only as a by-product, a visible eruption on the skin of a civilization in decay.

The promise-breaker war killed whom it freed,
And none living's the cleaner. Yet storm comes, the lions hunt

In the nights striped with lightning. It will come: feed on peace
While the crust holds: to each of you at length a little
Desolation; a pinch of lust or a drop of terror:
Then the lions hunt in the brain of the dying: storm is good, storm is good, good creature,
Kind violence, throbbing throat aches with pity.

From that general introduction Jeffers abruptly focuses on various minor characters whose lives will in some way be interlocked with the "passion" of Barclay. First there is Onorio Vasquez, "young seer of visions," who acts as a sympathetic counterpart of Barclay. Although he becomes a disciple of Barclay, he never desires power and is thus never harmful to others. Indeed, in *The Loving Shepherdess*, his kindness and consideration are in constant counterpoint to Clare Walker's self-destructive bent. Unlike Clare, he does not elicit our pity and hence disgust; he is probably the most thoroughly likable of all Jeffers's characters. Here in the "Prelude" he watches his brothers Vidal and Julio crucify a wounded hawk to the barn wall:

They prod his breast with a wand, no sponge of vinegar,
"Fly down, Jew-beak." The wind streams down the mountain,
The river of cloud streams over: Onorio Vasquez
Never sees anything to the point. What he sees:
The ocean like sleek gray stone perfectly jointed
To the heads and bays, a woman walking upon it,
The curling scud of the storm around her ankles,
Naked and strong, her thighs the height of the mountain, walking and weeping,
The heavy face hidden in the hands, the lips drinking the tears in the hollow hands and the hair
Streaming north. "Why are you sad, our lady?" "I had only one son.
The strange lover never breaks the window-latches again
When Joseph's at synagogue."

In the concluding lines of the nine-page "Prelude" Onorio envisions himself as replacing the hawk, as making the necessary blood sacrifice which life (or just man?) demands. And like Jesus in *Dear Judas*, Onorio realizes he must employ guile to induce his fellows to perform an act which the conscious mind must reject as barbarous. Put another way, Onorio realizes subconsciously that the symbol (and he reads the world only symbolically) can be kept alive only if he provides it with a new body. It is difficult, Jeffers seems to be saying, to believe in *things*; we can believe only in the representatives of things. Those representatives are part of my thought, and hence of my being. I think; therefore, I am. The world is my idea. Cartesianism ascending into the pure idea of Schopenhauer. A belief in shadows. The symbol is thus, in its inclusion of things, a shortcut for belief, a means of fusing the many into the one. The final lines of the "Prelude" attempt to express the wordless thoughts of Onorio:

Don't you see any vision Onorio Vasquez? "No, for the topazes
Have dulled out of his head, he soars on two nails,
Dead hawk over the coast. Oh little brother
Julio, if you could drive nails through my hands
I'd stand against the door: through the middle of the palms:
And take the hawk's place, you could throw knives at me.
I'd give you my saddle and the big bridle, Julio,
With the bit that rings and rings when the horse twirls it."
He smiles. "You'd see the lights flicker in my hair."
He smiles craftily. "You'd live long and be rich,
And nobody could beat you in running or riding."
He chatters his teeth. "It is necessary for someone to be fastened with nails.
And Jew-beak died in the night. Jew-beak is dead."

I read these lines as implying that the Christian God is dead, leaving those like Onorio in a temporary vacuum. For a time Barclay will fill that vacuum for Onorio, and when faith in that self-immolating god fails Onorio becomes physically sick and even begs to die.

In contrast with Onorio's visions, his fleshless desires, Myrtle Cartwright and Faith Heriot escape from the nothingness of their lives through a more commonplace outlet—sexual desire. Prayer temporarily prevents Myrtle from surrendering to the physical ache:

Prayer works all right: three times
Rod Stewart came down to see her, he might have been wood
For all she cared.

But she is young and life cheerless, her husband, Andrew, often away. Jeffers places all things in the seething cauldron of atomic strain:

Always the strain, the straining flesh, who feels what God feels
Knows the straining flesh, the aching desires,
The enormous water straining its bounds, the electric

Strain in the cloud, the strain of the oil in the oil-tanks
At Monterey, aching to burn, the strain of the spinning
Demons that make an atom, straining to fly asunder,
Straining to rest at the center,
The strain in the skull, blind strains, force and counter-force,
Nothing prevails . . .

As Myrtle Cartwright runs through the stormy night to her lover, another "marriage"—an inhuman wedding—takes place in Monterey. The lightning that frightens her signals the wild mating:

Black pool of oil hidden in the oil-tank
In Monterey felt the sword plunge: touched: the wild heat
Went mad where a little air was, metal curled back,
Fire leaped at the outlet. "Immense ages
We lay under rock, our lust hoarded,
The ache of ignorant desire, the enormous pressure,
The enormous patience, the strain, strain, the strain
Lightened we lay in a steel shell . . . what God kept for us:
Roaring marriage."

In one orgasmic gulp the one tank "roars with fulfilled desire, / The ring-bound molecules splitting, the atoms dancing apart, marrying the air," as Myrtle Cartwright finds the house of Rod Stewart, and as Onorio Vasquez dreams salvation through self-torture. Jeffers sets his stage well for the story that follows. His artistry in the "Prelude" is everywhere apparent, but what he brings together there with vigorous clarity threatens to fall apart in the poetic shards that follow.

Though I do not consider *The Women at Point Sur* the failure that many readers, some of them great admirers of Jeffers, have thought it, I do not think it as fine a work as several other of his narratives. It certainly has fine things in it, but it lacks the cohesiveness that his best work possesses. Though he omitted it from his *Selected Poetry*, as he remarked in the foreword, "because it is the least understood and least liked, and because it is the longest" of his narratives, Jeffers always professed a fondness for the poem, insisting that it was, in spite of grave faults, "the most inclusive, and poetically the most intense," of all his poems. Without disputing any of that, I still think the intensity is at times strained. Moreover, inclusiveness is not in itself a virtue; it can be an actual defect in the work of art, which depends upon ordering and condensation, above all, to appeal successfully to the mind and emotions of the beholder.

Not long after publication of the poem Jeffers wrote James Rorty about his intentions. Since his explanation was largely prompted by a review Mark Van Doren wrote for the *Nation* (27 July 1927), he sent a copy of the letter to Van Doren, who had, Jeffers wrote in a covering note, "been too kind to my verses to be left in the dark as to my intentions, whatever you may think of the book in question." The letter tells us much more than Jeffers's intentions in that one poem: it clearly reveals a great deal about the man and his general philosophy. Thus I feel compelled to quote the entire letter even though it has been reproduced several times before:

> You were right evidently about the need of an explanation. I have just read Mark Van Doren's article, and if he, a first-rate critic and poet and a good friend of my work, quite misunderstands the book, it is very likely that no one else will understand it at present.
>
> You remember a couple of letters ago I spoke of the morality—perhaps I said old-fashioned morality—implied in "Point Sur." "Tamar" seemed to my later thought to have a tendency to romanticize unmoral freedom, and it was evident a good many people took it that way. That way lies destruction of course, often for the individual but always for the social organism, and one of the later intentions of this "Point Sur" was to indicate the destruction, and strip everything but its natural ugliness from the unmorality. Barclay incited people to "be your desires . . . flame . . . enter freedom" [chapter 20]. The remnant of his sanity—if that was the image of himself that he met on the hilltop—asks him whether it was for love of mankind that he is "pouring poison into the little vessels?" He is forced to admit that if the motive seems love, the act is an act of hatred.
>
> Another intention, this time a primary one, was to show in action the danger of that "Roan Stallion" idea of "breaking out of humanity," misinterpreted in the mind of a fool or a lunatic. I take the idea to be what you expressed in "the heart is a thing to be broken," carried a little farther perhaps. It is not anti-social, because it has nothing to do with society; but just as Ibsen in the Wild Duck made a warning against his own idea in the hands of a fool, so Point Sur was meant to be a warning; but at the same time a reassertion.
>
> Van Doren's criticism assures me that I was quite successful in this intention and in the one about morality; only I proved my points so perfectly that he thinks—and therefore other intelligent people will think—that they are proved against me and in spite of me. I confess I didn't think of

this; I didn't think about myself at all. So I have written in these respects well but not wisely.

For the rest, the book was meant to be

(1) an attempt to uncenter the human mind from itself. There is no health for the individual whose attention is taken up with his own mind and processes; equally there is no health for the society that is always introverted on its own members, as ours becomes more and more, the interest engaged inward in love and hatred, companionship and competition. These are necessary of course, but as they absorb all the interest they become fatal. All past cultures have died of introversion at last, and so will this one, but the individual can be free of the net, in his mind. It is a matter of trans-valuing values, to use the phrase of somebody [Nietzsche] that local people accuse me quite falsely of deriving from.

I have used incest as a symbol to express these introversions, and used it too often, though it is the most appropriate symbol.

(2) The book was meant to be a tragedy, that is an exhibition of essential elements by the burning away through pain and ruin of inertia and the unessential.

(3) A valid study in psychology; the study valid, the psychology morbid, sketching the growth of a whole system of emotional delusion from a "private impurity" that was quite hidden from consciousness until insanity brought it to the surface.

(4) Therefore a partial and fragmentary study of the origin of religions; which have been necessary to society in the past, and I think remain necessary whether we like it or not, yet they derive from a "private impurity" of some kind in their originators.

(5) A satire on human self-importance; referring back to (1).

(6) A judgment of the tendencies of our civilization, which has very evidently turned the corner down hill. "Powers increase and power perishes." Our literature, as I said in answer to the New Masses questionnaire, is not especially decadent (because in general it is not especially anything); but our civilization has begun to be.

(Some of you think that you can save society; I think it is impossible, and that you only hasten the process of decadence. Of course as a matter of right and justice I sympathize with radicalism; any way I don't oppose it; from an abstract viewpoint there is no reason that I know of for propping and prolonging the period of decadence. Perhaps the more rapid it is, the sooner comes a new start.)

There were more intentions, but these are the chief ones that can readily be said in prose. Too many intentions. I believe they all carry over to an intelligent reader, as results though not as intentions, but no doubt I was asking him to hold too many things in mind at once. I had concentrated my energies for a long while on perceptions and expression, and

> forgot that the reader could not concentrate so long, nor so intensely, nor from the same detached and inclusive view-point.[2]

Six weeks later (on 21 September 1927) Jeffers wrote Benjamin De Casseres that he thought the book his best so far, "though perhaps unfit for human consumption." Its worst fault, he wryly noted, was that it caused people to come and ask him what it meant: "They'd think I was comparing it with its betters if I should ask them in return what King Lear means: so all I can do is to look grim and assure them that my hero was crazy but I am not."

Most readers will agree with Jeffers that the poem has "too many intentions." Given all the ideological layers in the poem, it is rather amazing that the characters possess any life at all. That his people do live is a tribute to his genius for characterization. I think it also apparent that the poem may be more readily understood today than it was fifty years ago. In numerous ways we are just now catching up with Jeffers.

As for his denial that he derived from Nietzsche, that too seems to me obvious. While there can be no doubt that he had read Nietzsche closely and even seemed to have him in mind while writing *The Women at Point Sur*, he actually seems to be attacking the Nietzschean viewpoint. Although it seems of little consequence to me, a strong case could be made for the view that Barclay was modeled on Zarathustra and thus should be taken as warning against Nietzsche's romantic savior. But while Zarathustra's overcoming of the all-too-human illustrates a triumph over human nature, which is paradoxically a triumph of humanity over supernaturalism, Barclay's overcoming is clearly a tragedy. Each book opens with its protagonist in a state of disaffection. Zarathustra speaks of the death of God and proclaims the advent of the overman. Barclay also begins on that note, telling his congregation that he had tried to cling to the ethic after the myths had died in his mind:

> *"The creed died in my mind, I kept the pastorate, I thought the spirit,*
> *The revolutionary spirit of Christ would survive, flame the more freely. There are many others*
> *Leaders of churches have sunk the myths and swim by the ethic. Love: and not resist violence: which one of us*
> *Holds to that now? Dared name it this time last year?"*

Last year the war still raged in Europe, and Barclay's son Edward died in that conflict. After preaching a dead creed for ten years, Barclay prepares to go off into the mountains, just as Zarathustra leaves his home in the mountains after ten years to return to mankind whom he has learned to love. Only when Barclay learns to love man, or rather decides that he must love mankind, does he return to the world below. (The love of both Zarathustra and Barclay is purely abstract; it is set in motion, so to speak, through an act of will.) Before leaving Barclay gives his hearers "ten years' / Thought in a moment's words":

> *"It is not possible*
> *To know anything while you eat lies: you half-believers, fog-people: leave that, wash the eyes, and who knows*
> *Now the earth draws to maturity, has taken the bloody*
> *Initiation of coming of age, you also grown adult*
> *May fish some flaming gleam of knowledge out of the netted ocean, run down some deer of perception*
> *In the dark wood: certainly it is hopeless, oh desperate; no man*
> *Down all the blind millenniums has known anything, no, not a scrap, not a dust-grain: I am calling you to that*
> *Blind adventure, I call you to take despair by the throat: I know you are fools and soft, woman-brained,*
> *I have lived among you, I have held my mouth not to despise you: I would set the sheep on the wolves to this end,*
> *The doves at the hawk's nest . . ."*

Thus he leaves behind an existence which has grown pointless: little more than an attendance on the marriages and burials of his flock, the gossip of newspapers, " 'the noise you keep up / Under the stars, your national quarrels and your observances, / Flags, fireworks, songs to dead Gods.' " In brief, all the petty affairs that make for a life of quiet desperation. He goes off alone to "gather [his] mind," to drive life into a corner, as Thoreau put it, and reduce it to its common denominator.

For a time Barclay settles into a passive state, a kind of nihilistic peace: "He seemed to have passed into a vacuum, no means, no resistance, valueless freedom / Like a vain ghost's in the air. Nothing solid, the roots out." This is but the peace before the storm, the gestation period when the savior-nihilist resolves the world into idea. His mind, a shell of stored energy, cannot be still, cannot avoid translating the world in some fashion, nor can it avoid asking and answering the questions posed by the ceaseless movement of phenomena. One part of his mind advises him to purchase peace through inaction (the Schopenhaueran way), but that, another part of his mind advises, is merely to will one's death. Moreover the mind is, Jeffers implies, as much a manuscript written upon by the world as it is an author writing upon the world. We are both makers and made, both partaking and partaken of. Given a glimmer of the truth, having seen man as a part of the cosmic flow, Barclay seeks to embody that truth through force of his will. He is betrayed by the same knowledge that blasted Melville's Ahab. A few lines of his interior monologue should help clarify this transmogrification from perceiver into perceived, from (quite literally) auditor into actor:

> *It came to him like a whisper from outward: "Plow the air, what harvest: take the earth in your hands.*
> *God thinks through action, how shall a man but through action?" "I have cut myself off, I acted when I cut myself off*
> *From action: I am only a wandering mind reaching at knowledge." But he thought "It is true that I have reached nothing.*
> *The presence I almost touched in the crowds . . . what was it I sought? . . . that came in flashes, vanishes derisive*
> *When the eyes focus. To mould one's thoughts from action. Give up sanity again, be mad enough to act."*

Having resolved to reenter the active world, Dr. Barclay realizes the need for disciples, the means to power; without power life is nothing. Power is the essence:

> *"The mind's powerless in vacuo, no one can dispense with disciples*
> *And burn to the essence.*
> *Those are the birds that are not caught but with confidence.*
> *What's honesty, the end is honest."*

He then descends from his lonely retreat. His journey has begun.

In chapter 4 we are introduced to the dramatis personae. After being refused lodging at a prosperous farmhouse, he is taken in by Natalia Morhead, who can use the money he pays for rent to help keep the ranch until her husband returns from the war. At the Morhead ranch are Natalia, her four-year-old child, Rachel, her crippled father-in-law, two farmhands, and Faith Heriot with whom Natalia shares a lesbian relationship.

In "Theory of Truth" Jeffers wrote that Dr. Barclay "touched" the answers to the questions he posed to himself, "but presently lost them again in the glimmer of insanity." He touched truth, Jeffers would say, when he concluded that the essence of life is strain or constant change. If this is true then humanity composes a part, albeit a rather insignificant part, of all that might be designated as natural and supernatural. There is nothing very earthshaking here. Indeed, the healthy individual might be expected to shrug his shoulders and then go about his business, none the wiser for having been informed of the all-too-obvious. In *The Unexpected Universe* Loren Eiseley, who admitted having been influenced by Jeffers, neatly expressed that truth in a single sentence: "As the spinning galactic clouds hurl stars and worlds across the night, so life, equally impelled by the centrifugal powers lurking in the germ cell, scatters the splintered radiance of consciousness and sends it prowling and contending through the thickets of the world."[3] Dr. Barclay, however, must pick at this truth until it festers and becomes injurious to his health. Above all, he must employ logic by which he attaches trailers to the truth, handles to which he might cling. In effect, he reasons thus:

"God thinks through action. There are only two ways: gather disciples
To fling like bullets against God and discover him:
Or else commit an act so monstrous, so irreparable
It will stand like a mountain of rock, serve you for fulcrum
To rest the lever. In vacancy: nothing."

What could be more logical (and more insane) than to conclude that if all acts are demonstrations of the divine essence then everything is permissible? The old values are made meaningless by such logic; and until new values are given, we cannot speak of good and evil. In the absence of moral postulates, we are free to follow wish wherever it might lead. Barclay says as much in a speech to Natalia, whom he suspects of a lesbian affair:

"When you go in,
Kiss Faith Heriot and tell her that what was right is wrong, what was wrong's right, the old laws are abolished,
They cannot be crossed nor broken, they're dead. The sanction is dead. This interval

There is nothing wicked, nothing strange in the world. What the heart desires, or any part of the body,
That is the law."

A moment later Barclay tells Natalia that "the world is changed," that what was once true (morally) is no longer so. He sounds more than a little like the author of "Song of Myself" when he seeks to allay Natalia's guilt feelings:

"Don't fear. Did I forget to tell you there is nothing wicked in the world, no act is a sin?
Nothing you can do is wicked. I have seen God. He is there in the hill, he is here in your body."

Ultimately he mocks those who try to enclose their lives with definitions of right and wrong and thereby place scruples in the path of discovery. Absolute freedom is the same thing of course as pure license. Any restraint in one's actions implies discrimination and sets up categories. As a test of himself Barclay goes to Maruca, the young Indian servant girl, and offers her money to have sexual intercourse with him. How much his decision was determined by physical desire and how much by his proclaimed need for deliverance from all restraint it is hard to say. At least, Barclay thinks that it is merely "a matter of deliverance," not just deliverance from animal want but from any moral reservation that still clings to his new being as fossil reminder of past enslavement to moral dicta. There can be no doubt, however, that he considers the transaction (he had to pay a few dollars for the experiment) a symbolic one—at least it is symbolic after the fact. And now having achieved the estate of symbol the act need never be repeated:

Maruca
Gathering the plates leaned over Barclay's chair
So that the great breast, through the oily brown cloth,
Lay on his shoulder, he overlooked his repugnance,
Unmoved, secretly smiling: the symbolic flesh
Had served him: the value of the symbol secured,
By-product amorousness, the ridiculous female
After-glow had no finger on; "I have cast the last fear:
Of being ridiculous."

When he leaves the room to walk in the night air, he is approached by Natalia, who wishes to confess her sin with Faith Heriot to him. In making him arbiter of her dilemma, she becomes his first disciple.

Like Nietzsche (and Blake and Wordsworth and Emerson and most other romantics), Dr. Barclay apotheosizes the child in man, the primordial innocence that now, for the first time in man's history, may be allowed to flame. All that man has done in the past or will do in the future, he has done as a child acting a role assigned him by nonhuman, and hence amoral, forces. Certainly no one, Barclay insists, can blame the child for following, or rather being, his own nature:

"Not the power but the soul
Crescents or wanes between the nights of the centuries.
Can a child sin? What's done is that child doing it, and what has been done?
War, torture, famine; oppressions; the secret cruelties; the plague in the air that killed its millions; that child
Reaping a fly's wings, innocently laughing
From the rich heart? Oh it has no laughter though a child. It is tortured with its own earnestness, it is tortured.
It is lonely: what playmate? It has no mother.
The child that is the stars and the earth and men's bodies, and the hollow darkness
Outside the stars, and the dark hollow in the atom."

In his rhapsodic rant, Barclay touches truth, as any student of history knows. In the final analysis one may object only to his conclusion that men may henceforth dispense with concepts of good and evil. If in the past those concepts have served as means to gull both the self and others, both victimizers and victims, they are still necessary to society.

In the following passage, the "awful voice not his own" is that of Nietzsche, or in any case the idea is thoroughly Nietzschean. Barclay asks if there is any substance in the "hollow and dark," that is, in the mindless workings of atomic energy. He answers his own query:

"There's power. What does it want, power?
It tortures its own flesh to discover itself. Of humanity
What does it want? It desires monsters. I told you it had changed.
Once it commanded justice, charity, self-continence,
Love between persons, loyalty: it was wise then: what purpose?
To hold the pack together for its conquest of the earth.

Now the earth is conquered, there is room, you have built your mountain, there is no competitor,
It says Flame! *it has sent me with fire, did you dream*
That those were final virtues? your goodness, your righteousness,
Your love: rags for the fire."
He groaned in his heart,
Feeling himself like a shell hollowed, the weakness,
The diminution, the awful voice not his own
Blown through his void.
"I have come to establish you
Over the last deception, to make men like God
Beyond good and evil. There is no will but discovery,
No love but toward that tragic child, toward the motherless,
The unlaughing, the lonely."
The fog had climbed higher and his head
Was hidden, only they heard his voice falling from above them
Until it had ceased.

The image of "fog" is used here, as elsewhere in his poetry (see his poem "Fog"), as a symbol of self-delusion. The greatest delusion, as I have remarked before, is that man may become God. And to puff oneself into such monstrous shape, one must employ the abstraction love. Nowhere else that I know of has the "God is love" absurdity been used with such scathing effect. When in the next section Barclay confronts his doppelgänger on the hillside (where the fog has thinned), he is forced to admit that his savior complex has grown from an inner need. His rational self mocks his irrational aspect, which now seeks its essence in the admiring eyes of converts:

Barclay climbed upward the slope. High up the gray fog
Was split in tongues, and over the bald summit blue sky. A man approached him
And said, "You've got outside humanity: you will not return.
Oh, let them feed and clothe you, you have money: but neither in love nor instruction
Lean to that breed." "Love?" he said, "what is love?" But the other: "To what purpose
Have you been dropping wine and fire in the little vessels?" When the buried sun
Rosed an arched banner of the mist, then Barclay saw the lean face, the stub of brown beard, the bar of the eyebrows,
His own mirrored; and the image: "If you did not love them would you labor to lead them?" He shaking and smiling:
"I see the devil is short of faces." It answered, "You could not fool yourself utterly. Your very body

Cried for companions; you stood like a moose bellowing for love. I listened all the while with secret laughter
The time we persuaded ourself we wanted disciples to bait the God-trap: their sweet persons you wanted;
Their eyes on our eyes. A filthy breed to refer to." And Barclay, "Here you are, madness.
The Magus Zoroaster thy dead . . . Where else does consciousness
Burn up to a point but in the bone lamps? I should be lonely." It laughed, "As the tragic child?" "He includes them.
And I though I choke, old portrait . . ."

At this point, Jeffers intercalates the first of three vignettes against Barclay's dialogue with self. Each of the brief counterpoints displays an aspect of love among the disciples: the vaquero Joe Medina forcing himself on Maruca; Natalia resuming her lesbian affair with Faith Heriot; and Onorio Vasquez peering at the scars on his palms, tangible evidence of his self-immolation. For such as these Barclay chose to "waste inward"; over them he unfurled the banner of love. Confronted with such sordid characters, the reader can only ask, as Jeffers intended him to ask, who is the more contemptuous: the savior or the saved? Between the evangelist and the evangelized there is little to choose.

In the following chapter (12), Jeffers steps outside his narrative to comment on the "idols" he has created. He admits that the vessels he has molded have "crackled" and gone mad—certainly an unnecessary admission. From this point, about midway through, we watch Barclay move from one perversion to the next, growing larger all the while in the minds of his motley followers. Until Barclay becomes convinced of his mission, he holds the reader as the ancient mariner held the wedding guest; but after that point he simply repels. He no longer disturbs us as tragic heroes or protagonists do, or even interests us very much, unless we have a particular interest in morbid psychology. Indeed, he resembles more the case study (out of, say, Krafft-Ebing) than he does the tragic victim of personal weakness or circumstance. The machinations of the moral hypocrite—a Tartuffe, an Elmer Gantry, or an Arthur Dimmesdale—can be extremely fascinating; such men can delight at the same time they appall, but the madman quickly palls. In the work of art, madness is better employed as a final state of being than as a cause for behavior. In the last half of the narrative, we are less concerned with the flesh-and-blood Barclay than we are with the uses Robinson Jeffers makes of him. He becomes a vehicle for the ideas of his creator, as Jeffers indirectly admits in the letter to James Rorty.

Moreover, Jeffers begins to repeat various of his charges against idealism. He shows again and again that Barclay's insanity is simply an extension or an exaggeration of the normal human propensity to reduce phenomena to symbols and finally to one symbol. His actions are little more than symbolic ratifications of his transcendental ideas. He violates the living in the name of love and commits the most flagrant of crimes in order to illustrate, or personify, an idea. For example, he feels that before he can become God (or take on the characteristics most people attribute to God) he must file away the last link that holds him to human morality. Since incest is one of the most horrible crimes against humanity, and perhaps the oldest of all tribal taboos, he chooses it for his deliverance from what he considers an outmoded moral enslavement; that is, he commits incest as symbolic gesture of his freedom from good and evil:

> *"I have got outside of good and evil, it needs a symbol, God thinks through action: when I cried on the hill,*
> *Love is more cruel than a wolf, hungrier than flame or the gape of water; your virtues, your nerves, your goodness,*
> *Rags for that fire."*

A moment later he tells his daughter, "I have given my mind to the future / In love, in love." Which is precisely what Nietzsche's Zarathustra did and what all saviors, secular or divine, have done.

Barclay sounds, incidentally, like a modern existentialist when he tells April that "the Stone has its nature, but a man / May become God." With such nonsense Sartre would be in complete agreement. In other words, actions are really symbols of being; one acts in such and such fashion in order to epitomize this or that symbol. To violate April was to remove all barriers separating him from all the people who were now part of his love:

> *The region people*
> *Were present in him, his mind contained them, and the others,*

Innumerable, covering the earth, cities and fields of humanity, the Americas, Asia, the ravenous
Billion of little hungers, the choked obscene desires, the microscopic terrors and pities,
All present in that intolerable symbol his daughter
With the bare bleeding wound in her.

And what message has the new messiah for his people? One that present-day counterculture freaks would approve: final overthrow of discrimination and objectification in the name of license and complete subjectivity. Standing above his tawdry band of freedom-seekers, "his arms extended and fists clenched holding them to stillness," Barclay delivers his sermon on the mountain:

"You here, you chosen,
Are the opening of love, you are the wedge in the block, the blast in the quarry, power and fire have come down to you,
This poor crack of the coast, between the ocean and the earth, on these bare hills. God walking in you
Goes north and gathers multitude and takes the cities to give you. What does he require, there is no commandment?
For love, for the broken order of the universe: nothing but acceptance.
That you be *your desires, break custom, flame, flame,*
Enter freedom."

In my limited examination of *The Women at Point Sur*, I have stressed Barclay's idealism in order to underline a recurring theme in Jeffers's verse: his attack on the anthropocentric view that invariably follows or accompanies any extreme self-consciousness. When Barclay exhorts his followers "to find God in each other," he does what most humanists, of whatever stripe, have been doing since the triumph of civilization in the Western world. Though it would be easy to show that Jeffers was himself an eminently civilized man in many ways, he believed, as did Freud, that the discontents of civilizations were ingrown and self-induced. Without attempting to define civilization—a hopeless task from which even so wise a man as Kenneth Clark has shied—I think we may at least be safe in saying that civilization is unthinkable except in relation to human reason. (I also admit the tautology of the phrase "human reason" since only humans reason.) Rational thought alone enables man to escape (or lose, as some would have it) his animal faith in the now. Civilization connotes a reverence for time past and a cultural or social concern for time future. Indeed, the more civilized the man, the more he will know of the past and the humbling lesson that it teaches about the future, no matter how unknown the future may be. Moreover, civilizations are given life or endurance by the necessary assumption that what one does, or even where one lives, will endure beyond the present. Were it possible to live only in the present—as do the lower animals, who, to use Nietzsche's phrase, live in an eternal present, without memory of the past or foreknowledge of the future—it would then be possible to abolish the *concept* of time (though not, of course, time itself) and thereby be free from man's greatest fear. Religious myths are essentially a device for escaping that fear of extinction. In subverting those myths, reason (or civilization) unhappily leaves man unprotected against the fear. It can be argued of course that the truly rational man will not fear death any more than he will fear life. That may well be, but then I do not say that civilization has made men rational; too obviously it has not. But it has done much to deprive men of those myths which once comforted them and helped allay their irrational fears. Jeffers expresses a thoroughly civilized (that is, rational) view in "Night" when he insists that the loss of belief in immortality has not only enhanced the value of life, made it more dear, but has shown that "death is no evil." To believe in immortality is, ipso facto, to believe that death is evil. Jeffers believed that death was often untimely—either too late or too soon—but to assign it a negative quality would be tantamount to decrying the very nature of things. And when the immortalist commits that folly he makes himself an alien from his only home.

More than any other of his narratives, *The Women at Point Sur* clearly reveals Jeffers's contempt for saviors, who misconstrue their personal sickness for a fault in nature, and who translate their hatred of mortality into an abstract love of humanity. But at the same time the poem illustrates his view that, for many people at any rate, some kind of salvation seems necessary. If in the light of "discovery," the way in which man must henceforth walk, the Christian myth (in this case) appears childish, efforts to replace that myth with an eschatology more congenial with reason have so far proved ineffectual. Though appreciation, or call it worship, of the world's beauty was sufficient for

Jeffers, he agreed with numerous other skeptics since the time of Euripides that "the many" demand shepherds and dogma. Instead of the world, which is too real for most people, they ask for symbols, man-made mirrors that reflect human shapes upon the world's body. Their fear of nothingness induces them to accept on faith—that is, against reason—the most preposterous and inflammatory form that supernaturalism can take: to wit, a belief in the superhuman. Such belief was evidence, Jeffers believed, of man's inherent hatred of the world. The beauty of things means nothing to the person seeking salvation from death; between his fear and trembling and the natural world he must interpose constructs of the mind, beliefs, and symbols, as buffers against the enormous multiplicity of things.

The Women at Point Sur offers no answers, except by indirection perhaps, to the elementary questions which humans have always asked. Its approach to man's inner need for worship is thus negative, unlike "The Inhumanist," which, for all its ridicule of humanity, is finally affirmative. The disgruntled and embittered, but still hopeful, old man of that later poem looked outward and found values—nonhuman values that humans might accept without injury to themselves. In Barclay, Jeffers shows in dramatic form the inception, working out, and final burning away of one rather typical answer: the enclosure of the world into the mind of the beholder. There Jeffers shows the danger of reading the world symbolically, of attempting to substitute the symbol for the thing symbolized. He shows moreover the sickness of those who strive to move beyond good and evil and thus be free from moral responsibility. In particular he reveals the horrific face of the savior who seeks solution for his private anguish through a transvaluation of values. That modern man needs new values is obvious; that those values must be founded on something far more stable and permanent than humanity is no less obvious.

III

In a letter to Arthur Davison Ficke (dated February 1929), Jeffers praised Ficke's poem "The Return of Christ" and then remarked that he (Jeffers) had written "a kind of passion-play" that would be published in the fall. His attitude toward Christ was similar to Ficke's, he added, except for a shift in emphasis: "you have made your Christ a little supernatural, preaching against religion, and I have made mine rather subhuman, at least all-too-human, founding one." The comment, even allowing for its element of jest, is instructive. Jeffers evidently considered the Jesus of the Gospels an extraordinary man, indeed a titanic figure of sorts, but at the same time he considered him less than human in so far as he was infinitely more noxious to mankind than any ordinary member of the species. As the founder of Christianity, Jesus was at once the cause (or at least the source) of more superstition and ignorance than any other human in history. And for Jeffers, unlike many of his contemporaries, ignorance and superstition are the two greatest enemies of man. (It is easy to say of course that it was not Jesus but his followers, particularly Paul, who gave Christianity its theology and no less its ethics. There are numerous such evasions, the final one being the well-known remark that we cannot know whether or not Christianity works since it has never been tried.)

For all their similarity in subject or theme, it would be difficult to imagine two poems more unlike than *The Women at Point Sur* and *Dear Judas*. Where one sprawls and rages, the other is compact, delicately devised, almost serenely resigned in its inevitability. It is no wonder that *Dear Judas* has been applauded far more extensively than the earlier work. Having deliberately chosen "the method of the Japanese Nō plays," as he wrote in a "Preface to 'Judas' " (in the drama section of the *New York Times*, 5 October 1947), Jeffers presents us with a place haunted by the afterglow of passion and inhabited by "two or three ghosts or echoes of life, re-enacting in a dream their ancient deeds and sorrows." The play opens on that note:

> *They have all died and their souls are extinguished; three remnant images of three passions too violent to vanish*
> *Still haunt the garden; they are nearly unfleshed of time: but if they were they would be eternal: they are fading.*

Jesus prompts the reluctant Judas, whose pitying love is necessary foil to the possessive love of his master. Knowing he can only obey, Judas nevertheless tries to break the already established pattern of the tragedy; he begs Jesus: "Let us go back, / To Galilee where the days were all glad." It is Judas, who is willed upon, that we pity. Judas and Mary, not the iron-willed Jesus, are pitiable. Jesus, like the Nietzschean overman, must first kill pity. He chides Judas for being fainthearted and then reminds him that what they are about to do has been predetermined:

I tell you freely that to-day will see done
What was determined before the rock was laid down under the towers of the mountains. This jewel of time
Laid in my hand, rejected once would be lost forever. All greatness is a wrestling with time,
And one who has got the grip of his gaunt opponent, if he lets go will not thrive, not again, but go down
And the dust cover him, sheet over sheet above his forgotten face, century on century. I feel
Signs in my soul and know my occasion. My soul is all towers.

It is noteworthy that Jesus at first believes his dominion over men can be bloodless:

I am making a new thing in the world,
I am making a kingdom not built on blood, I am making a power weaponed with love not violence; a white
Dominion; a smokeless lamp; a pure light.

Jeffers uses several contradictions in the Gospels to reveal the character of Jesus, to show, for example, his changing attitude toward the location of the kingdom he promised his followers. Judas recounts the change that took place in his master when it became clear that the city (the world, in other words) would not worship a mere man. At which point Jesus says, "Perhaps my kingdom is not of this world." And then in a fury he shouts,

This world is nothing. It is dust and spittle. All those that trust me inherit eternal life and eternal
Delight: all those that reject me shall scream
In fires a world with no end.

Not until near the end does he speak of himself as the son of God, and then it is his "private impurity" (see "Theory of Truth") that compels him to make the outlandish claim that he is God. When Mary will not tell him who his father is, he cleanses his blood by making the supernatural claim, which appropriately coincides with his growing desire for power:

JESUS: *I kept it*
Secret until I came to my power; I spoke of myself as the Son of Man, I told no one
Who was my Father, until this time was prepared of triumph.
MARY: *Misery, to see your power and your ruin*
Sprouting from the one root.

A few moments later Jesus admits that he wishes more than just power; he wants to possess the people and thereby gain a form of immortality.

And the means of power,
All clear and formed, like tangible symbols laid in my mind. Two thousand years are laid in my hands
Like grains of corn. Not for the power: Oh, more than power, actual possession. To be with my people,
In their hearts, a part of their being, inseparable from those that love me, more closely touching them
Than the cloth of the inner garment touches the flesh. That this is tyrannous
I know, that it is love run to lust: but I will possess them.

Knowing that the people love terror, if it does not touch them too closely, and that "pain's almost the God / Of doubtful men, who tremble expecting to endure it," Jesus chooses a symbol of suffering that will assure his triumph. Only the symbol can stand outside time and thus live eternally. Therefore the man-god must attach himself to that symbol to remain forever contemporary with the passing generations:

And I think the brute cross itself,
Hewn down to a gibbet now, has been worshiped; it stands yet for an idol of life and power in the dreaming
Soul of the world and the waters under humanity, whence floating again
It will fly up heaven, and heavy with triumphant blood and renewal, the very nails and the beams alive.
I saw my future when I was with God; but now at length in a flashing moment the means: I frightfully
Lifted up drawing all men to my feet: I go a stranger passage to a greater dominion,
More tyrannous, more terrible, more true, than Caesar or any subduer of the earth before him has dared to dream of
In a dream on his bed, over the prostrate city, before the pale weary dawn

Creeps through his palace, through the purple fringes, between the polished agate
pillars, to steal it away.

Judas then poses a question to Jesus that has doubtless been asked untold times since: having taught mercy, why would he not himself be merciful? That is, why insist on rousing the people to destruction when "to let the people alone is the mercy"? The answer of Jesus is that of all saviors everywhere: he serves an end which goes beyond any personal dictate and is beyond good and evil.

I tell you feelingly, it is the honor of all men living to be dupes of God
And serve not their own ends nor understandings but His, and so die. I that am more than a man
Know this and more, and serve and am served.

That Judas must serve him through betrayal is, Jesus avers, a foregone conclusion. He realizes moreover that his submission to the authorities "might appease them and lose me the cross," without which the "future world would never kneel down to slake its lusts at my fountain."

Only a crucified
God can fill the wolf bowels of Rome; only a torture high up in the air, and crossed beams, hang sovereign
When the blond savages exalt their kings; when the north moves, and the hairy-breasted north is unbound,
And Caesar a mouse under the hooves of the horses. . . .

By the time he makes his final decision and implores Judas to act out his part in the martyrdom, he realizes that the love by which he hopes to possess the people must be grained with violence, his dominion over men will be bloody. He foresees the injurious effect that his crucifixion and subsequent exaltation will have upon unnumbered "multitudes of souls from wombs unborn yet." And he foretells the bloody theological disputes of the future:

Oh, my own people
Perhaps will stab each other in a sacred madness, disputing over some chance word that my mouth made
While the mind slept. And men will imagine hells and go mad with terror, for so I have feathered the arrows
Of persuasion with fire, and men will put out the eyes of their minds, lest faith

Become impossible being looked at, and their souls perish.
. . . But what are men now?
Are the bodies free, or the minds full of clear light, or the hearts fearless? I having no foothold but slippery
Broken hearts and despairs, the world is so heaped against me, am yet lifting my peoples nearer
In emotion, and even at length in powers and perception, to the universal God than ever humanity
Has climbed before.

But in his mind there is still the lingering doubt, the nagging peradventure that he too has been gulled by the imagination. The doubt, indeed, saves him from being a fanatic or paranoid:

It is likely that all these futures
Are only the raving mind of one about to be killed, myself and my poor Judas alone
Will bear the brunt; I shall go up and die and be presently forgotten. I have been deluded again,
Imagination my traitor, as often before. I am in the net, and this deliberately sought
Torture on the cross is the only real thing.
Yonder the torches blink and dip among the black trunks.
They have lost the path, now they have found it again, and up the stone steps.
Dear Judas, it is God drives us.
It is not shameful to be duped by God. I have known his glory in my lifetime, I have been *his glory, I know*
Beyond illusion the enormous beauty of the torch in which our agonies and all are particles of fire.

He did, then, know the real God—the inhuman essence, the divine beauty. But he also knew in that clear moment that even though God may be known only through love of the world, most men demand a god that is human, all too human.

After the fashion of all romantics, Jesus sought selfhood in power, in extension of the self beyond the walls of nature. Finding no value in the material world, he sought to move beyond nature and locate himself in the realm of pure idea. He thus employs the Schopenhaueran means of escaping the confines of time and space. Such idealists, Jeffers implies, are the real pessimists, the haters of life, those for whom the life-cage is a prison. Such an idealized hatred of life is obviously an outgrowth of the fear of death. Jesus wishes to escape the matter-of-factness, the physicality of the present, which is of necessity filled with death, and move beyond death into the timelessness of past and future—that is, into abstraction. Jeffers's Tamar sought to purify evil, to remove from it any trace of goodness, and thereby gain a perfect freedom, which is to say, absolute nihilism. His Jesus attempted to gain absolute freedom through a purification of love, by washing away all its physical ingredients, thus making it impervious to time and change. Both Tamar and Jesus sought absolute power in order to possess (and destroy) the present world that both rejected as being inherently inimical to the self, for them the only thing of value. Titanic figures, they are the opposite faces on the coin of absolutism or idealism. In their kindred acts of purification—Tamar through the burning of the house, Jesus through the self-immolation on the cross—they cleanse self of all relations, of all shadings of relative quality. The purity—the fire—into which each leaps has the startling whiteness of nihilism.

A final note on the character of Lazarus, who appears at the poem's end. Having been dead for a few days, he has been released from the time-bound views of men. He is, in effect, out of the net (a word that appears again and again in Jeffers's poetry) that holds most men to their dying hour. The net of desires—for delight, for power, for posthumous glory, for gold, for all that is not life but is made to act as substitute for it. He tells Mary, who insists in the midst of her fear that her son is her joy, that there is "only one pathway to peace for a great passion":

Truth is the way, take the truth
Against your breast and endure its horns. So life will at last be conquered. After some thousands of years
The smoky unserviceable remainders of love and desire will be dissolved and be still. . . . Your son
Has chosen his tools and made his own death; he has chosen a painful death in order to become a God.

A moment later he tells Mary that her son has done what other men have not been able to do: he successfully chose and made his own fate.

The Roman Caesar will call your son his master and his God; the floods
That wash away Caesar and divide the booty, shall worship your son. The unconjectured selvages
And closed orbits of the ocean ends of the earth shall hear of him.

Lazarus "comforts" Judas by reminding him that his name will for many centuries be coupled with that of Jesus:

you enter his kingdom with him, as the hawk's lice with the hawk
Climb the blue towers of the sky under the down of the feathers.

Cold comfort for a man who never desired power or renown of any sort and whose pity for all suffering was a constant torture. The only one to escape the net of desires, Lazarus makes no effort to prevent Judas's suicide, but rather concludes the narrative on a note of resignation, unmarked by either hope or despair:

Let him go. He has done all he was made for; the rest's his own. Let him and the other at the poles of the wood,
Their pain drawn up to burning points and cut off, praise God after the monstrous manner of mankind.
While the white moon glides from this garden; the glory of darkness returns a moment, on the cliffs of dawn.

IV

Though Clare Walker of *The Loving Shepherdess* has none of the titanic fury of Jeffers's saviors, she possesses certain characteristics (that is, shortcomings) of those individuals who love inward or make of love a supernatural deity. Concerning the three faces of love to be found in the two long narrative poems of the *Dear Judas* volume, Jeffers wrote S. S. Alberts: "There is some relationship of thought between the two longer poems of the book; the shepherdess in the one, and Judas and Jesus in the other, each embodying different aspects of love: nearly pure, therefore undefiled but quite inefficient in the first; pitying in the second; possessive in the third."[4] Certainly Clare's love was "undefiled" in that she expected no return for it; her love was never employed as a wedge to separate herself from the nonhuman world or as a catapult to place her in a position of power over others. Her altruism is at the opposite pole from Jesus' possessiveness. But it is so "inefficient" as to make her as vulnerable to pity as was Judas. For all her insistence that she must protect life at all costs, she nonetheless sacrificed herself needlessly. Our attitude toward her must be condescending, as was Jeffers's when he referred to her as "a saint, I suppose, going up to a natural martyrdom." Her journey northward with the flock of sheep has all the pathos and pain of the Wagnerian *Liebestod.* Her love for all things is actually a kind of death wish, as is her fear of and loathing for all the little deaths that occur in nature to maintain balance therein.

Ironically Clare cannot comprehend anyone's committing suicide even though she knows that the fetus she carries will surely kill her. She first tells the young cowboy Will Brighton that she does not believe his story about the people who once lived in the now abandoned house near Point Sur. When Will tells her no one has lived in the house for eight years, she asks if something is wrong with the house. Will answers:

> *"Nothing. Our owner bought the ranch, and the house*
> *Stands empty, he didn't want it. They tell me an old man*
> *Claiming to be God . . . a kind of a preacher boarded there,*
> *And the family busted up." She said "I don't believe*
> *Any such story." "Well, he was kind of a preacher.*
> *They say his girl killed herself; he washed his hands*
> *With fire and vanished." "Then she was crazy. What, spill*
> *Her own one precious life," she said trembling,*
> *"She'd nothing but that? Ah! no!*
> *No matter how miserable, what goes in a moment,*
> *You know . . . out. . . ."*

Later when she meets Onorio Vasquez, who accompanies her to the end of her journey, she mentions the house at Point Sur. He tells her that "God lived there once and tried to make peace with the people," and that when no peace was made he (Onorio) had "bawled for death, like a calf for the cow. There were no visions. My brothers watched me, / And held me under the hammers of food and sleep." He adds that he wants "to hear nothing / Of what there was at Point Sur." Again Clare "thought certainly that no one / Ever had desired death."

A totally gentle man, Onorio is one of Jeffers's most vivid and appealing creations. Forced to live with his visions, which are "never to any point," he cherishes those moments of insight though he knows, now that his period of belief in Barclay is past, that they are without meaning or, in any case, beyond interpretation. In a brief history of Onorio's life, Jeffers remarks his peculiar personality:

A power in his mind
Was more than equal to the life he was born to,
But fear, or narrowing fortune, had kept it shut
From a larger life; the power wasted itself
In making purposeless visions, himself perceived them
To have no meaning relative to any known thing: but always
They made him different from his brothers; they gave him
A kind of freedom; they were the jewels and value of his life.
So that when once, at a critical time, they failed
And were not seen for a year, he'd hungered to die.
That was nine years ago; his mind was now quieter,
But still it found all its value in visions.
Between them, he hired out his hands to the coast farms,
Or delved the garden at home.

Onorio resembles Jeffers's Lazarus to some extent in that he is both in and out of the game, so to speak. He comforts and protects Clare in her journey; he makes practical decisions concerning lodging and the care of the sheep. His observations on various people they meet along the way are always perceptive. For example, when the old nihilist from one of the farms they pass comes to them with his madness, preaching annihilation for all those who have passed thirty, Onorio dismisses him as one of those "nothing-wishers of life [who] are never in earnest; / Make mouths to scare you: if they meant it they'd do it / And not be alive to make mouths." But at the same time his acquaintance (through his visions) with the temporal and spatial infinitude surrounding his finite being—his sense of vastation—prevents him from giving much importance to merely human affairs. It is almost as if his goodness grew from that coldness at the core of his being. Since he asks so little from life he can afford to be a virtuous man. Onorio loves life without demanding that it love him, an act that Jeffers considered the hallmark of goodness.

Near the end of the poem (in part 11), Onorio feels one of his visions growing or approaching. It is important to note that his vision, before it takes form, must first move through human shapes and history. And along the way he recalls a story told to him as a child, a story that relates to a practical problem of the present:

A part of his mind
Wished to remember what the rest had forgotten,

And groping for it in the dark withstood the prepared
Pageant of dreams. He'd read in his curious boyhood
Of the child the mother is found incapable of bearing
Cut from the mother's belly. Both live: the wound
Heals: it was called the Caesarean section. But he, fearing
Whatever thought might threaten to infringe his careful
Chastity of mind, had quickly canceled the memory;
That now sought a new birth; it might save Clare
If he could think of it.

A few lines later the "aquiline-headed Roman, who summed in his one person the powers and ordered science of humanity," becomes in the vision a symbol of human triumph, of man as measure. In Caesar, then, lay salvation? Not at all. No longer can man think of the earth as a separate unit, independent of the order and consistency that form the vision. Now there is simply eternal recurrence, no end of things, in fact, no real death from which new beginnings might be made. No salvation in a world that can only endure, that can never cease from change. Salvation means escape from change, removal from time, and violation of the consistency that appears in his vision. Vasquez sees what Jeffers saw, and Caesar loses in this new relativity even his symbolic status.

Jeffers seems to have had a curiously mixed feeling toward Onorio. While the vaquero's visions provide him with an escape from human anthropocentricism, they at the same time make him unfit for any true appreciation of the real world through which he must daily walk. Is there any meaning, for example, in the vision he has of the unity of things, of the spiral timelessness of all moving matter? None that Vasquez can comprehend. And nothing could be more vacuous than to keep returning to the *fact* of eternal recurrence, which can only reveal cosmic meaninglessness. Moreover Vasquez seems almost to be one of those "wild criers" of the poem "Fog" who are "slaves of the last peace, / Worshippers of oneness." Like all of Jeffers's visionaries (other good examples are Stella Moreland in *Tamar* and Mark Thurso in *Thurso's Landing*), Onorio pays dearly for his unearthly gift; the loss of normal joys of an earthly existence at least equals the gain derived from seeing beyond that existence. All such extrasensory knowledge, Jeffers implies, is finally short-circuited by the vision-seer's extraordinary subjectivity that fathered the visions in the first place. Which is to say, visions are always human in origin, and thus return upon the human eye. Jeffers was too much the naturalist ever to give any credence to a supernatural insight into the nature of things. Only through empirical evidence can we obtain knowledge of the natural world. Always an ardent student of astronomy, he nonetheless spoke of our "useless" knowledge of the stars. The adjective hardly fits, however, since he believed that astronomy was useful in deflating the human ego and in showing us how ridiculous, in the long run, are our dreams and aspirations.

Onorio's vision, which had to move through humanity before it could fully form and blossom, in the end moves back again to its human source:

The speckled tissue of universes
Drew into one formed and rounded light, and Vasquez
Worshipped the one light. One eye . . . what, an eye?
A dark mountain with an eye in its cliff? A coal-black stallion
Eyed with one burning eye in the mid brow?
Night has an eye. The poor little vision-seer
Groaned, that he never had wit to understand visions.
See all and know nothing. The eye that makes its own light
And sees nothing but itself. "I am seeing Barclay again,"
He marveled, as one should say "I am seeing God:
But what is God?" He continued gazing,
And beads of sweat spilled from his forehead into the fire-edge
Ashes. He saw at last, neither the eyed mountain
Nor the stallion, nor Barclay, but his own eye
In the darkness of his own face.

He knows that he must remain forever divided from himself, " 'gazing beyond the flaming walls, / Not fortunate enough, and too faint-hearted.' "

When Clare wakes she discovers that two of her sheep have strayed. After Onorio helps her find them (one has been killed and partially devoured by a mountain lion), she gathers about her those remaining to continue the journey. Vasquez begs her to go with him to his father's place in the canyon until she is well again. The picture he paints of his home would seem irresistible:

"When I have to go about and work on men's farms for wages I long for that place
Like some one thinking of water in deserts. Sometimes we hear the sea's thunder, far
down the deep gorge.
The darkness under the trees in spring is starry with flowers, with redwood sorrel,
colt's foot, wakerobin,
The slender-stemmed pale yellow violets,
And Solomon's seal that makes intense islands of fragrance in April."

But she insists on following the martyr's path to *her* "April," when parturition will end her life and the prenatal life she has jealously guarded. Realizing that nothing would change her mind, Vasquez, "still drunken with the dregs of his vision / To fatalist indifference," went for his horse, which had broken tether the night before in the hail storm. When he returned, Clare had already left.

He followed Clare the next morning,
But met another vision on the road, that waved
Impatient white hands against his passage, saying
"If I go up to Calvary ten million times: what is that to you?
Let me go up." Vasquez drew rein and sat staring.
He saw beyond the vision in the yellow mud
Prints of bare feet, dibbled about with many
Little crowding hoof-marks; he marveled, feeling no sadness
But lonely thoughts.

In the following final section of the poem, Clare makes her passion-journey to road's end. That journey, Jeffers implies, is as natural to her, and to others like her, as the upstream passage is to the salmon going to spawn. As Clare watches a salmon "row its worn body up-stream over the stones" in order "to find the appointed high-place and perish," she sees, "in a bright moment's passage of anxious feeling," her own fate reflected. In the stark conclusion pity and disdain are, for many readers, equally balanced. Onorio's response seems most appropriate: "he marveled, feeling no sadness / But lonely thoughts."

In *The Loving Shepherdess* Jeffers had gone as far as it was possible to go in depicting love. As he remarked, he had shown it in an "almost pure" form. In personifying love in extremis, Clare is as romantic as Tamar or Barclay or Jesus or, as we shall see, Hitler—and finally just as egotistic, though sympathically so. Though love, as an expression of the ego, is a necessary and positive quality of the human animal, it can, when carried too far, sever man from the very thing he wishes to possess or protect. Up to a point, the love of power or of self or of mankind or of life is salubrious. But beyond that point, a nebulous one to be sure, love can only be destructive. It is a matter of degree and balance.

V

In "Meditation on Saviors" Jeffers clearly denies that such a thing as free will exists. He then adds that our moral systems have their origin in magic:

How should one caught in the stone of his own person dare tell the people anything but relative to that?
But if a man could hold in his mind all the conditions at once, of man and woman, of civilized
And barbarous, of sick and well, of happy and under torture, of living and dead, of human and not
Human, and dimly all the human future:—what should persuade him to speak? And what could his words change?
The mountain ahead of the world is not forming but fixed. But the man's words would be fixed also,
Part of that mountain, under equal compulsion; under the same present compulsion in the iron consistency.
And nobody sees good or evil but out of a brain a hundred centuries quieted, some desert
Prophet's, a man humped like a camel, gone mad between the mud-walled village and the mountain sepulchres.

Still it is obvious that the protagonists of *Tamar*, *The Women at Point Sur*, *Dear Judas*, and *The Loving Shepherdess* chose the roles they played; they consciously "turned inward," as Jeffers would have it, rather than outward as Orestes did (consciously) in *Tower Beyond Tragedy*. And their choosing had definite consequences, which is to say that nothing occurs in vacuo, that all is process, everything following from antecedent forces and in turn being followed by resultant acts.

Still if our choosing a particular course of action is in no sense free—if, in other words, we must "choose" to do or believe only that which we are most strongly motivated to do or believe—there is an apparent (if not quite real) freedom in human affairs: simply by changing the weights and stresses that bear upon a decision, it is possible to influence that decision. No matter how "determined" the determinist, he will invariably make such allowances. Jeffers, for example, could express a deterministic theory of history in "Shine, Perishing Republic" and still conclude with advice to his children; he could even insist that "corruption / Never has been compulsory" without being in the least contradictory. Of course corruption in individual cases is quite often compulsory, but the cases vary according to circumstances. I think it evident that the Greek tragedians expressed such a view when they placed their protagonists in situations from which escape was impossible, and at the same time wrote their plays as warnings to the audience that all of us are susceptible to being caught up in similar chains of circumstance. Jeffers expressed a view not unlike that of the author of the Oedipus trilogy, and very much like the central view of Euripides, whose rationalism is most apparent in the insistent message (almost a sermon) that man is a good deal less the mover of things than he is moved by them. Like Euripides, Jeffers believed that reason was the only reliable guide of man, but at the same time wrote (in "Meditation on Saviors") that "reason is never a root, neither of act nor desire." Of course it isn't. Taken out of context the statement sounds like a truism; it is simply a rejoinder to a previous statement that the poet was contemplating doing something "that stands against reason." Such statements have caused some to assume that Jeffers was antirational after the fashion of D. H. Lawrence, or, in any case, that he was convinced that reason was qualitatively subordinate to feeling, after the fashion of Emerson, who always placed reason (which he called the "understanding") beneath intuition (which he called "Reason" with a capital letter). In fact he was not attacking reason or bidding us follow our irrational desires, but only avowing what the rational mind has been able to discover about the nature of human volition. Again and again he insists that in discovery lies our only strength, and then adds that our knowledge is still too little, that we are sadly still too unintelligent to realize that our desires lead us where no truly rational man would consider going.

All that by way of preface to a few remarks about "The Bowl of

Blood," included in *Be Angry at the Sun* (1941). For those who are so blinded by moral indignation that they can see Hitler and Nazism as nothing more than monstrous aberrations or mutations, the little mask (or masque) will be incomprehensible. It is, first of all, a splendid work of art, and hence neither more nor less moral than a violent storm (or picture of that storm) or a sunset (or a picture of that sunset). And it attempts to place Hitler, who is called The Leader, in a historical—that is to say, causal—context that will enable the reader to understand him both as an object shaped by various factors and then as a subject, shaping, or more precisely destroying, the nation he leads. As might be expected, a few critics believed they detected fascist sympathies in Jeffers—for example, Babette Deutsch in her reviews in the *Virginia Quarterly Review* (Winter 1942) and *New Republic* (23 March 1942), and Stanley J. Kunitz in *Poetry* (December 1941). Both those critics nonetheless praised *Be Angry at the Sun*, which was generally well received. Kunitz considered "The Bowl of Blood" a "magnificent accomplishment," calling it "the greatest masque since *Comus*." Still, the charge of fascism, idiotic as it certainly is, has lingered to the present. Writing in *Saturday Review* (22 May 1971) a journalist named John Hughes called Jeffers a "proto-fascist" who described Hitler as a "genius," implying that any such description could only redound to his discredit. As a matter of fact, Jeffers called Hitler a "genius" in "The Day Is a Poem (September 19, 1939)." The opening lines reveal quite clearly his attitude:

This morning Hitler spoke in Danzig, we heard his voice.
A man of genius: that is, of amazing
Ability, courage, devotion, cored on a sick child's soul,
Heard clearly through the dog wrath, a sick child
Wailing in Danzig; invoking destruction and wailing at it.

But I forget "The Bowl of Blood." The opening speeches by First Masker and Second Masker reveal the author's intentions and the response those intentions will probably evoke:

FIRST MASKER: *I do not know whether it is possible to present contemporary things in the shape of eternity.*

SECOND: *If it were, it would please no one. The present is always a crisis; people want a partisan cry, not judgment. No long views, for God's sake.*

Jeffers at once rejects the romantic theory that great men make history for the deterministic theory that forces make men. A Masker states the view (which was Tolstoy's in *War and Peace*) when he personifies power as the fathering force:

It [power] chooses one man almost at random
And clouds him and clots around him and it possesses him.
Listen: the man does not have power,
Power has the man.

The old woman, who gives counsel to those who ask it, is obviously the voice of history. As Colonel Weiss tells The Leader: "We know now that the dead live; we know they can help us with their counsel and their knowledge." For all his efforts to the contrary, Hitler can no more really believe in the soothsayer—that is, in history—than can any other such leader, but he is now desperate and hence willing to listen to "a solitude-crazed / Fishwife for prophecies." When the woman bends over a basinful of some dark liquid, Hitler demands to know what it is:

STEINFURTH: *Only blood, sir. It is not aesthetic but it is necessary. It is her method.*
THE LEADER: *That I don't like. I won't have it.*
STEINFURTH: *No show without it, sir: she inhales the vapor and drifts into her trance. It is only swine's blood. . . .*

We learn that The Leader has put on a mask himself, one formerly worn by others. Indeed all living things wear masks that can be put on or taken off. And when one dies, as the Second Masker remarks, "it is only someone dropping a mask. / A little personality lost, and the wild / Beauty of the world resumed." At which point the First Masker throws off his cloak and hood and appears in an old blue and red uniform: "I am Frederick the Great, who laid in sweat and blood the foundation stones of the German Reich." After disdainfully introducing himself—"Je suis le roi de Prusse. Et vous qui m'appelez en aide: qu'est-ce que vous êtes?"—Frederick reminds The Leader that *he* had always been a friend to England and then demands, "What have you done to England . . . Austrian?" Hitler can only answer that England hates his nation, but insists that he is not the cause of that hatred:

Ha? Not I but your own blood and successor,
The old outcast at Doorn burnt the roast.

> He *bungled them into hating us: mend it could no man.*
> *Where am I leading the Germans, King? From ruin to dominion.*
> *From degradation and poverty to honor, wealth, power,*
> *Vengeance and victory.*

Frederick contemptuously dismisses such nonsensical ideals: "Hm. Vengeance. Rache. . . . revanche. . . . This damned human race." Jeffers obviously sympathizes with, and probably admired, the great German, who was Hitler's opposite in most ways. While calling mankind (half in humor) "diese verdammte Rasse," Frederick laughed at utopias of benevolence and peace, just as Jeffers did. Indeed, in a letter to Voltaire he expressed a thoroughly Jeffersian view:

> Superstition, self-interest, vengeance, treason, ingratitude, will produce bloody and tragic scenes until the end of time, because we are governed by passions and very rarely by reason. There will always be wars, lawsuits, devastations, plagues, earthquakes, bankruptcies. . . . Since this is so, I presume it must be necessary. . . . The human mind is weak; more than three fourths of mankind are made for subjection to the most absurd fanaticism. Fear of the Devil and of hell fascinates their eyes, and they detest the wise man who tries to enlighten them. . . . In vain do I seek in them that image of God which the theologians assert they bear upon them. Every man has a wild beast in him; few can restrain it; most men let loose the bridle when not restrained by terror of the law.[5]

The Second Masker removes his cloak and hood, which the First puts on, and enters wearing the mask and attitude of Napoleon. He tells The Leader that he "would have unified all Europe"—the recurring dream of all leaders, as the idealist invariably dreams of unity. And even as he insists *he* will not commit the madness of Napoleon, "who embroiled himself in Russia before he had settled with the English," The Leader is disturbed by the worm of doubt that he, too, will fail in his noble mission, fail even "after all that hope and faith, the labor, the long preparation, the . . . crimes . . . / Blood, terror, treacheries in a just cause. . . ."

Though depicted as less a savior of men than as a pawn of forces, Hitler obviously has succumbed to the romantic, idealistic, incestuous crime of all those who presume to encompass the hopes and aspirations of humanity in their single separate being. In his moment of doubt he compares himself to the greatest of Western saviors: "This is my Gethsemane night, Christ's agony in the garden: only to great artists / Come these dark hours." The Maskers, who stand outside such folly, partaking in it only to illustrate its nature, comment bitterly on the self-deceit of the tragic actors:

FIRST MASKER: *It is necessary from time to time*
To turn the eyes away from mankind,
Frederick the Great's "verdammte Rasse,"
Or be choked with pity and laughter.
SECOND: *The posturings, not the wickedness;*
The poverty, not the excess.
Whoever thinks this man is more wicked
Than other men knows not himself.
THIRD: *If man must always have man in his eyes and nostrils*
Mass-suicide perhaps might be best.

In other words, as the Second Masker remarked, the inordinate egotism of the savior makes him less than human rather than more. His concentration on humanity reveals a poverty of imagination and wisdom. Or perhaps I should say that The Leader's inversion (according to the Maskers) makes him simply all too human. Most of us, I strongly suspect, would insist that Hitler was more wicked than we are; but that would be to say, according to the premises of the Maskers, that he was more patriotic, more determined to raise up his people, more convinced that ends justify means, and, above all, more gifted in the art of manipulating people than we are.

No matter where one places Hitler in comparison with humanity at large, it is important to realize that his shibboleths possess a power not to be found in the abstractions of prose. In their discussion of the sources of power, the Maskers remark that Hitler and those with him did "have a sense of the other world, the inhuman one." Unfortunately Hitler's sense of that world—the North Sea sunset, the Berchtesgaden landscape, the nature-dreams of Wagner and so forth—was too romantic to make it effective, that is, to make him abjure power over the lives of men. Still, the Germans employed the concrete language of poetry, while the West used the abstractions of prose. As one Masker put it: "They say 'blood and soil,' while the West says 'democracy.' Did you ever hear a prosier word? Democracy: the clay life-belt that sank Athens, and is sinking France. Blood and soil are poetry, you can fight for them; democracy is pure prose, abstract, indefinite, and, as they use it, dishonest."

After the meetings with Frederick and Napoleon, Hitler is more doubtful than ever that he will succeed in his plan for European unification (his euphemism for conquest). Only after conversing with the "mask" of a former friend named Friedenau, with whom he had served in the First World War, is he able to believe in final victory, and even then he must will the belief. In the meantime, the Maskers, wearing skull masks and black tights with white bones painted on them, begin a dance of death, chanting names of the cities that will be destroyed throughout Europe and Russia. Though Friedenau tells Hitler to pay no attention to the "spirits," he cannot shake the doubts that cling to his rational self. Which is to say, he knows enough history to realize that he can only lose. He also knows that there is now no turning back; once the Rubicon has been crossed there is no room for the play of free choice in the tightly woven web of events. He can, however, allow those events to run their full course, and thereby bring down his nation's roof as a memorial to his name.

THE LEADER: *Win or lose, I shall lose.*
I'll pull some down with me. I would have been Europe's saviour: now come destruction. The beautiful cities
That watch themselves in their waters will be burnt rubble
And homeless mounds.

Which is, as a matter of fact, precisely what he did—a romantic conclusion to his romantic dreams. In *The Rise and Fall of the Third Reich* William L. Shirer remarked the extreme romanticism of the Germans who liked to identify themselves with Siegfried and Kriemhild, Brunhild and Hagen: "an irrational, heroic, mystic world, beset by treachery, overwhelmed by violence, drowned in blood, and culminating in the *Goetterdaemmerung*, the twilight of the gods, as Valhalla, set on fire by Wotan after all his vicissitudes, goes up in flames in an orgy of self-willed annihilation which has always fascinated the German mind and answered some terrible longing in the German soul.

. . . It is not at all surprising that Hitler tried to emulate Wotan when in 1945 he willed the destruction of Germany so that it might go down in flames with him."[6] All that may, or may not, be true about the German mind and soul (I for one suspect that Shirer generalized from too short-term a view of German history), but it now seems evident that Germany never could have forced her will upon the whole of Europe, to say nothing of the Western hemisphere. The German military commanders knew as much early in the War, as numerous documents have since shown. Moreover, three weeks before Pearl Harbor, on 19 November 1941, Hitler admitted to a group of generals in his headquarters that he could no longer win the war. The most Germany could hope for was a negotiated peace, which Churchill refused to give him. After America's entry into the European conflict that thin hope was blown out the window.[7]

More important to the discussion of Jeffers's still controversial views about the war and our part in it is the question of whether Hitler posed a threat to civilization—of whether a German victory in Europe would have meant the death of all those qualities we attribute to civilization. To begin with, those who expressed such a view had somehow convinced themselves that civilization and democracy were the same thing, or were, in any case, complementary, even necessary one to the other. I know of no historical evidence that supports such a belief; on the other hand, a great deal of evidence flatly contradicts it. Although he praised our democracy for the freedom it allowed individual citizens and insisted he would fight fascism in this country, as well as Nazism or Communism, Jeffers always believed that the only excuse for going to war was self-defense. He clearly enunciated such a view in the address he gave at the Library of Congress and elsewhere in February and March of 1941. I consider it important that he did not use the word *civilization* in the following passage, but rather the word *culture*:

> Europe will be physically and morally exhausted after this second world war; and perhaps it will be our destiny to carry the heritage of European culture, and what we have added to it, across a time of twilight to a new age; as Byzantium carried the culture of Greece and Rome across the dark centuries, from that age to this one. Therefore we must guard what we

> have, for it is precious; and if we feel ourselves forced to intervene in foreign conflicts, we must consult the interests of our people first; and our generosity second,—we have always been generous; and ideology last. But sentimentality, never. We can still afford the material risks of sentimentality, but not the disillusion that follows it.[8]

It is not so much democracy, and it is never civilization, that Jeffers defended, but rather culture and its necessary ingredient, freedom. To him (and he resembles Eliot and Pound in this) civilization denotes decay; it is a hardening of the arteries of culture. That view is to be found everywhere in his poetry, and most explicitly in such poems as "Still the Mind Smiles," "New Mexican Mountain," "Hellenistics," and "Prescription of Painful Ends." In *The Decline of the West* Spengler described that process in great detail, stating his conclusion most succinctly in the following sentence: "Culture and Civilization—the living body of a soul and the mummy of it."[9]

Jeffers depicted Hitler as being less the enemy of civilization than a product of its discontents. In his person were embodied, symbolically as well as in fact, those frustrations, fears and hatreds natural to a proud people who have been defeated. He was to embittered Germans what Huey Long was to impoverished Louisianans, and, in many ways to be sure, what Roosevelt was to economically depressed Americans. Which is to say, he was a rallying point, a quieter of fears and dispenser of hope—in brief, a savior. To mirror the hopes of his people successfully it was necessary that he possess a touch of genius and at the same time be insufficiently wise. He perfectly illustrated the Caesar that Jeffers described in "Meditation on Saviors" in 1928:

> *Who is born when the world wanes, when the brave soul of the world falls on decay in the flesh increasing*
> *Comes one with a great level mind, sufficient vision, sufficient blindness, and clemency for love.*
>
> *This is the breath of rottenness I smelt; from the world waiting, stalled between storms, decaying a little,*
> *Bitterly afraid to be hurt, but knowing it cannot draw the savior Caesar but out of the blood-bath.*

The primary casualty of a German victory, Jeffers believed, would be man's dearest possession, freedom. I say *would be*: Jeffers never for a moment considered it possible for one nation to subdue all of Europe. Where, one must ask, would Germany find policemen enough to keep that continent in subjection to her wishes? Not even ancient Rome, a greater world power than Germany, could keep her possessions in thrall. Clearly, all those who believe in the right of humans to be free from civil oppression will oppose both Rome and Germany; that is, will try to prevent either Romans or Germans from overrunning *their* native soil.

But it is much too simpleminded to see their conquests as a triumph of barbarism over civilization, or, as Jeffers would say, a triumph of the greater evil over the lesser evil. After all, he associated civilization with imperialism, as did Spengler, who wrote, "Imperialism is Civilization unadulterated. In this phenomenal form the destiny of the West is now irrevocably set. . . . The expansive tendency is doom, something daemonic and immense, which grips, forces into service, and uses up the late mankind of the world-city stage, willy-nilly, aware or unaware."[10]

In contrast to the journalists and politicians, Jeffers believed (if we may assume the Maskers express his views) that civilization's "ripening / Is freedom's crisis." Accent the word *ripening*. There is greatness during the growth of a culture, but once the summit has been reached—that is, when a civilization has been formed—more and more restrictions of individual freedom become necessary to maintain an appearance of vigor and health. Ironically, the growth of imperialistic powers has been attended by a sharp increase in the power of the masses, which has led to a new kind of tyranny. In *The Sun Never Sets* (1940), Malcolm Muggeridge commented on the tyranny of the majority in a passage that reinforces (or at least repeats) the view of Jeffers: "The Sovereign People owe allegiance only to themselves; their enthronement must, therefore, result in their utter subjection to an abstraction—their own corporate existence, as embodied in the State, and, finally, in a demagogue who identifies his and the State's will. Becoming Sovereign, the People had to become slaves; and the Totalitarian State, whether in its classless, socialist society or Third Reich version, is the full realization of their slavery."[11]

In "Shine, Perishing Republic," written in the middle 1920s, Jeffers had described the movement from ripeness to decay in terms of natural process:

> *I sadly smiling remember that the flower fades to make fruit, the fruit rots to make earth.*
> *Out of the mother; and through the spring exultances, ripeness and decadence; and home to the mother.*

Though he believed that our decay was inevitable, that we had to become an empire, he still maintained that the individual could avoid the mass corruption. In "The Bowl of Blood," written fifteen years later, when everyone in the West was intimately concerned with the approaching war, he considered ways of delaying the inevitable. And then right after the war he attempted to expose what he considered the fraudulent reasons for our having taken part in the European conflict. If his historical sense formed a framework for both "The Bowl of Blood" and *The Double Axe*, the immediate concerns of our society were foremost in his mind.

If asked why civilizations cause such mischief and grief in the world before they begin their inevitable decline, Jeffers probably would answer that, for one thing, the restraints imposed by civilization must finally find release; and, for another, the civilized state, in order to prolong its life span, will always place a high premium on such abstractions as are necessary to give the social body an appearance (and it can only be an appearance) of both permanence and rectitude. Patriotism ranks highest on that list of abstractions, of course; and in patriotism, which is clearly a virtue up to a point, lie seeds enough for any nation to become imperialistic. No one would deny that the man who defends his land from foreign invaders is worthy of praise, but the man who invades another's land for patriotic reasons deserves our censure. The patriotic American who invaded Mexico in the 1840s is one thing; the patriotic Confederate who defended his soil against invading Union troops is something quite different. And yet the invading Union troops were sent to put down an uprising in *their* nation; and the Confederate, who must be praised for defending his plot of earth, was, by implication anyhow, defending slavery at the same time. This is to say that patriotism is good or evil depending upon circumstance. In its abstract form, it is irrational. When it blurs the vision of the patriot and causes him to defend an idea of something rather than the thing itself, it actually does more harm to his nation than it does good. When one of the Maskers remarked that the "costly luxury" of freedom could be maintained only by staying "at home" and protecting what is real—that is, what we then possessed—he was stating the limits of patriotism:

Men must keep in their minds
The one way to be free: that's to be better armed
And stronger than others, and not covet their goods,
And stay frugally at home, death to invaders: the Greek states flowered
While this was theirs.

In "The Love and the Hate" (the first part of *The Double Axe*) Jeffers attempted to refute the arguments of those who bear responsibility for our entering the war. In that bitterest of all his poems he cuts through all the sophistic reasons given for our second intervention in a European conflict. We had not, of course, remained at home; rather we sent millions of men overseas to help level European cities and thus, so illogic would have us believe, set them free from tyranny. Or as Jeffers might mockingly put it: we contributed our bit to the preservation of civilization by destroying as much of it as was possible in the four years we were given.

Near the end of the war Hoult Gore (in "The Love and the Hate"), an eighteen-year-old boy who was killed in the Pacific, returns home to speak for all those who had been sentenced to death by their governments.

"There are millions and millions, but as far as I know I am the only one
That has come back. It's unbelievable: how can they lie so still
After being gypped and killed? Gypped by their governments
And their fathers and their women: gypped out of life, fooled and despised and lied to, and stuck
Under the mangrove roots and the black mud, under the coral sand and the Russian snow,
And the cabbages in Europe. They're too submissive, they ought to damn patience and rise."

His adulterous mother, Reine, and his American Legionnaire father, Bull Gore, are symptomatic of the corruption and shallowness of American society. After listening to his father insist that we must have no mercy on the Germans once they have been pushed to their borders and must then "bomb hell out of Tokyo," Hoult erupts:

"Have you ever seen a flame-thrower? No, I suppose,
Not in your time. We roast them, you know, screaming, in their little nests. That was my occupation
For a time. But now I'm thinking of being a preacher, I got religion.
Under fire, you know." Reine came in and he glanced at her,
And said, "I'll go around and preach to the people: For Christ's sake amen. We must build gibbets
On every mountain-peak and every high hill,
All along the sky-line conspicuous gibbets, and if any person
Begins to say we have to save England or rescue France or avenge the Jews—take him up and hang him,
He is pimping for war. If he says democracy,
Remember they pimped for war and they will again—take him up and hang him. Or if he says we must save
Civilization: they said it: take them up and hang them. If they say, My country,
Right or wrong—they are pimping for war, take them up and hang them.
Higher than Haman. Hell, we'll have a fine orchard
When the sun ripes the plums."

Though admitting that "it is horrible / To hate, and hate, and hate, and go over their reasons again," Hoult damned those who condemned him to death:

"Because a German dog hoped to steal something
From a Russian dog. I know: I read his book: while we rotted
In Scofield barracks: and we were sold to death
By liars and fools. Now there is nothing left
But to envy and degrade life with our stinking bodies
And betrayed minds. I might have had joy and freedom, and someone
As beautiful as you, Mother, and loved her, even
If she were false as you. If she were still kind,
Who cares, who cares? But they pushed me down
Out of the sunlight, out of the decent air into dirt and darkness: and I fought back,
I am only a bitter will holding up a corpse
That walks and hates."

If in "The Bowl of Blood" Jeffers expressed a deterministic view of the causes of the war, here, just after the war had ended and the survivors (at least in those nations which were on the winning side) were celebrating their victory and, as is natural, forgetting the dead, he insists that we should never have become involved. Given the perspective from which his argument is sounded, it is difficult to refute Jeffers; it is nigh unimaginable that the dead would disagree with his censures of the living. Hoult mockingly tells his father that he will give him twenty-four hours to find just one reason for our going to war. Then, before his father can answer, he rejects those reasons that are invariably given:

> *"Don't say Pearl Harbor though.*
> *That was a trick, a dirty one. They had duped us*
> *Deep into war, they'd fooled us into doing everything*
> *Except declare it and send armies abroad: but if we were blooded,*
> *We'd be mad enough. Germany wouldn't attack*
> *Although we sank her boats and supplied her enemies:*
> *They needled the touchy Japs and they did it for them. And don't, for God's sake,*
> *Pretend that we had to fight while we still had friends*
> *In Europe: what do we want of Europe? We're stronger than the whole rats' nest*
> *This side of Russia, those that fight and those that lie down, and you knew it,*
> *And it's now proved. Oh, Oh," he moaned, "God damn you, haven't you*
> *One single reason? And I died for that? Nor don't say freedom:*
> *War's freedom's killer. Don't say freedom for foreigners,*
> *Unless you intend to kill Russia on top of Germany and Britain on Japan, and burn the whole world*
> *Into one bloody bubble-bath; don't say democracy;*
> *Don't talk that mush. And don't pretend that the world*
> *Will be improved, or good will earned, or peace*
> *Made perfect by blasting cities and nations into bloody choppets: if you believe* that
> *You'll believe anything."*

Jeffers would not deny that the war was inevitable; a year before our entry into it he had written that we would have to blindly follow our leaders who were intent on making war. All he says here (and I have chosen the most didactic passages in the poem) is that the reasons given were bad ones—no better than those that duped us into World War One. Needless to say, we have seen the same reasons touted in support of the ten-year conflict in Asia. That, too, was a *moral* war. All that is needed to justify the most heinous of war crimes is a few abstractions. Jeffers wrote "The Love and the Hate" out of pity for the dead and utter disgust and contempt for warmongers the world over. The poem suffers, as you might expect, from that intensity of hatred and pity, but it is an unforgettable narrative that only a great poet could have written. Not since Swift has anyone of the English-speaking world more effectively shown the horror of human folly.

But he does not stop there. What he takes apart in "The Love and the Hate," he puts back together in "The Inhumanist"; and human folly is but one of the parts. If individual parts are ugly, the whole remains beautiful. That is true of the world certainly. It is also true, I think, of the poetry of Jeffers.

SIX Coda

In his best poetry Jeffers provides us with a world that is beautifully and sometimes terrifyingly real—or real in the sense that any artistic creation is real; the world of every artist is, of course, visionary; the degree of his success is in proportion to the reader's or viewer's or listener's being convinced that the "world" is real and, in addition, has meaning for the auditor. In his tribute in *Ave, Vale, Robinson Jeffers*, Lawrence Clark Powell wrote, "This was his genius. To summon the spirit of place. To people the countryside with personages more real than its living inhabitants. To forge poetry on the anvil of thoughtful feeling with passion and certitude, the result and reward of which is quite simply literary immortality." Certainly no other American poet has approached him in the ability to endow character with life; his people, tormented and tormenting creatures, haunt the memory like grisly phantoms or spectral shapes rising from some atavistic depth of which we were unaware. Passing before the mind's eye, they reveal those gulfs over which we daily pass. In their strengths and weaknesses we see ourselves; they reveal to us, above all else, how slippery is our hold on reason and how tempting are the lures of irrationality in all its forms. Which is to say, Jeffers did what all great writers have done: he provided insight into the human condition.

Insight, above all else. And that insight does not stop with the human condition, but extends outward into the larger and, for Jeffers, more important natural world. No other poet of this century strove more successfully to "catch the inhuman God" in his lens. In this area, indeed, Jeffers had few peers in all of literature. The violence and extreme passion of the natural world color his lines in an unforgettable fashion. Though he protested in "Love the Wild Swan" that "this wild swan of a world is no hunter's game" and despaired of ever catching in his mirror "one color, one glinting flash, of the splendor of things," he knew that all such efforts by any poet were doomed to (relative) failure.

His failure to reproduce that beauty is attributable to the nature of things—to the primary fact that art can never be truly representative, that no attempt to reproduce or imitate can ever be totally objective. But that is a truism that, once admitted, need never stay us (it certainly never stayed Jeffers) from partaking in the sensual dance of life. Jeffers knew this, as he also knew that only death can perform the miracle of making us one with the divine substance—only at the dance's end do we become a part of what our senses imperfectly perceived and our artistry failed to reproduce. Man may and should worship the God, or divine substance, but only in a mineral sense can he become part of what he worshipped, and then he is without senses and mind to know and admire. He notes this truth again in "The Shears," one of the last poems he wrote, published posthumously in *The Beginning and the End* in 1963. There this almost painful love for the world of things, of which man is one thing only, is expressed with haunting tenderness:

A great dawn-color rose widening the petals around her gold eye
Peers day and night in the window. She watches us
Breakfasting, lighting lamps, reading, and the children playing, and the dogs by the fire,
She watches earnestly, uncomprehending,
As we stare into the world of trees and roses uncomprehending,
There is a great gulf fixed. But even while
I gaze, and the rose at me, my little flower-greedy daughter-in-law
Walks with shears, very blond and housewifely
Through the small garden, and suddenly the rose finds herself rootless in-doors.
Now she is part of the life she watched.
—So we: death comes and plucks us: we become part of the living earth
And wind and water whom we so loved. We are they.

In "My Loved Subject," from the same volume, Jeffers commented that though old age prevented him from walking the mountains as in the past, his loved subject remained unchanged:

Mountains and ocean, rock, water and beasts and trees
Are the protagonists, the human people are only symbolic interpreters.

The human drama, whether comic or tragic, is little more than a relief against what he called in an early poem the "divinely superfluous beauty" of the natural world. And "if the great manners of death dreamed up / In the laboratories work well" and humans do succeed in killing themselves off, that beauty will certainly remain. The poetry of Jeffers enables us better to see and understand both ourselves and the shining glory of the world.

Notes

Chapter One

1. George Sterling, *Robinson Jeffers, the Man and the Artist* (New York: Boni and Liveright, 1926), p. 2; W. R. Benét, "Round About Parnassus," *Saturday Review of Literature* 8 (16 January 1932): 461; *The Literary Notebooks of Winfield Scott* (Austin: University of Texas Press, 1969), pp. 20–21.

2. *The Selected Letters of Robinson Jeffers*, ed. Ann N. Ridgeway (Baltimore: Johns Hopkins Press, 1968), p. ix.

3. Printed on the dust jacket for *The Women at Point Sur* (New York: Boni and Liveright, 1927).

4. *Themes in My Poems* (San Francisco: Book Club of California, 1956), p. 28.

5. *Selected Letters*, p. 255.

6. Melba Berry Bennett, *The Stone Mason of Tor House* (Los Angeles: Ward Ritchie Press, 1966), p. 148.

7. *The Selected Poetry of Robinson Jeffers* (New York: Random House, 1938), p. 86. Unless otherwise noted, quotations from Jeffers's poetry are from this edition.

8. *The Passing of the Modern Age* (New York: Harper and Row, 1970), pp. 26–27.

9. Louis Untermeyer, ed., *Modern American Poetry* (New York: Harcourt, Brace and World, 1962), p. 359.

10. Ibid., p. 358.

11. *The Double Axe and Other Poems* (New York: Random House, 1948), p. 57.

12. *Roan Stallion, Tamar and Other Poems*, Modern Library edition (New York: Random House, 1935), p. 295.

13. "A Sovereign Voice: The Poetry of Robinson Jeffers," *Sewanee Review* 77 (Summer 1969): 487–507.

14. *The Failures of Criticism* (Ithaca, N.Y.: Cornell University Press, 1967), p. 17.

15. Two excellent books of photographs, accompanied by descriptive lines of poetry, have been published in recent years: *Not Man Apart* (San Francisco: Sierra Club Books, 1965) and *Jeffers Country* (San Francisco: Scrimshaw Press, 1971).

16. *Prejudices: First Series* (New York: Knopf, 1919), p. 44.

17. *Notes on Democracy* (New York: Knopf, 1926), pp. 102–103.

Chapter Two

1. *Selected Letters*, p. 16.

2. *Poetry, Gongorism and a Thousand Years* (Los Angeles: Ward Ritchie Press, 1949), pp. 8–9. The essay originally appeared in the *New York Times Book Review* (18 January 1948).

3. *Opus Posthumous* (New York: Knopf, 1957), pp. 158, 167.

4. *Character and Opinion in the United States* (New York: George Braziller, 1955), p. 20.

5. S. S. Alberts, *A Bibliography of the Works of Robinson Jeffers* (New York: Random House, 1933), pp. 109–114.

6. Melba Berry Bennett included this preface in her "family biography," *The Stone Mason of Tor House*. That work is a storehouse of important materials that would have been lost except for Una Jeffers's and Mrs. Bennett's care. Mrs. Bennett, who assumed full responsibility for the Jeffers papers after Una's death in 1950, notes in her preface that about that time she began transcribing the hundreds of notes and manuscripts Jeffers had written "on bits and pieces of envelopes, on discarded grocery lists, on the backs of advertisements, and even on the backs of other manuscripts or typescripts."

7. Bennett, pp. 106–108.

8. Alberts, pp. 150–51.

9. As a matter of fact, the transcendentalists or romantics (see the quotation above from Santayana's *Character and Opinion in the United States*) would deny not only that understanding should be, but that it *could* be, a concern of the poet. After all, poets are human, and no human can understand in the deepest sense of the word anything—except, strangely enough, that he cannot understand. In other words, the human does understand, at least, that he cannot in fact do what he is doing. My colleague Morse Peckham, an incorrigible romantic, takes great delight in arguing that such doublethink actually makes sense. In his *Beyond the Tragic Vision* (New York: George Braziller, 1962) he denied that an individual can know anything beyond self, or even imitate that which is real (even assuming that such a thing as reality exists): "[The artist] does not imitate reality, because he cannot; but the images which he uses as signs of that reality are so controlled by cultural tradition that they are seen by himself and by his audience as copies of reality" (p. 345). Unless one knows what reality is, I fail to see how one can say what it is not; and until something more persuasive comes along, I shall continue believing that I do reside in a real world.

10. Melba Bennett wanted to include "Rhythm and Rhyme" in *The Beginning and the End and Other Poems* (New York: Random House, 1963), but she was unable to decipher the word *toggle*, which appeared to her to be *tazzle*. Donnan Jeffers later deciphered the word correctly, and the poem was pub-

lished in a limited edition of 500 copies in 1966 by the Peters Gate Press of Monterey.

11. *The Loyalties of Robinson Jeffers* (Ann Arbor: University of Michigan Press, Ann Arbor Paperbacks, 1963), p. 65.

12. *Hungerfield and Other Poems* (New York: Random House, 1954), p. 105.

Chapter Three

1. *The Classical Tradition* (New York: Oxford University Press, 1949), p. 356.

2. Ibid., pp. 227–28.

3. *The Aristos* (Boston: Little, Brown and Company, 1964), p. 37.

4. *Poetry, Gongorism and a Thousand Years*, p. 11.

5. In commenting on the character of Charles Eliot Norton in the introductory note to his *The Classical Tradition in Poetry* (Cambridge: Harvard University Press, 1927), Gilbert Murray might have been describing Jeffers as well. Not a word from the following sentences would need changing: "Distinguished, critical, courteous and a little aloof, breathing an atmosphere of serenity and depth of thought, he possessed to an exquisite degree the taste that is rightly called classic; that is, his interest lay, not in the things that attract attention or exercise charm at a particular place and moment, but in those that outlive the changes of taste and fashion. His eyes were set toward that beauty which is not of to-day or yesterday, which was before we were, and will be when we are gathered to our fathers."

6. Squires, p. 69.

7. *Existentialism and Humanism*, trans. Philip Mairet (London: Eyre Methuen Ltd., 1948), p. 44.

8. *The Myth of Sisyphus*, trans. Justin O'Brien (New York: Vintage, 1959), pp. 44–45.

9. *The Life of Reason*, one-volume edition (New York: Charles Scribner's Sons, 1954), p. 57.

10. *The Myth of Sisyphus*, pp. 45, 46, 47.

11. Commenting on "Margrave" in a letter to F. I. Carpenter (31 March 1932), Jeffers admitted that he had been "irritated into extravagance by the excessive value that people seem to attribute to human consciousness." See *The Selected Letters of Robinson Jeffers*, p. 195.

12. *The Concept of Nature in Nineteenth-Century English Poetry* (New York: Macmillan, 1936), pp. 545–46.

13. *An Essay on Man: An Introduction to a Philosophy of Human Culture* (New Haven: Yale University Press, 1944), p. 25.

14. *Rats, Lice and History* (Boston: Little, Brown and Company, 1935), pp.

20–21. By 1963 this remarkable book had gone through thirty-three printings.

15. Ibid., pp. 21–23.

Chapter Four

1. *Selected Letters*, pp. 159–60.
2. Ibid., p. 116.
3. Bennett, p. 112.
4. Obviously, a life without some aspect of the Dionysian would be as savorless as a life without Apollonian order would be insane. The most complete life, Jeffers believed, is that in which the two polarities are in equilibrium. Out of the tension between the two comes the heightened awareness that makes up the greatest quality of human existence. As replacements for "the cross" (symbolic of self-immolation and romantic excess) and "the hive" (symbolic of the communal welfare state of regimented lives and kept souls), he proposed in "Rock and Hawk" new emblems "to hang in the future sky":

Here is a symbol in which
Many high tragic thoughts
Watch their own eyes.

This gray rock, standing tall
On the headland, where the seawind
Lets no tree grow,

Earthquake-proved, and signatured
By ages of storms: on its peak
A falcon has perched.

I think, here is your emblem
To hang in the future sky;
Not the cross, not the hive,

But this; bright power, dark peace;
Fierce consciousness joined with final
Disinterestedness;

Life with calm death; the falcon's
Realist eyes and act
Married to the massive

Mysticism of stone,
Which failure cannot cast down
Nor success make proud.

Notably, Jeffers chose nonhuman symbols—emblems in which man could find no reflection of himself. There may be guides in nature, but there are no mirrors there.

5. *Themes in My Poems*, p. 24.

6. *Beyond Good and Evil*, trans. Walter Kaufmann (New York: Vintage, 1966), pp. 115–16.

7. *Be Angry at the Sun* (New York: Random House, 1941), p. 151.

8. In a prefatory note to that volume, Jeffers lamented "the obsession with contemporary history that pins many of these pieces to the calendar, like butterflies to cardboard. Poetry is not private monologue, but I think it is not public speech either; and in general it is the worse for being timely. . . . Yet it is right that a man's views be expressed, though the poetry suffer for it. Poetry should represent the whole mind; if part of the mind is occupied unhappily, so much the worse. And no use postponing the poetry to a time when these storms may have passed, for I think we have but seen a beginning of them; the calm to look for is the calm at the whirlwind's heart."

9. *Be Angry at the Sun*, p. 153. The lines are from the title poem of the volume.

10. Sara Bard Field, "Beauty Dedicated to Reaction," *Pacific Weekly* 3 (11 November 1935): 226–27.

11. *Selected Letters*, p. 234. Una's long letter, dated 13 November 1935, to two close friends reveals a great deal about Jeffers's attitude toward the growth of dictatorships in Europe during the thirties.

12. *The Life of Greece* (New York: Simon and Schuster, 1939), p. 470.

Chapter Five

1. An excellent study of the poem has been made by William Everson, who considers it Jeffers's central masterpiece. See his *Robinson Jeffers: Fragments of an Older Fury* (Berkeley, Calif.: Oyez, 1968), pp. 99–162.

2. *Selected Letters*, pp. 115–19. This version of the letter differs slightly in wording from the one in Alberts's *A Bibliography of the Works of Robinson Jeffers.*

3. *The Unexpected Universe* (New York: Harcourt, Brace and World, 1969), p. 79.

4. Alberts, p. 57.

5. Quoted in Will and Ariel Durant's *Rousseau and Revolution* (New York: Simon and Schuster, 1967), pp. 496–97.

6. *The Rise and Fall of the Third Reich* (New York: Simon and Schuster, 1960), p. 102.

7. See John Lukacs, *The Last European War* (Garden City, N.Y.: Anchor Press / Doubleday, 1976), pp. 157–60.

8. Bennett, p. 177.

9. Oswald Spengler, *The Decline of the West*, trans. Charles Francis Atkinson, 2 vols. (New York: Knopf, 1926), 1:353.

10. Ibid., 1:36–37.

11. *The Sun Never Sets* (New York: Random House, 1940), p. 278.

Index